W9-DHT-475

Dallas

RELUCTANT EMPIRE

By George Fuermann

RELUCTANT EMPIRE
HOUSTON: LAND OF THE BIG RICH

RELUCTANT EMPIRE

by

George Fuermann

Melvin

With Drawings by E. M. Schiwetz

Doubleday & Company, Inc., Garden City, New York

1957

Library of Congress Catalog Card Number 57–13017

To

My Mother and Father

So anxious is every one in Texas to give all strangers a favourable impression, that all statements as to the extreme profit and healthfulness of lands must be taken with a grain of allowance. We found it very difficult, without impertinent persistence, to obtain any unfavourable facts.

Frederick Law Olmsted
A Journey through Texas (1857)

Friday Mountain Ranch near Austin

Preface

This is a book about Texas now. It could be called *The Mind of Texas, 1946–65,* for in it the last decade is tracked and the next one is guessed at. If the conclusions of Chapters 1, 3, and 4 prove to be substantially correct, no years since 1836–46 have been so important to the state as the decade after the Second World War, not even the years of Civil War and Reconstruction. Anyone wanting to know about the state's history or romance, anyone wanting a guide to Texas, will find nothing here. Some of history helps explain Texas now, but history is otherwise absent from this book except as the years 1946–57 are the past. Nothing is in this book, either, about many aspects of today's Texas. What then is this book about?

It is meant to be a contemporary, critical appraisal of a state—critical in the Matthew Arnold sense of evaluation—and its effects on the United States. I have tried to show Texas and its probable immediate future in terms of mentality, politics, and culture, of strengths and weaknesses. I have tried to separate fact from popular conceptions that are drugged with myth and error. Mr. Justice Holmes once said, "All I mean by truth is what I can't help thinking." Something of the kind has masked the state's reality for decades, and trying to get around such an obstacle is not without difficulties. "People are inclined to argument when you talk about their homeland in terms of its shortcomings," Walter Prescott Webb told me. I expect that.

My hope from the outset has been to describe Texas today as Mark Twain, in the suppressed passages of *Life on the Mississippi*, said Mrs. Frances Trollope described the United States of more than a century ago: "She knew her subject well, and she set it forth fairly and squarely, without any weak ifs and ands and buts. . . . She did not gild us; and neither did she whitewash us."

My debts—my borrowings from other minds—are many, for many have given me enough help to have written a better book than this. Three men especially tried to instill in me a consciousness of diction, economy, and grace of writing that shuns journalese. What they tried to do takes years, and the result of their pains and hopes will be shown, I think, in some later book. They are J. Frank Dobie, Walter Prescott Webb, and Frank H. Wardlaw, each a subject of Chapter 17. I do not see how any writer could have been better served than I have been by Frank Dobie. No Texan has stronger convictions than Dobie or is more willing to fight for them, yet he never sought to change my ideas but only my want of precision and clarity in writing. No matter that this book is sparing of excellences, it is incomparably better than it would have been if Dobie, Webb, and Wardlaw had not tried to hog-tie my roll-outs of words, words, words. Mrs. Gilbert Wrightsman could not by any stretch of the imagination be called my secretary; she is more important to my work than that. She did type the manuscript and do a lot of other work of that kind, but her brilliance, which she does her best to conceal, and her sure grasp of my illusions were a tonic for five years. Finally, I have always wondered why many male authors take up space in prefaces to thank their wives. Now I know why, and I suppose that Betsy Walters Fuermann could write an essay of interest on the benefits of being married to an insurance man, say, without ever mentioning money.

The translations of various parts of Guido Piovene's *De America* were made by Bruno Bagnoli, vice-consul of Italy in Houston and a remnant of a past age's civilization, who was my friend until his death in 1955. E. M. Schiwetz, whose drawings appear throughout this book, is a mischief-maker in his late fifties who would seem to be descended from extremely talented pixies. His work will soon be the subject of a retrospective book to be published by the University of Texas Press, or it will be if he can ever manage to cope with the inconvenience of deadlines. Schiwetz is in some ways to Texas painting what Frank Dobie is to the state's writing, and his work here will make the book welcome in many places where the text may seem out of place. Professor Earl Fornell, formerly of Rice Institute and now of Lamar College, in Beaumont; James E. Maloney, of the Houston *Post;* and Miss Geraldine Carlton, of Houston and Ganado, were of material help to me. It is a pity that a newspaper may possibly be embarrassed by a member of its staff who writes books. I have been served with kindness and good fortune by the Houston *Post*, its publishers, editors, and the members of its staff, with whom I have worked since 1941 with the exception of four years of army service during the Second World War.

I follow another custom of prefaces with more than customary cause. This book and especially its conclusions are my own and the people who helped me are in no way to blame for novelty and eccentricity of thought. Most of the people who helped me would not care to be mixed up with many of this book's ideas. I have tried, as Matthew Arnold said of other things, "to see the object as in itself it really is," and I say of this book what Heywood Broun used to say: "That's the way I saw it."

G.M.F.

Houston, June 3, 1957

CONTENTS

V TEXAS IS ITS OWN REWARD

I THE MIND OF TEXAS

THE CAPITOL BUILDING FROM EIGHTEENTH STREET

Cotton Picking by Hand and by Machine

1 Enigma Variations

All Texas is divided into three parts. On the right, or conservative side, is Rural Texas. Also conservative, but moving
from the right to a void on the liberal side, is Urban Texas.
The third division, Mythical Texas, is everywhere. Rural
Texas, second in population and first in the legislature, commands Urban Texas, which grew from the Spindletop gusher
to become two out of three Texans by 1950. Mythical Texas
roots in the dime novel and grows in the flamboyance of oil
riches. It lingers as an American legend, dominating the state
and much of what others think about it. Few words arouse
impression as "Texas" does. The word is understood in the
instant, however differently by each person. It once meant
cowboys, longhorns, and land. It has come to mean bragging
and *bizarrerie*, oil and millionaires, and the closed mind. The

closed mind works both ways in this case, though that says nothing of the state's vulnerability.

The tang of the word that means "friends" or "allies" was first seen in the 1830s because of a political issue: annexation of the Republic of Texas. Soon the Anti-Texass Legion was formed in the North to deter the Union from taking in another slave state. More than a century later the legion is still busy, in a way, but with other goals: to cut the state's brag and bark to size, to trim the state's millionaires of their Tory lust. Texas does not keep time with the rest of the land. It is often at sixes and sevens. Its troubles are infected part by reality and part by myth. The reality is the theme of much of this book. The myth, however, was never a product of Texas alone, and it is not one now.

On March 2, 1844, during the debate on Texas annexation, Rufus Choate, of Massachusetts, was called from his seat in the United States Senate by the son of an old friend.

"I am going to Boston, Mr. Choate. What shall I tell my father?"

"Tell him we are beaten, Mr. Hale—we are beaten, *magno proelio victi sumus*. We have been beaten in a great battle."

The father who awaited this news from Washington was Nathan Hale, editor of the Boston *Daily Advertiser*. The messenger was Edward Everett Hale, a young clergyman whose life would be oddly interwoven with Texas and who was to write "The Man Without a Country." Young Hale's outrage at the prospect of Texas annexation erupted in his first political pamphlet, a sixteen-page, three-penny tract, *How to Conquer Texas, Before Texas Conquers Us*. The pamphlet cited six dangers, two of which are not unheard of today. Admit Texas to the Union, Hale wrote, and the United States would have:

"The introduction into the Union of an unprincipled population of adventurers, with all the privileges of a State of naturalized citizens.

"The creation of an enormous State, in time to become the real Empire State of the country. Texas, with three hundred and ten thousand square miles of territory, is admitted as one State, into the Union. If she remain such, she will prove the Austria of the confederacy, to overrule all opposition."

Hale's plan to overcome some perils of admitting Texas to the Union—it was too late, he thought, to avoid them all—was for Northerners to emigrate to Texas as swiftly as possible until they outnumbered the Texans. "May not the North pour down its hordes upon these fertile valleys, and bear civilization, and Christianity and freedom into their recesses?" he asked. One need go to no pains to see that Hale's notions still prevail in newspapers and magazines. It is an exasperation for a state that has fulfilled at least one prophecy: its wealth, vastness, and effects have made Texas an empire state in Hale's meaning of the phrase. So the myth is as old as Texas— a myth made of heritage, spurious legend, and fact.

What then *is* Texas, this source of relish and annoyance, this stimulant, this irritant? It is a dogma made of two parts: the most intensively tracked state history in America and a state patriotism that has caused the Texas flag to be flown above the American. (The history, however, attracts more than Texans: the five-volume *Bibliography of Texas,* published by Harvard University Press, is the work of Thomas W. Streeter, of New Jersey; several notable collections of Texana have been made by other than Texans.) The state is the hungry heart, out of breath in its bigness and its extremes of pride, riches, and political mediocrity. But it is also the high heart, a symbol of individualism, even now that individualism goes against the democratic grain. Texas is religion, mainly the restrictive religions of Southern Baptists and Methodists. The state was influenced by cotton and religion until the Civil War, by cattle and religion to the end of the century, by oil and religion since then.

Texas is materialism, longing for the images of the 1920s. Even while giving big majorities to Franklin Roosevelt, Texans elected two governors who cut his throat. The state is governed by men who respond to the needs of wealth, which they respect as representing the sanctity of property. The state is influenced by an oligarchy of oilmen whose force is such that Price Daniel, when he was attorney general of the state in 1952, could publicly imply, without contradiction by any Texas newspaper, that every Texan is an oilman. The Democratic state has a Republican press that favors property rights in any showdown with human rights.

Texas is demagoguery. In 1938 a candidate for governor offered the Ten Commandments as his platform, the Golden Rule as his motto, and won the election against twelve opponents in the first primary. He was re-elected, was twice elected to the United States Senate, and retired to sell insurance. He was W. Lee O'Daniel, a charlatan. In 1951, weathervaning his formula in the hope of becoming a candidate for President, he said, "Only God can save this nation. I'm willing to help Him." In 1956 O'Daniel was again a candidate for governor, praying on the radio for

> Men of honor, true and great,
> To fill our offices of state;
> Strong men, wise men who'll fight
> For everything that's just and right;
> Men who will not lie or steal,
> Or double-cross on any deal.

It may have been a prayer for self-improvement, for O'Daniel prayed for qualities he lacks. The state showed its advance in mentality, for at last O'Daniel lost an election. Though he got 346,355 votes, he ran third in a field of six. Three months later, when he fouled his way to a second chance, he got more than a hundred thousand write-in votes in the general election.

Texas is one-party politics, a state without political choice, one price of which was O'Daniel's successes. It will be argued later that Texas is several-party-minded within one party, but the want of two-party cleavage has weakened the state. One-party politics has given Texas low voter-participation ratios and frequently unopposed candidates, has been a factor in maintaining the poll tax, and is one reason the people reacted ineffectively to a succession of disgraces and lootings in state government in the 1950s. Of the state's deficiencies, one-party politics is the least sensitive to change. Texas, like the South, is stuck with it for years. The essential, however, is that Texas, in effect, has been Republican in intrastate affairs from 1949, when Allan Shivers became governor, to 1956, when the Democrats showed the first signs of returning to influence.

Texas is oil—it may be that above all since the Second World War. Oil is an even larger concern than racial segregation. In 1956 John Ben Shepperd, then attorney general of the state, made a statement in which he briefly abandoned interposition as a method of preserving segregation, but he added, "Texas may want to employ interposition as a means of protecting its regulation of natural resources." He meant oil and gas. Oil makes many Texans, and through them all of Texas, rich. It pervades the state, causing boom's intoxication to be par. In 1955 the state's mineral production—mostly oil and gas—was valued at more than four billion dollars, *one fourth* of the nation's total.

Oil: "Oil has saved us," said the postmaster and general storekeeper of Glen Cove, a hamlet in central Texas. "No crops were made this year [1952], and people had to sell a lot of their stock because of the drought. I don't know what we would have done without oil." *Oil:* The Humble Oil & Refining Company paid the town of Liberty, near the Gulf coast, $55,750 in 1956 for mineral rights on city streets, a substantial aid to tax relief in a town of five thousand people. *Oil:* By the middle of 1956 the University of Texas owned 2776 producing wells in West Texas, up to which time oil and gas had given the university an endowment of $259,872,602. *Oil:* In 1955 oil and gas accounted for $187,876,000 of the Texas government's revenue. That does not include taxes paid to counties, cities, and school districts. A survey by the Texas Legislative Council found that 36 per cent of the state government's annual revenue comes from direct taxes on petroleum and its products, and from such other petroleum sources as royalties, leases, and bonuses. Other states must find other ways to get tax money that Texas gets from oil and gas.

Such are random examples of oil's economic good to Texas. Yet oil, more than ever in the public mind in the middle 1950s because of an American sectional quarrel, encumbers the state. The quarrel is between states with gas and those without it; the latter want the government to control the price of gas. It is partly a result of that dispute, and of the oil industry's shenanigans in trying to prevent regulation of gas prices, that oil—and thus Texas—is thought of with distaste in many states. Older causes for this stigma include attempts by a few Texas oilmen to influence elections in other states, the playboy monkeyshines of those oilmen who yearn for the limelight, and the fact that the oil industry exerts what Richard H. Rovere, writing in *The New Yorker* in 1956, called "the most spectacular political power in the country. . . . No industry has ever found itself in a more advantageous position for getting what it wants from legislators." Possession of nearly half of America's oil and gas reserves, ironically, has become in some ways a liability.

These developments have come mostly since the Second World War. Their legacy could be a melancholy future for Texas, to which oil has given importance. Wall Street was the nation's antipathy in the years between the Great Depression and the Second World War. Since then, with Wall Street braced by government security regulations, the Texas oil millionaire has cornered this antipathy. The state puzzles, as America takes it in with a mixture of envy and derision. A trivial note in *The New Yorker*, in 1956, showed that the switch from Wall Street to Texas was by no means confined to the United States: "A friend who lives in Rio de Janeiro tells us that when the movie called 'The Barefoot Contessa' was shown there, the line 'He owns Wall Street' was rendered '*E o dono do Texas*,' or 'He owns Texas.'" Texas has become what Hale said it would. It has won an empire's dimension, and, unexpectedly, some of an empire's responsibilities. The price of this gain, but especially of the obligations, is changing Texas from a willing to a reluctant empire.

. . . it is an empire, an entity, totally its own. John Gunther, 1947, *Inside U.S.A.*

Texas has not yet reached maturity. When it does, it may be wise enough to cast off its adolescent ways and accept its responsibilities as a member state of the United States and a part of one sovereign world. J. A. Burkhart, 1949, *Antioch Review.*

The rain of scorn falling on the state has caused Texans to take cover under a glass umbrella of indifference—a gall to a people who are traditionally unabashed. Most, having no clue to the historic roots and only a superficial notion of the proximate causes, are baffled by the nation's temper. They conclude that their state is being misrepresented by magazines, newspapers, and other influences on opinion, and that the people of other states envy Texas. There is some truth in such balm—great size and apparent wealth may not invite affection even when their possessors do not take them seriously—but not enough to account for the aggressiveness of America's mood to discipline Texas.

The state is being misrepresented, not so much by writers, as by a few oilmen of extraordinary wealth who have reversed the principle of *noblesse oblige.* These worthies have made it seem that their political goals are those of the majority of Texans. The whole state is held to account for the adventures in influence of three Texans[1] and a few others of like mind but smaller means. It is an idle fancy, of course, but Texas could use an unconventional regulatory body with a rather abstract function. It should be made up of wise and meaty

[1] H. L. Hunt, Clint W. Murchison, and H. R. Cullen, whose ambitions and effects are concerns of Chapters 3, 4, and 6.

men who could forestall affronts to the state's conscience. This good would be won by counseling the less gifted, but articulate, rich inside the state and, if possible, some journalists outside of it.

The use of oil wealth to buy political influence in states where the purchasers do not have the vote is a thorn to Texas because there is no way to cope with it or the bitterness it causes. One cannot manage a fog. As existing legislation is not concerned with this aspect of political spending, courts can give no relief. Texas finds itself diplomatically immobilized for want of a way to restrain these Tory crusaders, for want of a way to subdue the professional Texan in and out of the state, and for want of objective inquiry by its own and some of the Northern press. The state's press does not trouble to evaluate, or even to take up, most issues concerning these problems. At times such concerns are skipped in the hope that they will go away if nobody stirs them up; at other times it is not in the interest of the dominant class that they be taken up. Yet the chief bone of contention—attempts to stunt the democratic process in other states—does not represent action by, or even the plan of, the dominant class, but by a few who are of the class.

Some of the reporting on Texas by Northerners is tuned with haste, preconception, and excessive liberalism. The zeal of these journalists often enlarges the ills complained of to such giant size that truth is either obscured or forced into a blind alley. Texas has been a lure to journalists more to its cost than benefit. One solution to this bother might be for the state to pare down its size—Texas is beset by size—and divide itself into the five states it has the right to become, admittedly an unlikely event. It is a possibly faulty theory, anyway, since the new states, like dividing amoebae, might become *five* states like Texas.

Texas is more at odds with its own extremes than with the world. It is one American state that might make its way as an independent nation. Only politically can Texas be treated as a state. Texas is a region; in Europe it would be a nation. It is almost exactly central between the Atlantic and the Pacific. Its 370-mile seacoast is the third longest among the states. It has a longer border touching a foreign nation whose civilization, language, and dominant religion are different from its own than all the rest of the states together. It is a land of extremes, and of such almost inconceivable variety that there is no way to compare it with any other state, *not even with any other equal land area in America.*

"By accident Texas stands in the physical path of a special destiny," Walter Prescott Webb wrote in 1944. He said the accident is a cultural triangle in which three natural environments, three molds of separate cultures, meet and oppose each other in Texas: the woodlands, the plains, and the desert. There is also a fourth—the sea. The state's size and variousness create troubles of equal proportion and diversity. Merging in this one state are seven regions that are united politically but conflict in instincts and customs, even in different religions and standards of living in some cases.

One state: East Texas, spared the mildew of William Faulkner's Deep South by the fertility of its oil; the Gulf Plain, a golden littoral of energy and cities; the Rio Grande Valley, the almost-tropics, where energy is more in sun and soil than in men; the Border, indelibly Mexico and the valley's cast-off kin; the Trans-Pecos and West Texas, the former the desert, the latter the Old West, one within the other but sharing only drought's poverty of spirit and purse; the Panhandle, with nothing to lean the eye on, not even a tree, except the surprise of cities rising from the Great Plains; finally, the vast central region, pragmatic and more stable than the others. Here in the center the other six merge and lose their identities in what, in the small towns, is still the heart of Texas—rural civilization. Thus the extent of a Texas problem—size and variousness. But that problem, though vaguely comprehended, is not so vexing as another, also inherited from the past.

*Friends, I tell you the promised land is a reality. I didn't
believe it. I didn't come looking for it. We have seen it and
explored it.*   Victor Considerant, 1852, *Au Texas.*

*. . . a central obsession in the [Texas] fantasy [is] . . . the
castration-anxiety that seems to be endemic in the Lone Star
State.*   Bernard De Voto, 1952, *Harper's.*

No issue—not oil, not segregation, nothing—concerns Texas
as does states' rights. The one issue blankets all the others.

Chief of the state's stimulants of conservatism is the Dallas
Morning News. Hewing to a philosophy slightly to the left of
the one that distinguished the Chicago *Tribune* of Colonel
Robert R. McCormick's time, the *News* may be regarded as
the spokesman for Texas conservatism. The editorial mind of
the *News* is by no means singular—conservatism is the rule
of Texas newspapers—but the conservative leadership of its
editorial page will thread this book. One of its editorials, in
March 1957, typified Texas conservatives' wish to be free of
the federal government at nearly any cost. The *News* com-
mented on a proposal that Alaska be made a commonwealth
rather than a state: "Texas would jump at the chance to have
our present state become what a . . . congressman proposes
for Alaska. . . . The main difference would be that Alaskans
would not have to pay any federal income tax . . . Everything
else would be the same . . . except that Alaskans would have
no voting representatives in Congress . . . but it might not be
too high a price to pay."

Some Texans have come to regard the victory at San Jacinto, the bizarre climax of the state's fight for independence
in 1836, as a fruit of questionable flavor in the light of later
events. Most of their alarms arise from issues that blossomed
after the Second World War. A little less than ten years after
winning independence from Mexico, Texas voluntarily surrendered this responsibility to become the twenty-eighth
state. In spite of so natural an affiliation, Texas has sometimes
felt obliged to continue fighting for independence, not from

the United States but from the American federal government, a peevish distinction that is necessary here. This feeling is caused by a number of grievances, but especially three: federal aid to education, the government's attempt to take the Texas tidelands, and its insistence that segregation be abandoned in the public schools.

A statue to Confederate heroes on the grounds of the Texas capitol is inscribed, "They died for States' rights guaranteed under the Constitution." States' rights, a generally South-wide conviction that is disdained by many Northerners, is the state's creed. The issue antedates the Union itself. Texas is not the South, and only the eastern part of it ever was, but the mind of Texas is of the South more than of the Southwest or the West. The state is Southern in political reaction; its union with the South is physical, not chemical. But having been a member of the Confederacy, Texas was subject to Reconstruction, which meant being occupied by the enemy for a decade. Writing in *The New Yorker* in 1956, Edmund Wilson, a Northerner, interpreted this background as part of a reappraisal of James Branch Cabell, a Southern writer.

"We Northerners do not . . . really grasp the state of mind of the Southerners," Wilson said. "We have always made a point, in our relations with them, of disregarding what we call the Civil War, they of remembering it and calling it the War Between the States. We like to assume that the United States is an integrated, homogeneous, and smoothly functioning nation . . . Except when an issue arises so troublesome that it cannot be ignored—such as that of the recent Supreme Court ruling against racial segregation in the schools—we hardly realize how deep and how virulent, from a long-standing sense of grievance, runs the instinct toward repudiation of any responsibility on the part of the South to that federal government of states which are by no means so completely united as the Northerner likes to suppose. The Northerner does not take account of the extent to which the Southerner—if not overtly, at least among other Southerners and in his own most intimate being—disassociates himself from the North."

Wilson said the Southern writer—it would apply to Southerners other than writers—"however intuitive, intelligent, imaginative, well travelled, well read—may fail to accept our [Northern] assumptions. . . . We do not realize that he lives in a world in which planning, progress, reform, making the world safe for democracy, laying the foundations for a classless society, promoting the American way of life do not really mean anything at all. What makes his indifference possible, and even tolerably easy, for the Southerner is the fact that such phrases as these are often the merest cant and may disguise other interests less worthy."

It would be consoling to argue some of Wilson's reasoning, but the point here is not that he puts the bee on the South *and* the North. What he does is illumine the motives of the South's danger—estrangement—in the modern world. And he brings into focus the North's failure to comprehend the character of the South's theory of states' rights. As Texas is politically a part of the South, Wilson's interpretation may be applied to it. The newer phase of Texas history that began in 1901—that is, the predictable results of riches quickly won—has changed the state's stance. It has not, however, materially altered the inherited traditions of thought and prejudice, and the instinctive modes of reaction, arising from the state's roots in the South's past. One other point must be made: insistence on states' rights, in Wilson's words, also is "often the merest cant and may disguise other interests less worthy."

The validity of the states' rights doctrine will not be a concern here, but a Supreme Court ruling of Chief Justice Salmon P. Chase, in 1869, would seem to show that it is not unpatriotic, as is sometimes heard. "Not only, therefore, can there be no loss of separate and independent autonomy to the States . . . but it may be not unreasonably said that the preservation of the States, and the maintenance of their governments, are as much within the design and care of the Con-

stitution as the preservation of the Union and the maintenance of the National Government," Chase wrote in the
historically vital case of Texas vs. White. The case grew out
of the Civil War; in effect, Chase's decision reunited the nation. Chase added: "The Constitution, in all its provisions,
looks to an indestructible Union, composed of indestructible
States."

"One of the great historic constitutional conflicts in the
United States—federal vs. state authority—is shaping up for
the sharpest test since the Civil War," began an editorial in
the *Christian Science Monitor* in October 1956. By the end
of the decade after the Second World War, the states' rights
issue was a mixture of conviction and political opportunism
in Texas. "We must raise funds [for education] from state,
municipal, and private sources unless we want to turn it all
over to the Great White Father," Governor Price Daniel said
in a Houston speech in 1957. States' rights is the Holy Grail
of modern Texas aspirations.

*It has the cult of heroes. . . . The qualities of Texas are its
good heart and a certain amount of bigness of soul, its generosity, its solidarity, and its promptness to help. It is still the
land which welcomes the man who wants to do well.* Guido
Piovene, 1954, *De America.*

*Thanks to those who have congratulated us on our removal
into civilization. We are indeed very happy to have escaped
from the Texas nightmare.* Charles F. Heartman, on the
cover of his book catalogue for December 1951, the first he
published after moving from Texas to New Orleans.

There are other formidable problems in the state's way—
the internal problems, the ones affecting Texas alone rather
than national or sectional areas as well, are a later subject.
One, like states' rights, has been shared with the South for
more than a century. Texas is an economic colony. To the
North, and especially to some of its leading financial inter-

ests, Texas is worth more alive than dead. Texas produces a
variety of wealth for itself, but a case could be made to show
that it enriches the North more than itself. The degree of
economic dependence on the North has diminished considerably throughout the South, and especially in Texas and
Florida, since the Second World War. One thing, however,
makes the problem of the state's need of Northern capital,
and its role as a supplier of materials with which things are
made elsewhere, of more importance than to any other
Southern state: Texas has so much oil, gas, and sulphur to be
owned elsewhere.

Even with such spasms of troubles, Texas is not a complain-
ing state. Blame for the nest of enigmas must be shared by all
Texans in that they have not risen up to overwhelm the causes.
It is in the nature of things, however, that Texans disagree as
to what should be risen up against. Still populated by more
cattle than people in 1957, Texas is a fourth dimension among
the states, and there's the rub. To be different is to attract
attention but does not of itself inspire esteem or tolerance.
The state's richness of spirit and economy, its haleness, and
its instincts for compassion and co-operation are marred by
droughts of curiosity, altruism, and response to reality. The
mind of Texas is not contemporary with itself except in certain urban milieux. But the state's overlong adolescence is
fading; adjustment is a disease to die-hard illusions. An
East Texas saying, "He's running around like a blind dog in a
meat house," in some ways describes Texas in the middle
1950s. The attractions are ideas, change, motion. Texas is being retreaded with modern principles. The stigmas are being
alloyed by a shift in ideals that is owing to the rise of the
urban mind. Long a monotony of one theme, Texas is becoming contrapuntal.

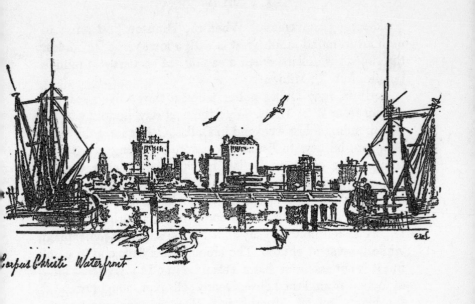

Corpus Christi Waterfront

2 Millionism: Time Capsule

A few days before Christmas of 1955, Bailey Balken, a Dallas oilman, was called by a reporter for the Dallas *News*. The *News* had received an Associated Press story saying Balken had inherited $552,000 from the estate of his grandfather; did Balken have anything to say? It was the first the oilman had heard of the windfall, and he paused to consider the sum. "That's not much money around here, is it?" he said at last.

Two years before, when Roy Hofheinz was mayor of Houston, he called a press conference to disclose that he had made his first million dollars. He could not, however, pin down the exact date he had done so. "You just don't notice things like that," he said. H. L. Hunt, a Dallas oilman whose wealth is such that at times he seems to think of it as play money, has said that "money is nothing; it is just something to make bookkeeping convenient." When the Houston *Post* refers to millions in round numbers, it is with a lower-case "m" unless the subject is dollars, when a capital "M" is used—"3 million people" but "$3 Million."

Early in 1957 Dallas police jailed a thirty-seven-year-old oilman from West Texas. Sober the next day, he told why he was spending a lost weekend in Dallas. Celebrating the birth of a son, he flew to Dallas for a spree. Having heard that things were costly in Dallas, he said, he brought enough money to see him through. Police then returned his pocket money, which they had kept overnight in their safe: $55,-474.44 in cash. In Houston some months earlier Paul D. Denny called police to say that his house had been robbed while he was at church. The amount was $130,000 in cash, but it is not essential that a Texan be in oil to have that kind of money around the house; Denny sells pies, doughnuts, and the like. Clint W. Murchison, of Dallas, once was trading some oil and insurance properties with Toddie Lee Wynne. Being nearly half a million dollars apart on the deal, they flipped a coin to settle it. Wynne won the $498,000.

In 1951 a man identified as "a Texas millionaire" called a Cadillac dealer from Fort Worth's Blackstone Hotel. *The New Yorker* reported the conversation as follows: "You got a Cadillac with the top that goes up and down?" the caller asked. "Got it in blue?" Told that one such was on hand, he asked about various extras, all of which were available. "Well, put 'em on, fill her up with gas and oil, and have the car brought around to the hotel in two hours," he said. The salesman asked about payment. "Just charge it to my hotel room here," the man said. The salesman called the manager of the hotel, who said it would be all right. Two hours later a boy drove the Cadillac to the hotel, left its keys at the desk, and received $4270 in cash from the room clerk. "We receive more and more evidence that life in Texas is not stultifying," *The New Yorker* said two years later. It told about a man in the St. Regis Hotel barbershop who was asked by his barber what he used on his hair. "Don't remember," he said. "Call my barber in Beaumont, Texas, and find out." It was done.

J. M. West, Jr., an oil heir who takes his own butter with him when he dines out, was staying at the Ambassador Hotel in Los Angeles one night in 1955. He wished to get up at a certain early hour the next morning. With a logic that is peculiar to West, he made sure of a prompt awakening by making a long-distance call to a man on his staff in Houston and telling the man to call him in Los Angeles at the specified hour the next day. West is eccentricity's pride. For one thing, he has more than fifty telephones in his house. Known as Silver Dollar West, he keeps two thousand silver dollars in stock for a Negro to shine and put in racks built for the purpose. He carries with him 160 cartwheels at a time, eighty in each of two specially lined pockets prepared for all his trousers. He throws away the dollars as though they were confetti, and yet he manages to do so with discretion.

At a cost of many thousands of dollars, West had a Jeepster rebuilt into a luxury hunting car for use on his ranch, part of which is enclosed by a fence fifteen feet high and thirty miles long. He put two 2500-watt, 12-volt airplane landing lights on the back of the Jeepster and nine 200-watt floodlights on the front so he can turn night into day when he hunts after dark. West likes to eat more than the next man, but he does not care to scout around for food. Once, when he was to make a two-hour trip from Houston to his ranch, he laid in a larder of ten steak sandwiches, five pounds of peanuts, five dozen doughnuts, two five-pound boxes of candy, and a case of soft drinks, though but one friend was to make the trip with him and the ranch is well stocked.

On Page 13 of its 1956 Christmas catalogue, Neiman-Marcus, a specialty store in Dallas and Houston, pictured a stuffed and jeweled tiger, price one million dollars, including tax. From time to time, however, one-dollar bills have allure in Texas. The actor William Bendix appeared on a radio show in Bryan in 1955. Several people who had watched the show asked Bendix for his autograph, but paper for him to write on was wanting. Brazos Varisco, the owner of the building in which the radio station has its studio, took a roll of currency from his pocket and Bendix signed one-dollar bills for all. The actor, who seems never to have autographed money before, was shaken by the experience.

A biography of H. R. Cullen, a Texas oilman, was published in 1954. Through the Texas Medical Center, a beneficiary of his philanthropy, he sent 108,000 copies of the book to individuals, newspapers, and libraries over the United States. The cost of this urge was $216,000, plus mailing. Clara Driscoll, the daughter of a Texas rancher whose land flowed millions of dollars' worth of oil, was provoked to a more costly urge. She was the author of two novels and a Broadway musical comedy in the early 1900s; in 1903 she bought an option on the Alamo, controlling the shrine long enough to prevent its destruction; and she was the National Democratic Committeewoman from Texas for sixteen years. Piqued by the manager of the Plaza Hotel in Corpus Christi, she told him, "I'll build a hotel tall enough to spit on your damned old Plaza!" As a result of this rage she spent more than three million dollars to build the higher Robert Driscoll Hotel next door to the Plaza.

Robert A. Welch, who died at the age of eighty, in 1952, was unknown to the public in his home town in spite of having made a fortune of more than twenty-five million dollars. He was well known, however, to leaders of the United Fund and other Houston charities. With the exception of his barber, to whom he gave a dime after each haircut for nearly forty years, he was not known to have given away a cent in his lifetime. His thrift was a near cry to that of New England's Hetty Green, but Welch left 85 per cent of his fortune to a foundation for research in chemistry and 15 per cent, plus the same percentage of future profits, to the twenty-nine employees of his oil and sulphur firms. Employees got from around two thousand dollars to four hundred thousand dollars each.

Glorious Texas! what if thou art a little too much given to the Bowie-knife and revolver, and what if grass-widows are somewhat frequent in some of thy localities, thou art all right at heart! Admiral Raphael Semmes, 1869, *Service Afloat During the War Between the States.*

When a ranch house owned by L. M. Josey, a Houston oilman, burned to the ground in 1951, the Houston *Press* reported that Mrs. Josey fought the fire while wearing a mink stole. Mrs. Josey's secretary later called the *Press* to correct an error. "Your story says Mrs. Josey battled the blaze clad in nightgown, robe, and mink stole," the secretary said. "We wish to correct this. Mrs. Josey was wearing her marten furs." Lloyd Hilton Smith, an oilman whose pride is his scorn of the state's *nouveau riche* eccentricities, flew to New York early in 1957 with his pet, a Chihuahua, so the dog could be treated by a New York veterinarian. At about the same time a social-ite widow of grace and wit wore a woolen coat to a party of Houston elite. She put her coat on a bed with other guests' minks. Leaving the party early, she found her coat segre-gated. It was in a corner of the bed, alone, away from the richness of minks.

W. T. Waggoner, one of ranching's legends, was for a time the richest man west of the Mississippi when his ranch chanced to produce more than fifty million dollars' worth of oil. One of his sons was Guy, who took for his seventh wife a woman of charm and culture some twenty years younger than the groom. They went to Europe for their wedding trip, spending several weeks in France. The seventh Mrs. Guy Waggoner's taste ran to painting, Guy had the means to in-dulge her taste, and they returned to Fort Worth with a num-ber of paintings of the Fauve school. Eventually the marriage went on the rocks and Guy moved to the Fort Worth Club while they worked out the terms of a divorce. "You can have the house, the paintings—everything," he said one day. "Just send me that picture of a graveyard." The painting of a

French cemetery was the only one Guy liked, and she sent it
to him a day or so later. First, using indelible ink, she wrote
his name on the rump of a donkey in the painting's fore-
ground—and the names and marriage dates of his seven wives
on seven tombstones.

J. B. Wilson, of Dallas, owed his fortune to frugality and
real-estate clairvoyance. A group of women once called on
him to ask for a donation to a civic project. Wilson was
shocked by the request. "Ladies," he said, "I have nothing to
give you, but if you ever want to sell your gall, I'd like to bid
on it." He was a stickler for staying on top of his due, and
years ago the head of the Dallas streetcar lines became an
authority on this aspect of Wilson's method. Wilson agreed
to lend the firm $365,000 at 10 per cent interest—$100 a day.
He did not, however, want the interest paid annually, quarterly, or monthly. He wanted it every day. One term of the
loan was that he was to get the first $100 collected in fares
each day. Every morning until the loan was repaid, Dallas
streetcars were relieved of nickels until there was $100 worth
for Wilson.

One Texan of note spurned more than a hundred thousand
dollars he had earned. Jesse H. Jones never had a personal
servant and rarely entertained. The allure of Cadillacs, said
to be the Texas merit badge, was a mystery to Jones, who
never owned one, but he refused to sell an old Pierce Arrow
long after it was of any use to him. A few years before his
death, in 1956, a reporter asked him why he held on to the
Pierce Arrow. "Sentiment," the financier said. The leading
conservative of the Roosevelt New Deal, Jones was named
a director of the Reconstruction Finance Corporation by President Hoover in 1932. His friends said at the time that he got
the job because he was the only man who had more cash than
the government, but his enemies said he went to Washington
to fill his pockets with gold. In any event, Jones reacted to his
enemies: in thirteen years of service as head of the RFC and
Secretary of Commerce, he refused to cash his government

pay checks—more than a hundred thousand dollars' worth of souvenirs. They are still among his papers.

In the early 1950s the ladies of a New England garden club visited a number of gardens in Texas cities. A Boston lady, admiring the beauty of one garden's azaleas, asked the owner the secret of her success. "Mink manure," the matron said.

A year or so later C. O. Girard, an officer of Linz Jewelists, a Dallas firm, got a telephone call from a customer in town from Houston. The visitor asked Girard to meet him at the store right away. First off, when Girard arrived, the man fired a pistol at him three times. No harm done; he was shooting blanks. He had come to pay his bill, he said, and was using the gun to guard the money. He owed the store nearly six thousand dollars and had every cent of it with him —six thousand silver dollars in tin boxes.

In 1955 Paul Crume, of the Dallas *News*, wrote of a wealthy El Paso man's son who was in Dallas for consolation. He was carrying a cashier's check on an El Paso bank for $125,-000. The check was made out to his wife, but by misfortune the man was not married. His father, deciding the son ought to get married, offered him and anyone he married $125,000 each. He gave the son the future wife's check and said he would turn over the other one at the wedding ceremony. The offer suited the son to a T; he already had the girl picked out. He called on her and showed her the check. She turned him down.

Another instance of money's occasional futility was the climax of a series of practical jokes two Houston oilmen played on each other. While one was in Europe the other had a fair-sized roller coaster built in the traveler's back yard. Unknown to the stay-at-home, however, his friend had put his mansion on the market before leaving town. It was sold soon after the roller coaster was completed and the realtor gave the stay-at-home twenty-four hours to have it dismantled and the grounds repaired.

Clifford Mooers, whose taste and means ran to yachts and

race horses, died in New York, at age sixty-seven, late in 1956. He studied law, hunted gold in Alaska, and raced automobiles before he started wildcatting in Texas in 1918. Sixteen years later he moved to Houston, where he was something of a mystery. It suited Mooers to live by his own lights instead of the crowd's, and five years after he came to Houston he built for his second wife, a Cuban beauty, the most extraordinary house in the city. Though the house, built on a hundred-acre tract, was then far from the city, Mooers shut out the world with finality by surrounding it with an electrically charged fence. The house was sometimes known as Penguin's Folly. The source of the epithet was Mooers's private zoo, which included such rarities in Texas as dwarf Australian barking deer, or muntjacs, and some penguins. Mooers had no more luck raising penguins than the Houston zoo was to have fifteen years later. He built an air-conditioned pen, but the Antarctic birds gave up the ghost during their first summer in Houston.

The mansion's cost, $164,000, was a sum of consequence in 1939, and one of its attractions was its seven larger rooms. Each was a precision replica of a room that had caught Mooers's fancy in a hotel or mansion somewhere in the world. The mansion's other feature was its formidability. Mooers's concern for the floodwaters of nearby Buffalo Bayou caused him to build a fortress. Bulkheads sealed off the lower level in case of need, which did not develop, but water could have risen to a height of twenty-four feet without effect. Expecting the worst, however, Mooers put two great pumps in the basement to spray floods from the rooftop. Every room faced a lake Mooers built, for the bottom of which he shipped in tons of white California sand. He sold the house when he left Houston in 1946, and it has since become the clubhouse of the Lakeside Country Club. One of his favorite horses was buried at the place, and in 1952 he had its bones sent to his Texas ranch and the gravestone to his Kentucky farm. The horseshoes were sent to the ranch, too, so Mooers could have them gold-plated. At the time of his death he owned more than two hundred race horses; eighty-seven of them were auctioned early in 1957 for three quarters of a million dollars.

Verbatim quote, taken down on the spot, from a broad-hatted nabob who was getting off the Santa Fe's Texas Chief at Houston: "It's been a hard day all around. First, my wife's pet kangaroo has to go and get poisoned, and then somebody stole my midget butler's stepladder." Stanley Walker, 1956, *The New Yorker.*

Stanley Walker, a Texan who lived New York to a draw for years, may have coined the quote. Pet kangaroos and midget butlers have come to measure up to the state's millionaire legend. Some kinds of reality provoke legend. This chapter's memoir of caprice and pungence is fact, up to this point, not legend. But legend is not concerned with the dimension of its source, with whether fact represents the whole or the exception. The Des Moines *Tribune* has said that Texans like to send Cadillac get-well cars to sick friends. The legend prompts such a frame of mind about a whole state. The belief that Texas could never be as arresting as something made up about it has root in reality, but such a legend overtakes and then intimidates reality.

Worth Gatewood, a latter-day Lord Chesterfield of Texas life, distinguished for his poverty and bohemian gentility, was for many years a savant of the Houston *Post*. At last, when poverty went to his head, he became an editor of the New York *Sunday News*, from which refuge he described, in a story for the *Post*, the extravaganza of legend's Texan, circa 1955. He told of an oil tycoon who stuffed five million dollars in his valise and set out for a year of sport in Manhattan. "The parties he hosted in his suite at the Waldorf Towers were the talk of the town," Gatewood wrote. "The canapés came gift-wrapped in $100 bills and champagne spouted from a miniature oil derrick wrought in platinum. . . . One day he was strolling along Fifth Avenue, a picture of magnificence —solid-gold Stetson, a suit of shimmering mauve gabardine with lapels five inches wide, and a tie hand-painted by Grandma Moses."

Thus, in three sentences, America's notion of the modern Texan. One Fred Majdalany, a film reviewer for the London *Daily Mail*, wrote: "I have gained the impression [from a movie titled *The Last Command*] that Texas was originally a vast expanse of nothing. That it then became a battleground on which cattlemen and growers fought over whether it should be crops or pasture. That dispute (I have been led to believe) was amicably solved by the discovery of oil . . ." Edna Ferber, the state's old maid aunt, has described Texas as "exhilarating, exasperating, violent, charming, horrible, delightful, alive." Texas excites writers to such runs on adjectives.

The Texans-from-life who dance a hornpipe in this chapter helped smooth the way for Gatewood's, Hollywood's, and Miss Ferber's Texans—the legend's blossom. Legend's Texan is the one Americans expect, the Texan who diverts and annoys the other forty-seven states. Wealth's clowns, however, are the part of the iceberg that shows. Texas is harassed by other than a millionaire legend of little validity.

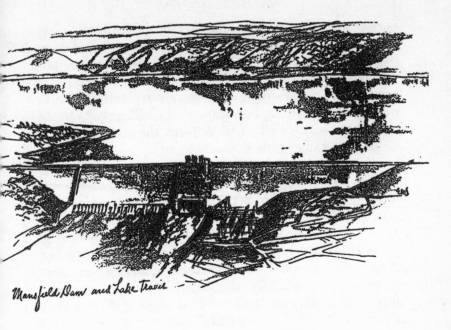

Mansfield Dam and Lake Travis

3 The Power of Fate

Mrs. John Wells Heard, the widow of a San Antonio oilman, might be known as a dowager but for her likeness to a bride's mother the day before the wedding. This fixed condition of Mrs. Heard's outlook causes her to attack each of several interests as though it were the only thing under the sun. She will fly the length of the land to make motion pictures of a symphony orchestra, a flower show, an art festival. Taking up deep-sea fishing in 1950, she subdued the sport with such gusto that she was named to fishing's hall of fame three years later. Her formidability as a patron of music is a subject of marvel in New York and a number of European cities, which, judging from the frequency of her visits, she feels are right next door to her ranch.

In 1952 Mrs. Heard chartered an airplane to fly nine of her friends to New York to attend the opening of the Metropoli-

tan Opera's sixty-eighth season. That she did not have tickets
for the event was not a misfortune in her case. "The Metropolitan's directors rose to the occasion by giving up their private box to Mrs. Heard and her party," the New York *Times*
reported the next morning. The opera was Verdi's *La Forza
del Destino,* which may be translated as *The Power of Fate.* In
the light of nature's gift of oil to Texas, the title is prophetic
of the state's affair with its money legend.

Oil overwhelms Texas, and so Texas is rich—and is said to
have an oil and money civilization. This view has taken some
of its strength from the "Big Rich" fantasy, which is less than
skin-deep in the state's character. As a combination of adjectives expressing a quality thought of as properly belonging to Texas, "Big Rich" has become the state's private epithet.
A more damaging one is hard to conceive, and it is important
to know if it describes Texas.[1] "Big Rich" seems to have been
first applied to Texas by *Fortune,* in April 1948, in a story
titled "The Land of the Big Rich." At that time, however, the
term was used to describe the Southwest, which *Fortune*
defined as being New Mexico, Colorado, Kansas, Oklahoma,
and Texas. The *Time, Life,* and *Fortune* group of magazines,
notably *Time,* afterward pared the term's geography to
hound Texas alone. The implication is that as the state is rich,
rich, so it must be host to a mentality that conceives of cash as
the measure of culture. The result is two-edged: the epithet,
inspiring envy, has pepped up the anti-Texas mood and it
has served Texas liberals as a label of convenience.

The "Big Rich" legend is a newer penalty of being Texas.
By the 1950s the state could not escape a legend it did not
conceive, did not want after the novelty of early experience,
and does not seem to be able to oppose. The legend does not
fit the state except as it draws out grotesquerie. It is a shadow,

[1] A few Texans, on reading this paragraph, will recall that the title
of my first book, published by Doubleday & Company, Inc., in 1951,
is *Houston: Land of the Big Rich.* I regretted the title, and some parts
of the book, a few months after I began working on *Reluctant Empire*
in 1952.

blurred and exaggerated, supported by the reality without which a shadow cannot exist. Chapter 2 reflected the reality's exception, not the rule. The legend was born, nearly full grown, of the number of new rich created by the state's oil and the uses some of these people make of eccentricity and money's command. It was also born of a national longing for such a legend after the Second World War. The state's most widely known symbol, developing for a century and a quarter, is the Texan spirit. The "Big Rich" legend, developed in the five years between 1946 and 1950, has come to be second in the public mind, and in many Texans' minds, as a state symbol.

Dr. W. R. White, president of Baylor University, announced in 1954 that the university had received three million dollars during the first year of a drive to raise much more. He said he had asked some men to help raise the rest of the money and told of one man's hopes. The committeeman said he "met a Houston taxi driver the other day who confessed to me that he had more than a million dollars in real-estate holdings, and I'm telling him about Baylor University." It may be that some Houston cab driver is a millionaire; one cannot say for sure. But a university president thought well enough of the report to tell the press about it. Thus the legend's acceptance in Texas.

Most of the millionaires, of course, are aware of the legend's deceit. Sid W. Richardson, of Fort Worth, is one of several Texas oilmen whose fortune has been called the largest in America by newspapers and magazines. "Out here in Texas," he has said, "we judge a man's worth by how much he owes." Robert E. Smith, a Houston oilman, was asked what he thought about newspaper reports of various Texans' wealth. "That's just paper money," Smith said. The legend's insistence, however, causes opposite facts to be shunned, or to be received as inventions. Texans' per capita income in 1956 was $1686—$254 below the national average. In 1929 Texas was the thirty-fourth state in per capita income; by 1955 it had advanced to only twenty-seventh place. Seven Texans had taxable incomes of a million dollars or more in 1951. The same year nearly half a million Texans paid taxes on incomes between $2000 and $3000, and more than four hundred thousand paid taxes on incomes between $1000 and $2000—together nearly 40 per cent of Texans who paid taxes that year.

"In the history of history, a myth is a once valid but now discarded version of the human story, as our now valid versions will in due course be relegated to the category of discarded myths," Carl Becker, the historian, once said. Thus may the state shake off its "Big Rich" legend, but history takes a long time. As the legend has been nourished outside of Texas more than in, history will have to deal with a spew of rhetoric that has bullied reality out of focus. ". . . the Lone Star State is one of the few places left in the world where millionaires hatch seasonally, like May flies," *Time* said in 1950. ". . . wealth is not news in Texas," *Fortune* said in 1953. "Having made his millions in oil, [Murchison] is now using them to further the popular Texas ambition of buying up the rest of the U.S.," *Time* said in 1954. The London *Daily Mirror* columnist Cassandra (William Connor), in the United States in the summer of 1956 to attend the national political conventions, came to Texas beforehand. He wanted to meet and write about a "real Texas millionaire." He implied that a millionaire from some other state would not do. In 1954 the Los Angeles *Mirror* published a series of four articles titled "The Texas Jillionaires." In 1952, when A. Harris and Company, of Dallas, sent models to France for the Riviera's Texas Week fashion shows, the French Communist press said the fashions were for the wives of oil millionaires only and that the Texans were in France to shoot the peasants.

One Bert Wiggins wrote from Hopewell, Virginia, to the Houston *Post* in 1956 to ask for help. "Being from Houston, I'm getting the business from the local and New York State fellows regarding . . . Texas Millionaires," he wrote. "If you have any information regarding Texas Millionaires that may

assist me in my arguments that Texas has more than any other
state, please rush it to me." The *Post* advised Wiggins to talk
about Angora goats, or pecan trees, or any of the other things
in which Texas *is* first, because the state does not lead in
millionaires. Since the Cadillac automobile became a syno-
nym for "Texas millionaire"—a phrase *The New Yorker* once
described as an instance of tautology—it is hard to persuade
some people that Texas was not first but seventh in registra-
tions of new Cadillacs in 1955. California, New York, Michigan, Illinois, Pennsylvania, and Ohio led Texas in this distinction. The disclosure had one effect in Texas—publication of a
jingle:

> Though Texas lacks
> For Cadillacs,
> It's rolling in
> Petroleum.

*We have no real objection to these [magazine] articles
about solid-gold Dallas. We actually like them because, after
all, everybody likes to read about some place he has never
been.*   Paul Crume, 1953, Dallas *News*.

The effects of the nonsense and distortion inspired by the
"Big Rich" legend have been trivial compared with the legend's unexpected result. Texas has become a liability in national politics in spite of the dominant roles of Texans
Lyndon Johnson, the Senate Majority Leader, and Sam Rayburn, Speaker of the House. In this case, however, "legend"
is an inexact word. A legend, as a rule, defies verification or
is estranged from fact. The source of the liability is all fact.
Horace Busby, at different times an aide to Texas Senators
Johnson and Price Daniel and a speech writer for Governor
Allan Shivers, wrote of the problem in the Houston *Post* in
1955:
   "National politics is where the Texas reputation has suf-
fered most severely. . . . Some Washington advisors re-

gard it as 'unsafe' for political figures to let it be known that they number Texans among their friends. . . . It may be unpleasant for some Texans to face, but a long list of positions of importance in national affairs could be drawn which, under prevailing conditions, no Texan is likely to fill simply because he is a Texan. Secretary of the Treasury, Secretary of the Interior, Federal Power Commissioner, and Commissioner of Education are typical posts where a nominee with a Texas background would have trouble being confirmed. . . . In Maine and Oregon, and points in between, 'anti-Texanism' was a winning issue [in congressional elections of 1954], and promises to whittle Texas down to size had charm for voters in such implausible places as Delaware and Rhode Island."

The causes of this animosity are complex, but the yeast is that a few Texas oilmen have tried to control elections in other states. Most of the state's oilmen give money to party campaign funds—Republican, usually. The money is spent as the party sees fit, and the use of this traditional means of political spending has not been criticized. Some of these oilmen, however, have contributed to candidates in state primary elections from coast to coast. State primaries are commonly thought of as the exclusive concern of the voters in each state. To put the shoe on the other foot, Texans would rage if Pennsylvania coal money, say, were used to influence their choice of a senator or congressman in the state's Democratic primaries. Indeed, the Dallas *News* and many other Texas newspapers denounced Walter Reuther, the CIO, and the United Auto Workers during the state's 1956 primary elections, claiming that out-of-state unions contributed to Ralph Yarborough's campaign for governor. The shoe *was* on the other foot that year, or so many of the newspapers said.

Dominating activities that created this aspect of the anti-Texas mood have been three oilmen: H. R. Cullen,[2] H. L. Hunt, and Clint W. Murchison. The three men, with little

[2]Cullen died, at age seventy-six, in July 1957, shortly after this book was completed.

help from others, have made Texas oil, and thus Texas, a national antipathy. They are among the wealthiest of the state's
oilmen, but except for their wealth, and the type of their political action, they are dissimilar. Of the three, mainly because
of his attempt to mold the mass mind through his Facts Forum, Hunt has been the most damaging and also the least re-
warding to the state; he has shown no interest in civic works
or philanthropy. Cullen's philanthropy, on the other hand,
has been enormous; he has benefited Houston and Texas with
his wealth, having built a large part of both a university and
an important medical center. Murchison is neutral between
the Hunt and Cullen extremes of citizenship; his philanthropies and civic works are trifles, but he has no Facts Forum,
either. Murchison, it seems, is content to increase his fortune
while humoring a fading penchant for the late Senator Mc-
Carthy's brand of Republicanism. His brilliance and fairness
in financial manipulation have become a contemporary American business legend, and oil, the beginning of his wealth,
was less than a fifth of it by the middle 1950s.

An illustration of the trio's type of political action—though
they are often involved in the same campaigns, the three
have always worked independently—was the campaign of one
Robert L. Jones, who opposed Senator Margaret Chase Smith
in Maine's Republican primary in 1954. As Jones was unem-
ployed at the time of the campaign, many in Maine specu-
lated as to the source of his campaign funds. It was said that
Jones was put in the race by Senator Joseph W. McCarthy, a
Republican of Wisconsin, and that some of Jones's money had
come from Senator McCarthy's friends in Texas. These
friends were several, but mainly they were Murchison, Hunt,
and Cullen. It will be shown later that Texans' attitude toward Senator McCarthy, when the latter was the central
American news figure, was not what it was reported to be,
but thus did Texas become a bone of contention in a Maine
primary election. Jones, who lost the election, said that his
campaign funds came from Maine alone. In affidavits made

later to the clerk of the House of Representatives by Cullen and Douglas B. Marshall, a Cullen son-in-law, the Texans said each had contributed $500 to Senator Smith's opponent.

Official records show that Cullen and members of his family contributed a total of $75,750 to political campaigns in 1952, making the Cullen family second only to the Rockefeller family, and followed by the Du Pont family, in political spending that year. Cullen himself spent $53,000. Among Murchison's contributions have been $10,000 to the campaign of John Marshall Butler, a Democrat of Maryland, who, with Senator McCarthy's aid, defeated Senator Millard E. Tydings in a notorious campaign in 1952. Murchison also gave $15,000 to the campaign of William A. Purtell, a McCarthy Republican of Connecticut, who defeated Senator William Benton. Senators Smith, Tydings, and Benton had it in common that Senator McCarthy opposed each. Hunt seems to be third in the amount of spending of this type, but he is alone in a different enterprise to achieve a similar end—a subject of Chapter 6.

The political ambitions and alarms of these three men have been largely responsible for what may be called a congressional legislative campaign against Texas. Oilmen are allowed to reduce their taxable income by 27½ per cent, up to 50 per cent of the net, before computing their income tax, because production of oil depletes the asset permanently. The aversion to Texas oil caused by Murchison, Hunt, and Cullen has been one of the main causes of proposed legislation to reduce the depletion allowance. Perhaps the trio would be less exposed had they been lucky enough to support only winners. Their candidates have lost more often than won, and there is no mystery about the disposition of a senator or representative who has been elected against the odds of money contributed by Texas oilmen.

The situation is no mystery to many members of the Texas congressional delegation, either, though not one has been even mildly critical of the oil industry. "Frankly, I don't know how much we can do about it [defense of states' rights]," Congressman Brady Gentry wrote to the East Texas Chamber of Commerce in 1955. "One of the contributing causes to the deplorable state in which we find ourselves . . . is caused by the tremendous publicity that has been given the 'big rich' of Texas. . . . If it still continues I feel certain that the time will come when the [oil] tax depletion will be greatly lessened, if not entirely eliminated." The congressman's conclusion was wise, though his reasoning was incomplete. The publicity has been a factor, though not an important one in this respect. Congressional opposition stimulated by the Murchison-Hunt-Cullen activities has not been directed solely at oil. In 1954, for example, Senator John Williams, a Republican of Delaware, asked the Senate to investigate "millionaire ranchers in Texas or other areas" who were accepting government drought relief. He mentioned $32,585 in drought relief to the King Ranch. The "King Ranch, a fabulously rich outfit in Texas, is now on relief," the senator said, adding that the drought-relief program "was never intended to be a relief measure for millionaires."

Texas is not braced to withstand its vulnerability to this trio of oilmen and a few others of the same stripe. The three men condemn the federal government for interfering with states' rights, yet their actions prove that individuals can abridge these rights, too. The important effect of their political action is not the eagerness with which part of Congress wants to discipline the oil industry but the severity with which many states have come to regard anything Texan. The attitude toward Texas of the states affected by this pressure on their primary elections is obvious—an off-with-its-head temper. It does not matter that most Texans are not in sympathy with the cause of the trouble. The Texas public, by and large, is unaware of the problem's dimension and is thus unable to react to it in any way. No metropolitan Texas newspaper has inquired into the trouble, or formed a judgment

about it, let alone condemned any aspect of a Texas dilemma
of more consequence, perhaps, than any other.

The increasing suspicion of Texas oil has made it seem to
others that oilmen are dishonest and crafty, yet the customs
and operations of independent oilmen are among their chief
merits. In 1948, when the "Big Rich" legend was beginning
to hold the public fancy, and the political action of Murchison, Hunt, and Cullen was incipient, *Fortune* magazine said
"the boom in the Southwest bears none of the shadows that
have darkened prosperity elsewhere. It is astonishingly free
of the gray and black markets, the chiseling, and the trading
in misery that have marred the recent accumulation of
quick wealth both in Europe and in the U.S."

"Have you noticed the way Texas millionaires are being
used as villainous types lately in fiction stories and in television dramas?" began a story in the Dallas *News* in 1955.
Many wealthy Texans, at any rate, seem to have noticed the
unpopularity of the Texas millionaire symbol. Evidence of
individual Texas wealth was being secluded by the middle
1950s, and there are fewer anecdotes to feed the "Big Rich"
legend. The legend has become obnoxious; being from Texas
has become a distinction for some to worry about. The president of an oil tool manufacturing firm in Texas, himself a
wealthy man, no longer lists his home address as Texas
when he registers at hotels in New York. He gives his home
address as New Orleans, where his firm has an office.

*And what is Texas? . . . This new republic . . . has been
called a Farce. But the tragic element prevails so much over
the farcical . . . that we cannot laugh at it.* William E.
Channing, 1837, *A Letter to the Hon. Henry Clay, on the Annexation of Texas to the United States.*

Texas is riches, but of all that Texas is, riches typify it
least. When W. L. Moody, Jr., died in 1954, his fortune was
more than four hundred million dollars (and thus, inciden-

tally, the largest Texas fortune was made with little help from oil). In 1955, when one of Moody's former secretaries died, a spinster named Marguerite Collins, *she* left more than two million dollars. Both she and Moody were eighty-nine when they died, and in their wills both cut off members of their families with $1.00—Moody his only living son and Miss Collins her nine blood relatives. Mrs. Clark W. Thompson, the wife of a Texas congressman and one of Moody's two daughters, described her share of the inheritance as "a little driblet of two hundred thousand dollars," which is conceivably a fair appraisal when compared with a treasure of four hundred million dollars. The Moody-Collins story is "Big Rich" enough, but the state's millionaire legends are Sunday-supplement Texas. They are typical of Texas as they are of New York and Pennsylvania, which have more millionaires than Texas but which have had them for decades instead of years.

Texas is not typed by its millionaire legends but by habits and projects, by characteristic day-to-day activities, and by expressions of individuality which are obscured by the pungence, the attractiveness of the "Big Rich" lore. The state is in focus in the fetes of its people: the Dogwood Festival at Woodville, Old Maids' Day at Denton, the Cowboys' Christmas Ball at Anson, Charro Days at Brownsville, the Tomato Tom-Tom Festival at Yoakum, the Turkey Trot at Cuero, the National Cow Calling Contest at Miami, the Rose Festival at Tyler, the Spinach Festival at Crystal City, the Fiesta de San Jacinto at San Antonio, the Strawberry Festival at Poteet, Buccaneer Days at Corpus Christi, the State Fair at Dallas, the Rattlesnake Derby at McCamey, the Sidewalk Cattlemen's Association at Madisonville, *Cinco de Mayo,* Juneteenth, the Blackberry Festival at Lindale, the Easter Fires in the Fredericksburg hills, the *Gebirgsfest* in the Hill Country, the East Texas Old Fiddlers' Contest at Athens, Mother-in-Law Day at Amarillo, the fish fry of the Fraternity of the White Herons at Anahuac, the Shrimp-O-Ree at Aransas Pass, Splash Day at Galveston, fat stock shows at Houston, Fort

Worth, San Antonio, and smaller cities. Festivals for forests, yams, cantaloupes, and grapes.

Texas is less "Big Rich" than it is the custom of black-bordered handbills on the streets of small towns when an old resident dies, or the tolling of church bells to indicate a dead person's age. Revival meetings, rodeos, barbecues, and square dancing are more of Texas than millionaires are. Drought and irrigation, wetbacks and border patrols, Fort Sam Houston and Randolph Field, black-eyed peas and corn bread, tamales and chili, deep-sea fishing and football, "Watch for Livestock" highway signs—those are Texas.

The House of Representatives—
Texas State Capitol

4 "Beautiful, Beautiful Texas"

In no other American state has the liberal-conservative issue
been so intensified, since 1946, as in Texas. "Conservative,"
"reactionary," and "right wing" will be made synonymous
and called "conservative" in this book; "liberal," "progressive,"
and "left wing" will be made synonymous and called "liberal."
"Conservative" will be taken to mean opposition to the administrations of Franklin Roosevelt and Harry S. Truman,
plus the hope of restoring certain values which dominated
Texas before the Second World War. "Liberal" will be taken
to mean approval of the Roosevelt-Truman administrations,
plus the hope of speeding the acceptance of certain values
which are likely to dominate the state in good time.

The state has been bullied by its political extremes. It has
seemed that no one in Texas with the gift of articulateness is
familiar with the uses of compromise, or favors an issue of

fact if one of emotion can be found, or respects any shade of
political thought that is not at one extreme or the other. The
conservative mind—in Texas a meringue of oil, rural, and Republican ideologies—governs Texas. The liberal mind—a less
crusty meringue of oil-be-damned, urban, and Democratic
ideologies—may possibly begin governing Texas in the 1960s.
It does not seem to be more prepared to do so with wisdom
than the conservatives are doing it. The liberals need a giant;
the conservatives, overwhelming more than governing Texas,
could win with a midget.

For four years, beginning in 1890, the people of Texas were
governed by James Stephen Hogg, a man of integrity, vision,
and action—a man whose heart and mind were always in liaison with each other. Hogg was the great governor of modern Texas history. With few exceptions since Hogg, and with
none since W. Lee O'Daniel took office in 1939, the conservative mind has governed Texas. Texas conservatives have been
successful in spite of generally mediocre candidates. The liberals have failed to be successful because of generally mediocre candidates and a want of discipline, even of unity, among
large groups of voters whose economic interests cause the
same groups in the North to support liberal candidates. Effective politics is said to be made of boldness and craftiness
in mysterious proportions. Texas liberals seem not to have
divined the proportions, possibly because they have been
unable to get the experience of office-holding.

The Dallas *News* is the chief spokesman for conservatives. The *Texas Observer*, a weekly newspaper published
at Austin, is the only newspaper-spokesman for liberals. By
reading both papers, but not by reading one or the other,
a Texan may learn what is going on in politics. Most of the
state's metropolitan newspapers are of the same mind as the
News. The fault of the Texas press is not its conservatism but
that as a rule it masks the essence of issues that do not dove-
tail with the theories and goals of the property class. The
want of a matured, inquisitive press—a deficiency that is com-

mon to many states, especially in the West—has made possible
Texas politics' preoccupations with oil and money rather than
government and people. All that good government requires
is an enlightened press.

Despite the extravagance of magazine and newspaper reports about the state, Texans are similar to the newer-model
Americans everywhere. There is the difference, however, that
broader opportunity has enlarged those traits which are
common to areas of new chances and methods. The traits are
characteristic of frontiers, where goals are personal rather
than community—the acquisition of money and identity to
the exclusion of aesthetics and reforms. A frontier in spirit
need not have the rusticity of a Western movie; it can
have skyscrapers and symphony orchestras. The frontier instinct is conservative, not liberal. Thus Texans have been tol-
erant of people but not of ideas, and thus Texas liberals have
not coalesced with the speed that immigration statistics and
urban growth would seem to have caused. Not all the liberal
element has been liberal.

Though Texas is said to be a Democratic state, which it has
been through most of its history, there has been some question
about it since 1944, when the Texas Regulars organized to
defy the New Deal. The Regulars were a group of extreme
conservatives who planned in vain to disfranchise Texas Democrats by diverting the state's Democratic electoral vote to
the Republican candidates. Since 1952, when Governor Allan
Shivers led the state in delivering the nation's sixth largest
electoral vote to the Republican party, the Texas political
complexion has eluded definition. Writing in the *Reporter*
magazine in December 1955, Douglass Cater said the state's
multiparty politics "almost rivals that of France in its com-
plexity." There are other similarities in the politics of Texas
and France, but the essence of Texas politics has come to be
this: Texas liberals want the Democratic party of Texas to
conform to the national party; conservatives want the national

party to conform to their branch of the Democratic party in Texas, which is Republican in principle.

Texas has been called Democratic in state politics and Republican in national politics since 1952. So long as Texas conservatives are in power, that is a distinction without a difference. In 1952 Texas was either a no-party state or a four-party state—Texas Democrats and national Democrats, Taft Republicans and Eisenhower Republicans, though the first and last were virtually the same. In 1951 the Austin *American* said there were four divisions of the Texas Democratic party alone—Truman Democrats, Anti-Truman Democrats, Fence-Jumping Democrats, and Anti-Democrats.

The several groups under Governor Shivers's leadership were known as Shivercrats or Donkephants. Their motif was "Principle Before Party," the governor taking the position that the Democratic party of Texas and that of the nation were unrelated, as indeed they were from the Shivers point of view. In a letter to the Harris County Democratic Club, in April 1952, in which he capitalized all the letters of the word "Texas" in each reference, Shivers explained himself: "I consider myself a member of the Democratic Party of TEXAS and an office-holder in the Democratic Party of TEXAS, and will be a candidate for nomination as governor of the Democratic Party of TEXAS. I will follow the instructions of the majority of the Democrats of TEXAS."

With Governor Shivers and most other Texas Democratic officeholders of importance supporting the Republican candidate for President, Texas Democrats who favored the Democratic candidate were obliged to take the name of Loyal Democrats. The general election of November 1952 showed there were 133,650 fewer of the Loyalists than of the Shivercrats; Dwight Eisenhower got 1,102,878 votes and Adlai Stevenson 969,228.

Lynn Landrum, a Dallas *News* columnist and editorial writer, suggested a solution to the anomalies of Texas politics. "We shall have to build our own party," he wrote in 1952.

"The parties we now have are all sore backs and no brains." His suggestion was not acted upon, and the one change of substance in Texas politics between the presidential elections of 1952 and 1956 was the growth of liberal influence. In 1954, however, Landrum explained the distinction of Texas politics: "Long ago Texans gave up trying to riddle out what is the Democratic party and fell hilariously to cutting each other's throats to determine by force and arms who is the Democratic party." Two years earlier he had written, "We Texans simply aren't sensible about our politics. We have quit shooting out the lights in the saloons and we have quit riding Old Paint into the lobby of the hotel. But what fools we make of ourselves in election year!"

We have only two or three laws [in Texas], such as against murder before witnesses and being caught stealing horses, and voting the Republican ticket.   O. Henry, when he was a Texas newspaperman in the 1890s.

"In Texas the vague outlines of a politics are emerging in which irrelevancies are pushed into the background and people divide broadly along liberal and conservative lines," V. O. Key, Jr., wrote in *Southern Politics,* an important book on the subject, published in 1949. "A modified class politics seems to be evolving, not primarily because of an upthrust of the masses that compels men of substance to unite in self-defense, but because of the personal insecurity of men suddenly made rich who are fearful lest they lose their wealth. . . . Imbued with a faith in individual self-reliance and unschooled in social responsibilities of wealth, many of these men have been more sensitive than a Pennsylvania manufacturer to the policies of the Roosevelt and Truman Administrations."

The argument that Texas millionaires are a novelty as to the source of their fears of the New and Fair Deals has come to be commonplace in explaining Texas conservatives. The inference is that the motive for conservatism in other states is different and, compared with that in Texas, noble. Except as the argument applies to being "unschooled in social responsibilities of wealth,"[1] however, the argument has become a cliché, a bridge for getting onto other ground with convenience. Apprehension of the central government's power is known in the other forty-seven states, and the type of alarm that gave short life to the Texas Regulars was similar to that which created the South's Dixiecrat maneuver of 1948—the race question alone did not account for the Southern revolt —and the Old Guard of the Republican party in the North.

The motives for fear and defiance of the Roosevelt and Truman theories of government, except for the principle of racial integration, are fairly uniform among conservatives throughout America. The logic of a conservative millionaire in Maine, Oregon, and Texas, say, is such that it would be difficult to discover which was which if all three philosophies were printed side by side without identification. An editorial in the Dallas *News* in August 1956 and an excerpt from Lynn Landrum's column three months later may be said to summarize the views of Texas conservatives. Landrum wrote: "Most of the South is solid for a Democratic Party which doesn't exist any more. Franklin Roosevelt killed that Democratic Party deader than the celluloid collar and arm garters for shirtsleeves. Some of the South never did get to the funeral and some don't know yet of the demise." The editorial said: "The Democratic Party is still the party of Franklin Roosevelt and Harry Truman, of Harry Hopkins and Lee Pressman. That it is now the party of Hubert Hum-

[1]One form of social responsibility in which wealthy Texans excel, however, is philanthropy—endowing universities, art museums, churches, and foundations whose aims are sociological, scientific, agricultural, and municipal researches. Such other spending for the public good as underwriting the cost of books and art portfolios and buying works of art for public institutions is a commonplace of the state's philanthropies. Largely a result of oil fortunes, philanthropy is a subject of Chapter 6.

phrey and Walter Reuther, of Paul Butler and Thurgood
Marshall, alters the situation no whit. . . . But [Adlai]
Stevenson is not going to offend the NAACP or the AFL-CIO
or the UMW. To heck with principles, what this party needs
is votes!" Thus the position of the state's conservatives: opposition to the national Democratic party, opposition to
organized labor, and opposition to racial integration. Only
the latter issue is not a common denominator of American
conservatism.

The rise of a class politics in Texas has been aggravated
in the years since Key's book was written. Class against class:
statements by the two gubernatorial candidates in the second
Democratic primary election of 1956 suggested that the election would determine whether Texas was to be governed by
the National Association for the Advancement of Colored
People and the head of the United Automobile Workers in
Detroit or the "Texas Association for the Advancement of
Millionaires." The candidates were United States Senator
Price Daniel, who did not resign from that office to run for
governor, and Ralph Yarborough, who had been defeated by
Allan Shivers in the governor's races of 1952 and 1954. Senator Daniel, who supported President Eisenhower in 1952,
was the conservative candidate; Yarborough, who supported
Adlai Stevenson, was the liberal. Senator Daniel often gave
the impression that his opponent was not Yarborough but
Walter Reuther, the Detroit union leader. Yarborough made
no bones about the identity of his opponent, but he implied
that the senator was a toy belonging to unnamed oil millionaires. Quotations from their campaign speeches show how
the rich man and the worker, plus the Negro, were pitted
against each other.

Daniel, August 18, speaking at Pittsburg and other villages
in northeast Texas: "Walter Reuther and the National Association for the Advancement of Colored People are attempt-
ing to dictate to the people of Texas how they should vote."

Yarborough, in several talks late in the campaign: "The

TAAM—the Texas Association for the Advancement of Millionaires—is the backbone of my opponent's campaign."

Daniel, July 27, in a television talk the day before the first primary election, asked Texans to vote for him instead of "turning the state capitol into a way station for Reuther and the NAACP."

Yarborough, August 15, at Austin: "They tell me that the big boys have outbigged themselves this time in their lavish display of spending money."

Daniel, August 7, at Longview: "Walter Reuther has been fighting Texas and he has been fighting me for years. He fought me on the tidelands issue and now he has paid organizers in Texas trying to block my election as governor."

Yarborough, August 11, at Lufkin: "Shivers and Daniel are representatives of the monopolistic big-business Republicans [who are] scheming to control the [Texas] government by infiltration."

Daniel, August 22, at Galveston, asked his campaign workers to assure that the margin of his "victory will be loud enough so that Walter Reuther will hear it in Detroit and the NAACP will hear it in New York." (Daniel, however, may be said to have won honors in felicity. To campaign workers he once said, "Don't do anything that will bring heartache to my opponent's wife and son." Later, at a rally in a small town, he said, "This has been a family campaign. My wife and children are home washing so they will have enough clean clothes to wear next week.")

Yarborough, August 26 (the day after the election, when the result was still in doubt), said the people had "the power of all the wealth of Texas arrayed against them" and "all the large daily newspapers in all the cities arrayed against them . . ."

There was no question about Yarborough's comment on the newspapers' editorial support of the senator. No metropolitan daily newspaper endorsed Yarborough's candidacy, which was one of several indications that the political mood of the majority of Texans was coming to be at odds with that of the newspapers. Daniel, whose attempt to make Walter Reuther an issue in a Texas election included frequent showings of a photograph of Reuther giving a $75,000 check to officials of the N.A.A.C.P., was elected by a majority of three thousand out of a total of 1,392,703 votes. The senator and his supporters were shocked at the narrowness of his victory. He led five other candidates in the first primary, when he got 165,498 more votes than Yarborough, the second high man. "Senator Daniel's lead [in the second primary election] is expected to be between 175,000 and 200,000 votes over Mr. Yarborough," the *Christian Science Monitor* reported three weeks before the election, and the *Monitor's* estimate was that of most Texans. Conceivably the liberals might have won their first important election with a giant. The state's gubernatorial elections are hungry for giants—for liberal and conservative candidates with the gift of altruism and the talent to make the gift effective.

You have only three friends in the world—God Almighty, Sears-Roebuck, and Jim Ferguson. James E. Ferguson, rural demagogue and Texas governor who was impeached in 1918 but regained the office, in effect, when his wife was twice elected governor.

The annual gridiron show of the Women's National Press Club, performed before President and Mrs. Eisenhower in 1954, included a skit in which Texas millionaires were caricatured. The members of a quartet in the skit were identified as Clint W. Murchison, Sid W. Richardson, H. R. Cullen, and H. L. Hunt. At one point "Murchison" and "Richardson" sang:

> They [Texas millionaires] like to hunt for Commies
>   And pinks of every hue,
> But if they can't find Commies,
>   Plain liberals will do.

The character of Texas politics was transformed with a vim between the time of the duet in Washington and the popularity of a different type of song, composed by W. Lee O'Daniel as an aid to selling his flour, in the 1930s. The first line of O'Daniel's song—sung by thousands of Texans until the Second World War—was "Beautiful, beautiful Texas"; the last lines were:

> So let us all smile, for life is worth while
> When we live in this beautiful state.

The Great Depression had begun to melt by 1938, when "Beautiful Texas" was O'Daniel's campaign song. American liberalism was losing the nearly unanimous appeal it had had a few years earlier. O'Daniel succeeded James V. Allred, a liberal, as governor in January 1939. From that day through the date of this book Texas has had a succession of conservative governors who have been at odds with the Democratic party's leadership in Washington. Life in "Beautiful, beautiful Texas" has become more and more worth one's while, but the increasing savageness of Texas politics has caused smiles to be rationed. Neither good humor nor the complacency of O'Daniel's song has been in the air since O'Daniel's first term as governor.

Businessmen, industrialists, and men of wealth have alone commanded Texas. Men whose luster is the intellect have had virtually no share in Texas government. "It [Texas] is basically distrustful of the intelligentsia in matters of government," Lynn Landrum wrote in the Dallas *News* in 1956. Texas conservatism, like the New Deal, was extended to twenty years of power when Price Daniel was elected governor in 1956. Also like the New Deal, Texas conservatism was weakened by scandals, venality, and, until the narrowness of its victory in 1956, a disposition to regard itself as permanent. The state's conservatism may in some ways have made a hostage of the state's future, as is suggested by the total effect of the following profiles of excess:

§ A chart of the voting records of Southern Democratic senators in the sessions between 1933 and 1945, made by Dr. Key in *Southern Politics*, shows O'Daniel as the most Republican of Southern Democrats—more Republican, even, than most Republicans. In 1954 Governor Allan Shivers proposed the death penalty for anyone in Texas convicted of being a member of the Communist party. (In this, but in few other things, the Dallas *News* and the Houston *Post* opposed Shivers.) Two organizations, Democrats Opposed to Socialism and the Anti-New Deal League of Texas, were formed in the First Congressional District, in 1952, in an attempt to defeat Representative Wright Patman, who had defended the Truman administration. In 1955 State Representative Joe Pyle, of Fort Worth, proposed an amendment to the Constitution of the United States that would have given the government three years to get out of any business not authorized by the Constitution, including the Federal Housing Authority.

§ A testimonial to the efficiency of Texas conservatives was given by Robert Oliver, legislative director of the CIO, in 1955. In a speech before a convention of the Texas State CIO Council, Oliver called Texas labor laws "the worst in the nation." The laws to which he referred were passed between 1941 and 1955. The closed shop is banned in Texas. Picketing for union recognition is banned unless the union can prove that it represents a majority of employees. A striker who uses force to prevent a strikebreaker from entering a plant is subject to a two-year penitentiary sentence, but the law does not affect strikebreakers who use force and does not limit the activities of employers. In 1952 Grady Ivey, an AFL ironworker and the father of two children, was sentenced to a year in the penitentiary for fighting near a Dallas picket line. He went to prison on Thanksgiving Day that year and was released the following March. Had a non-union man been involved, the offense would have been a misdemeanor with a fine of $5.00 to $25.

§ Labor unions may not contribute to political campaigns; employers are not so affected. Union locals must submit annual financial statements to the Texas secretary of state. Picketing may not be done by groups of more than two, each group must be at least fifty feet from another, and no more than two pickets may be within fifty feet of the entrance to a plant. Unemployment compensation is denied to union members who are laid off at a subsidiary plant because of a strike at a parent plant, but non-union workers may be compensated. The latter law grew out of a situation at the Dallas plant of the Ford Motor Company when men were laid off because of a parts shortage caused by a strike at a different Ford plant. The restriction of organized labor in Texas was such that in 1952 a Texas chamber of commerce published a booklet to show why Texas was a desirable place for industry. The single subject of the booklet was eleven Texas labor laws.

§ In 1956 the Paul Carrington Chapter of the Sons of the American Revolution, in Houston, sent 10,911 copies of a book by John T. Flynn, *The Decline of the American Republic*, to governors and legislators of the forty-eight states, congressmen, editors, educators, and businessmen. The chapter also sent 7500 copies of Fulton Lewis, Jr.'s, *The Fund of the Republic* to libraries throughout America. Flynn and Lewis won their distinctions as anti-New Deal writers. The books were bought by H. R. Cullen, a member of the chapter. Distribution on such a scale of the Flynn and Lewis books may be thought of as a peculiarity of Texas conservatives, but the national society of the Sons of the American Revolution thought well of it, giving the Houston chapter the President General Trophy. The basis of the award—the highest the national society could bestow on one of its chapters—was the distribution of the Flynn book.

§ A chrestomathy of quotations from H. R. Cullen's speeches, public statements, and interviews with the press is as descriptive of the thinking of Texas conservatives as are editorials in the Dallas *News*. Cullen's quotations are used as illustrations rather than those, say, of Hunt or Murchison because Cullen is the Texas millionaire with the least inclination to conceal his opinions. His condemnations, his approvals, even his views on manners and morals, health and religion, are willingly disseminated.

§ "But suppose my grandfather or your grandfather of the Texas Republic should return [today] and stay awhile with us. . . . I've wondered what he would say after having . . . to support the most extravagant and wasteful government on the face of the earth, in all its grand schemes of bottle-feeding the voting population of this country from the cradle to the grave, and grub-staking the rest of the world. After a taste of that, I wonder if our grandfathers wouldn't decide it was time for another Texas Declaration of Independence. And by the time he put up with a few years of it, he might be in favor of another Texas revolution. . . . Really, those early Texans fought for less than we are tolerating today." From a speech at the San Jacinto Monument on San Jacinto Day 1949.

§ The tidelands controversy is more important than "national politics, the budget, our international commitments— even the tragedy of [war in] Korea." From a letter to all United States senators, February 1952.

§ "The kind of reception he [President Eisenhower] gave a committee of three women, representing a patriotic organization fighting for the Bricker amendment, shows that the pressure he is under is having an ill effect on his nerves." From a letter to United States Senators William F. Knowland, Lyndon B. Johnson, John W. Bricker, and Walter F. George, February 1954.

§ "I told them . . . that I thought Senator McCarthy is the greatest man in America." From a press interview after two University of Texas students delivered a student petition asking Cullen to reconsider his invitation to Senator Joseph W. McCarthy to speak at the 118th anniversary celebration of the Battle of San Jacinto, April 1954.

§ "In order to hold the fort against socialism . . . the true Democrats of the South must again join with the right-thinking Republicans of the North and re-elect President Eisenhower." From a public statement, May 1956.

§ ". . . every member of the Supreme Court could be impeached. And I say they should be, for the Supreme Court's usurpation of the power to legislate . . . smacks of fascism, nazism, and communism." From a speech to graduates of the South Texas College of Law and Commerce, June 1956.[2]

The evidence above—the Republican voting record of Democrat O'Daniel through the Cullen quotations—is that the conservative mind in Texas and that of the Republican Old Guard in the North are virtually identical. And the evidence of all this chapter has been that Texas conservatives, unlike the hard-shell Republicans of the North, have succeeded. Beginning with the Jester-Rainey campaign for governor, in 1946, however, liberals became a nuisance to conservatives. By the end of the next decade liberalism had become a competitor of endurance and growing power. The latter part of Chapter 10, a comparative essay on Dallas and Houston, contrasts the voting record of the most conservative of Texas cities with that of the most nearly liberal. Houston's suggestion of non-conformity is a sign of the rise of liberal influence in Texas, but there are more signs than that.

Texas has two state Democratic conventions in presidential election years. Delegates to the one in May 1956, at Dallas, approved an anti-poll-tax resolution. It was an action without effect, but it was a sign of emerging liberal principles. Earlier in May, at more than five thousand precinct conventions throughout the state, Texas Democrats gave Governor Allan Shivers the first defeat of his political career. Party leadership was transferred from Shivers to Senator Lyndon Johnson, who is thought of as a liberal only in comparison with Shivers. It was a setback of consequence to Shivers, meaning that for once a governor did not control the state's delegation to the national Democratic convention. It was thought that

[2]Not all of Cullen's public statements are conservative. In 1952, speaking at ground-breaking ceremonies for an Episcopal church in Houston, he made a plea for a universal church.

"Religious people of the world could face their common enemies of atheism and communism with all their strength if they were united," he said. In 1956 he sent telegrams to Democratic and Republican congressional leaders asking them to urge businessmen to increase their contributions to the nation's schools and hospitals.

Shivers was paying the price of his defection to the Republicans in 1952, yet the following November Texans gave President Eisenhower a larger majority than they did four years earlier.

A man of adroitness and political competence, Allan Shivers was governor of Texas for seven and a half years—longer than anyone else. No one since Hogg, well over half a century earlier, formed the state in the mold of his own leadership as Shivers did. But Shivers was governor too long for his own good, and the conviction grows that he was governor too long for the state's good. Texas was punished by the most pernicious scandals in its history, since Reconstruction, in the last years of Shivers's terms. Many of the scandals involved men appointed by Governor Shivers, and their effects could have been reduced had the governor acted with determination. Not only was he repudiated at the May convention, but conservatives of his choice were ousted from both National Democratic Committee posts. The new National Democratic Committeewoman, Mrs. R. D. Randolph, an heir to an East Texas lumber fortune, is another sign that liberalism is taking effect, however tenuous that effect may prove to be. She won the post in spite of determined opposition by Senator Johnson, who favored a conservative.

Once again the Democratic party has saved the nation from Texas. Former United States Senator Tom Connally, of Texas, quoted by the *Texas Observer*, when the Texas delegation at the National Democratic Convention of 1956 voted without exception for candidates who were not nominated.

Sometimes it looks in Texas as if it would be easier to integrate white folks and black folks than it would be to integrate Texas Democrats. Lynn Landrum, 1956, Dallas *News.*

Any definition of Texas politics is imperfect. The amorphousness of its politics is another result of the state's great area and diversity. A politics appealing to the Border region may offend the Great Plains area, hundreds of miles to the north. El Paso is not concerned with the dreams of Orange, nearly nine hundred miles to the east. Years of striving for a politics of state-wide unity has deformed the state's political character. Politicians who manage to umbrella the state's vote often have a good deal in common with Jack of the nursery rhyme—"Jack be nimble, Jack be quick."

The newer leadership of Senator Johnson has been an enigma at best. Politically, the senator has a split personality. In Washington he is a conservative liberal. In Texas he is a conservative who is sympathetic with the liberals when it suits his purpose. He won his first election to the Senate, in 1948, by a margin of 87 votes out of a total of 988,295, one of the closest elections in American history. He has been an exception to the rule of Texas congressmen, having been a national more than a regional or state leader. He has been the Great Conciliator of the Senate, a moderate on every issue but oil and civil rights. He is a politician of skill whose success may be attributed to his artfulness in finding the common denominator of party accord in the Senate. He has won the respect, or at any rate the sympathy, of the Senate and a gravity of mixed emotions in Texas. That he is no great shakes at pulling Texas Democracy back toward national Democracy is owing to the opportunism and expediency which are large in his character. The senator's tenuous leadership of Texas Democrats is something of a paradox. It is an article of faith among both liberals and conservatives that no good can come of his leadership. Each side feels that the senator will bear watching, much as a chained mastiff keeps an eye on a postman who enters the yard.

Senator Johnson is teamed in his leadership of both the state and national Democratic parties with another Texan, Sam Rayburn, who has been Speaker of the House of Representatives longer than any other man in history. Mr. Sam is made of sternness, pragmatism, rural ideology, and a degree of party discipline that seems eccentric to a state of Texas's mood. Speaker Rayburn has been a liberal in Washington and, as a rule, a model of discretion in Texas. In 1956, however, his anger erupted at the likelihood that his state would again favor Dwight Eisenhower: "There are too many big-rich oil men there, and too many fat-cat newspapers, all of them Republican." He has become a political figure of national dimension through skill, instinct, and representation of a rotten borough—one of the most thinly populated congressional districts in the United States. The Dallas *News*, Speaker Rayburn's nemesis, has long yearned to have his district reapportioned into the conservative predictability of east Dallas.

The outcome of the state Democratic convention of September 1956 was an instance of the Johnson-Rayburn expediency. When the liberals were in danger of getting the upper hand, Senator Johnson and Speaker Rayburn, who are thought to represent the liberal mind in national politics, sided with Price Daniel, leader of the conservatives. The convention's distinction was that it multiplied the uses of adversity. "It must be apparent even to the most Pollyanna-minded apostle of harmony that when the delegates streamed out of the convention hall [in Fort Worth] after 14 hours of wrangling the Texas Democratic Party was split as widely as it has ever been in its history," the Houston *Post* said in an editorial. Senator Daniel, then governor-elect but for the formality of the general election in November, was booed with such vigor that he made his speech with difficulty. The liberals booed Daniel, the conservatives booed Speaker Rayburn, and both sides pitched in to boo Senator Johnson. Mrs. Randolph, though one of the highest officers in the state party, was barred from the convention because she was a member of the liberal delegation from Houston, which was thrown out of the convention. The Houston liberals were barred when the city's conservatives were permitted to vote on which group would be seated. Such a novelty is second to none in assuring conservative dominance.

Even with such odds, however, the conservatives cornered the convention by the skin of their teeth, managing a majority

of 137 out of 1875 votes. William H. Gardner, writing in the
Post, felt that the convention may have been a draw. "To illustrate the confusion, nobody seems to be exactly sure who
won," he wrote. A spokesman for the conservatives said the
liberals won because a few labor leaders were named to the
State Democratic Executive Committee. This conclusion,
Gardner said, was apparently based on the theory that the
only safe majority for conservatives is 100 per cent. In any
event, the conclusion of the *Post* editorial was a prophecy:
"The convention may have pointed up more clearly than ever
before that the Democratic Party [in Texas] has become so
divergent in its makeup, so far apart in its political extremities, that it is no longer possible for everybody to crowd under the same tent."

In 1956, for the third time in less than thirty years, Texas
voted Republican, giving President Eisenhower a majority of
220,661 compared with one of 133,650 four years earlier. Yet
in 1956 Governor Shivers and W. Lee O'Daniel were virtually
alone among the state's Democratic notables in supporting
the President. Price Daniel supported Adlai Stevenson this
time, but he did so from the necessity of politics caused by
the urgency of liberal demands. In April 1957 Ralph Yarborough was elected to fill the unexpired twenty months of
Daniel's term in the Senate, but his election did not signify
that the state had yet turned its back on conservatism. Yarborough got 38 per cent of nearly a million votes for twenty-
two candidates, most of whom were conservatives. He ran
well ahead of Congressman Martin Dies and a strong Republican contender, Thad Hutcheson. "Texas conservatives
elected Ralph Yarborough," the Dallas *News* said in an editorial. The point of the editorial was that the conservative
vote was split by the prevalence of conservative candidates.

The contrast of rising liberalism and the Eisenhower victo-
ries raises a number of questions. Will Texas Democrats who
supported President Eisenhower rue the day? Will Texas become Republican? Will the influence of the newer industrial

class return the state to the Democratic party? The conclusion of this book is that of the Houston *Post* editorial quoted above —that sooner or later *two* tents will have to be pitched—and of William G. Carleton, writing in *Harper's* in 1955: "The truth is that Texas . . . has developed a fairly healthy political life under its own private brand. It has gone farther than any other Southern state in building a two-party system within the ancient framework of the Democratic party. The very aggressiveness of the conservatives has sharpened the issues and called forth bold counteraction by the liberals. . . . Ultimately it seems inevitable that the industrialization of Texas . . . will result in a considerable strengthening of the liberal and pro-labor elements."

In the long run the state's conservatives will be forced to take refuge in Old Guard Republicanism. They were disillusioned with President Eisenhower by 1957, when the state's Republican party was hard put to raise enough money to pay the debts of its 1956 campaign. The state's millionaires were divided about 80–20 in their support of Eisenhower and Stevenson in 1956, a proportion that would apply to millionaires generally. But the 80 per cent is coming to suspect the President. His appointment of Earl Warren as Chief Justice of the Supreme Court, his opposition to the Bricker Amendment, his veto of the Harris-Fulbright bill, and his approval of increased Social Security benefits have dismayed the conservatives' backbone of wealth.

The liberals' road is uphill all the way. More than a thousand of them met in Austin, in May 1957, to organize a group, called Democrats of Texas, with the aim of getting party control from conservatives. Mrs. Randolph, the National Committeewoman, was named chairman of the group's executive committee and Senator Yarborough was a speaker, but no other leading political figure would have anything to do with the convention. The State Democratic Executive Committee, in a newsletter a month later, scorned the meeting as a "labor-dominated convention" and a "left-wing movement."

Reprisals against D.O.T. members were swift. In July, Dr. Byron R. Abernethy, a professor at Texas Technological College who had been the convention's keynoter, paid for his liberalism when he was discharged by the college's board of directors. His nemesis was J. Evetts Haley, a member of the board, director of the college's Institute of Americanism, and state organizer for the For America group. A candidate for governor on a white-supremacy platform in 1956, Haley did not resign from the board when he was in politics but later seems to have reasoned that such freedom was in poor taste for a liberal. Calling the board into executive, or closed, session, Haley saw to the discharge of Dr. Abernethy and Dr. Herbert M. Greenberg, a blind assistant professor, who had publicly favored racial integration in the schools. At the same time Haley persuaded the board to abolish the college's adult-education program, apparently because it was sponsored by the Ford Foundation. In Texas the liberals' road is not only uphill but risky.

Few Texans could be called independent politically. Even trivialities of the state's politics are fraught with danger, being as contentious as larger issues in the fury of the liberal-conservative debate. Rural Texas and conservative urban elements have combined to resist change in a swiftly changing state. But the big cities are coming to contain a majority of the votes—a development that came to the North years earlier—and an eventual balance in the state's political mood seems certain. "In one of the most significant changes in Dixie politics, Lone Star State Democrats have revamped their party into an organization more nearly resembling the big-city-dominated Democratic parties of the North and East," Bicknell Eubanks wrote in the *Christian Science Monitor* after the state's Democratic convention of May 1956. "It was a 180-degree turn from conservatism to liberalism." The conclusion seems premature for long-range purposes, but Texas is destined to lose its distinction of being a no-party state and return to national Democracy.

II OIL

OFFSHORE OIL OPERATION · TEXAS COAST

Cotton Stripping—Scurry County

5 Virtue's Baggage

Late in 1956 the FBI disclosed the theft of more than a million dollars' worth of oil-survey maps from the Gulf Oil Corporation. The maps were Gulf's evidence of undiscovered oil —buried-treasure maps, an oil company's hope chest. Later, announcing that it would sue anyone making use of the stolen maps, Gulf compared such use to "stealing another man's wife." The harvest of no other natural resource, save possibly gold itself, arouses such emotion. Oil has the power to enrich more swiftly and abundantly than anything but dreams, to which its triumphs often bear a resemblance.

Wildcatting success—finding oil where it is not known to exist—infects the oil business with its lure: the chance of great riches in the instant. Success may spring a man from hope to millionaire, or from millionaire to dream-wealth's authority. But another aspect of oil is of greater importance to its attraction: it enriches not a few but many. One oil well may turn the trick for a man, and there are more oil wells than forests or coal mines or gold, copper, or uranium lodes, more than all the others together. Twenty thousand oil and gas wells were completed in Texas in 1954. Perhaps half of them *could* have made new millionaires, as some wells did.

The last sentence needs a tedious explanation. Of the 20,123 wells completed in Texas in 1954, 13,150, or 65 per cent, produced varying amounts of oil and gas; 6973 were dry holes—failures. The majority of the successes were by no means wildcats; they did not create thirteen thousand new millionaires. Many were drilled by major oil companies and individuals in areas where the presence of oil was already proven. Wildcat successes may not have been more than 10 per cent of the thirteen thousand, and major companies as well as individuals drill wildcat wells. The cost—losses—of the 6973 failures was at least $244,000,000, based on a conservative average of $35,000 a well. Fortunes lost in dry holes are camouflaged by the color of wildcat successes.

One oil well: George W. Strake, born in St. Louis, Missouri, in 1894 and educated at St. Louis University, went to work for the Gulf Oil Corporation in Mexico after the First World War. Leaving Gulf later, he stayed in Mexico as a lease buyer and driller until 1925, when he had made nearly a quarter of a million dollars. He went to Cuba, lost most of his money in an automobile agency, and moved to Houston in 1927. By the time the Great Depression had dropped the price of oil to a few cents a barrel Strake had become convinced that there was oil near Conroe, a town thirty-five miles north of Houston, and he started buying oil leases in the area. This seemed nonsense, or eccentricity, to the major companies and independent oilmen, and none would hazard any money on Strake's hope. In despair, he tried to persuade members of Houston's Elks Club to invest in the well, promising to enrich them all, but at last he had to drill it alone. On December 13, 1931, he brought in a gas well of modest production, and six months later he struck oil with his second well. He had discovered the Conroe Field, third largest in the nation, in which he owned a third of the acreage. His first lease trade in the field brought him $5,000,000 in 1932. With depression dollars' command, he was one of the richest men in the world.

It is said that Strake later set a price on other acreage in the field—and a deadline for major companies to meet it. Each day for three days a company was late in agreeing to buy the leases, and each time Strake is said to have penalized the company by adding $1,000,000 to the price. The company was prompt on the fourth day and the deal was made, Strake presumably having gained $3,000,000 by his aversion to tardiness. In 1951, when his interest in the Conroe Field was small, Strake estimated his oil reserves—oil still in the ground—in Louisiana and West Texas at more than 250,000,000 barrels. At the price of oil at that time, his estimate gave him a theoretical fortune of considerably more than half a billion dollars.[1]

One oil well: The mystic Edgar B. Davis, though he was penniless in 1922, had been a millionaire. He had been treasurer of a New England shoe manufacturing firm and later an officer of the United States Rubber Company, where he made his first fortune. That he no longer had the fortune was his penalty for drilling a number of dry holes near Luling, Texas. Fifty-two in 1922, Davis was a cherubic bachelor, six feet three inches tall and weighing more than 325 pounds, born and reared in Brockton, Massachusetts. He belonged to no church but believed, without sham, that God had given him the mission of finding oil at Luling. He also saw in the mission an obligation to return such wealth to the impoverished area. By August 1922 his faith in Providence had made him an intimate of despair. "I was broke," he said, years later. "I had to sell my fine New York office furniture, and my Packard car . . . We could not meet the payroll." Then,

[1]See Chapter 12 for Strake's theory of his success.

"providentially, I have always thought," his secretary in Massachusetts found "a block of securities which I had forgotten . . . and which kept us going for a while."

Luling, in the cedar and post-oak country fifty-four miles east of San Antonio, had a population of fifteen hundred. Its sidewalks were wooden, the ground was its streets, the sun was an agony in summertime. Luling had nothing but Davis to recommend it—Davis, his astonishing faith in Luling's geology, and his United North and South Oil Company. He named it that to help salve the memory of the Civil War. On the afternoon of August 9, 1922, Davis visited his Rafael Rios No. 1 well. He was to return to New York that afternoon, hoping to borrow enough money to complete the well. He did not make the trip. When his back was turned for a moment the well came in, flowing around two hundred barrels daily. He had discovered the Luling Field.

Davis's life was a melodrama of alternating rapture and despair, but he high-nooned in 1926, when he sold his Luling oil interests to the Magnolia Petroleum Company for $12,100,000, half in cash and half in oil payments. Soon afterward, having bought and cleared a hundred acres of cotton land for one of his few personal extravagances, he invited friends from all over the world to a barbecue at Luling. More than fifteen thousand people came—the population of Caldwell County was less than thirty thousand—to see New York stage stars and to hear Davis make a talk.

He said that every employee of the United North and South Oil Company would be given a bonus. Those with a year of service got 25 per cent of their total pay, two years 50 per cent, three years 75 per cent, and four years 100 per cent. Five men on his staff were given $200,000 each—a million dollars. Later he gave Luling $50,000 and the land for a golf course, $50,000 for a Negro clubhouse, and $50,000 for the maintenance of both. He gave $53,000 in prizes for three annual art contests. Finally, in 1929, he gave $1,000,000 to establish the Luling Foundation, a demonstration farm, and

$1,000,000 to the Plymouth Foundation in his native Massachusetts. Of the $6,050,000 cash paid by Magnolia, Davis soon gave away more than $4,000,000 without the stimulant of the tax advantage of a decade later. And he said he would live and die in Luling.

The Depression, a lawsuit, and possibly Davis's largest benefaction sieved his second fortune. The benefaction— many would call it a lark—was a Broadway play written by Davis's boyhood friend J. Frank Davis. Kenneth Foree, Jr., has written that Edgar met Frank in San Antonio soon after selling out to Magnolia. Frank Davis was a mediocre fiction writer, a romancer, later head of the WPA's Texas Writers Project. Frank's luck was ailing at the time, so Edgar suggested that he write a play and promised to produce it. Frank obliged with *The Ladder*, a dismalness about reincarnation. Edgar was a missionary for the reincarnation theory, and it is likely that he suggested the theme. The play's fate was bizarre, even for Broadway. "At an average performance there were all of six persons in addition to the ushers," Foree wrote. Yet *The Ladder*, nourished by Edgar Davis's cash and conviction, was given 789 performances beginning October 22, 1926. Unable to sell tickets, Edgar gave them away, and the play is believed to have cost him $1,500,000. The plunge was by no means motivated by Broadway fever but by Edgar's will to promote a message.

With the Depression nibbling his fortune, Davis was sued by the state of Massachusetts for state income taxes. Massachusetts claimed he was a citizen of the Bay State for many years after he moved to Texas. The verdict of a Massachusetts jury was a $750,000 judgment against Davis. He countersued, and a Texas jury awarded him a $1,000,000 verdict. Two years later the Supreme Court overruled the Texas verdict and Massachusetts offered to settle its $750,000 judgment for $25,000. "Not a cent!" Davis said. "When I said I was a citizen of Texas, not Massachusetts, I lied or I didn't lie."

Continuing the oil hunt after selling his Luling Field, Davis organized the United North and South Development Company. Again he wildcatted with success, but the Depression outwitted his success and the company was declared bankrupt in 1935. Davis continued as the company's president, without salary, while men appointed by a court were in command. As the Depression faded and the Second World War prospered everything, Davis regained part of his fortune without getting a chance to spend it: the Massachusetts lawsuit tied up his assets. Still he refused to pay the judgment. At last, aged eighty-one, this tranquil zealot died in 1951, a rich man who was virtually a pauper. After his death Massachusetts agreed to a $200,000 settlement of its judgment, but the state got more through an irony. Davis's dismay at the thought of death caused him to die without making a will. His fortune, free of Massachusetts' bonds, went to nephews and a niece who paid taxes in Massachusetts.

My mother has no faith in the presence of oil under her acres. She has always hoped that nobody would drill a well on the ranch and thus conclusively prove the absence of oil. So long as land is not absolutely condemned by direct drilling, leases "and money from them" are possible. J. Frank Dobie, 1948, *Holiday.*

Oil enriches, in moderation, without even showing itself. The owner of land that might conceivably bear oil hopes to lease it, for as much money as possible, to someone who will chance the cost of drilling to find out. The landowner risks no money in such a venture, losing nothing if the well is a failure but gaining whatever he is paid for the lease. If the well succeeds he gets a minimum of one eighth of every barrel of oil produced on his land unless he has sold an interest in his minerals or royalty. How much an owner is paid for a lease may depend on the distance of his land from land that is already producing oil, the nearer the better.

No oil well: Herbert Doerre's family has lived at Klein, a

community twenty miles northwest of Houston, from the beginning. The hamlet probably was named for Adam Klein,
Doerre's grandfather. A bus driver and maintenance man for
the Klein School, Doerre owns 150 acres, next to the school,
that were deeded to him by his father in 1917. He had leased
the land two or three times, never for more than ten dollars
an acre, but no oil had ever come of it and none had been
found nearby. Early in 1954, however, oil was found half a
mile east of the school. Then began a hare-and-hounds race
that is a custom before an oil well is drilled in hope—in land
that *may* produce oil. Doerre was the hare, lease buyers were
the hounds.

Lease buyers came to a grocery and feed store, owned by
Doerre's sons Victor and Leonard, to make their offers one
Saturday afternoon. The result shows what a man can get
from oil without troubling to invest in it. Doerre leased the
land for $15,000 cash, plus a $25,000 bonus if enough oil were
found, and a one-sixth royalty on all oil produced. If the well
were a dry hole, Doerre still had his $15,000 and the hope
that someone else would lease it again. If oil were found and
as many as four wells were drilled, he would get the $25,000
bonus and could expect to make around $25,000 a year in
royalty payments, probably for more than a decade, perhaps
longer.

Buying leases is a competition of craft and shrewdness. An
oilman's urge to lease a certain property depends on his geologist's clairvoyance and his own hunch. The subject of buying leases is a sensitive one and is easier to illustrate from a
distance. Robert Lee Blaffer, a Texas oil leader of importance
who was later president of the Humble Oil and Refining Company, was buying leases in Louisiana in 1910. He was competing with E. A. Sims, founder of the Louisiana Land and
Exploration Company, in the Anse la Butte area. Arriving in
the area a day or so ahead of Blaffer, who was named for
Robert E. Lee and whose father was an officer in the Confederate Army, Sims rumored that Blaffer's father had been

a captain in the Union Army. This was a grave charge in Louisiana at the time and the result was a cold shoulder for Blaffer and leases for Sims. Blaffer, however, was the victor in the long run: every one of Sims's wells was a dry hole. Nearly half a century of experience since then has not notably altered the ruse and ploy of buying leases.

The oilman feels, often with cause, that he is at the mercy of anyone who owns land to be leased. The lease demands of a farmer, say, may be based on advice from people as green to oil as he is. As a rule oilmen give in to such demands; someone else may otherwise get the lease. In October 1956 Mike Riordan, a lease buyer for Ray M. Southworth, a Houston oil-man, revenged himself on all the landowners who had com-plexed his life. He was trying to lease some land owned by a Louisiana farmer. Someone had told the farmer not to sign a lease unless it gave him the right to see electric logs, sand cores, and other data the farmer would not understand. See-ing that the man was not educated, Riordan drew up and inserted in the lease the following paragraph:

"If a well should be located on the surface of the land herein leased, then in lieu of Lessor being furnished an elec-tric log, Lessor shall have the right to be lowered head first down the casing equipped with a two cell battery flash-light, to a depth of 7,000 feet, or some lesser depth if heaving shales be encountered. Lessee agrees that Lessor will be lowered at a rate of speed not to exceed that rate which any prudent operator would lower his Lessor into a well bore. It is further understood that if lowering line should part, immediate fishing operations shall be com-menced, and in no event shall Lessor be cemented in plug and abandoned."

The lease is recorded in Jefferson Parish, Louisiana.

Buying leases may involve pitfalls of consequence. The buyer must beware, as two Texas firms discovered in the early 1950s. Two wells drilled by the firms in East Texas were plugged and abandoned though one produced oil and the other was drilled to the contract depth. Someone in each firm's lease department made a mistake: the land was owned by the state. A resident of the area waited until both wells were completed and then reported them to the General Land Office. He was well rewarded for his pains. The law provides that the informer gets the one-eighth royalty in such cases. Each company's loss was around eighty thousand dollars.

The importance of an oil lease to a landowner is twofold. A man who leases his land does not lose its use. He can still farm most of it, or use it for grazing, or put it to whatever profit he had of the land before it was leased, for most Texas oil wells are spaced one to forty acres and gas wells one to 160 acres or more. Lease money is extra money. And lease money has bread-and-buttered thousands of Texans who have never hazarded a dollar in oil and whose land has never produced a barrel of oil.

Bacon described riches as the baggage of virtue. The foregoing was a primer of oil's dazzle—how this baggage is won: wildcatting for daredevils and lusters; lease pay for those who are, more often than not, accidents of fortune. The fragrance of Texas oil's successes hides the reverses. Oil's gloom—$244,000,000 worth of dry holes in 1954—bores, and investors in thousands of dry holes are unencumbered by the baggage of riches. As will be shown, however, Bacon's evaluation of riches applies to Texas.

Oil Operator: Man with leather coat, Ford car and a wild woman. Anonymous, 1924, *Runnin' Wild*, a booklet about oil, published in Houston.

The great number of Texas oil fortunes—a few are false-fronted as fortunes—has created a seemingly high proportion of boobs and show-offs. Yet Texas oil's ratio of clowns to men of decorum is probably no higher than that of Pennsylvania's steel in its Carnegie heyday, of the nation's railroads in their nineteenth-century bloom, or of the filigree aristocracy of

Massachusetts until the First World War. The difference is one of numbers, a conclusion wanting either the comfort or embarrassment of statistics. Put another way, however, there were not at one time several thousand trusts for Boston Brahmins to manage, or that many railroads for speculators to pirate, or steel mills to own.

There are possibly twenty thousand independent oilmen in Texas and six times that many oil wells. Most of the oilmen are toned to reserve and restraint in public conduct, whether from dismay at the spectacle of the few, from an instinct for thrift, from heritage, or from inclination. But the fluff-minds —youths of middle age and more—profile Texas oil in the public mind by competing with the absurdities, follies, and bacchanalia of Petronius's *Satyricon*. These Texan tableaux, as the public has come to identify them, are staged chiefly in Los Angeles and New York, and they have antagonized a nation since 1930. Their effect on Texas is illumined by the activities of D. D. Feldman, a Dallas oilman whose life style may be influenced by the philosophy of Peter Pan.

Six feet four inches tall, free of malice and busybodyness, Feldman was born in Fort Worth in 1904. He was graduated from Cornell University in 1925 and was in business in Miami, Florida, until 1929, when he came to Houston and oil. He seems to have succeeded early, meanwhile moving to Dallas. An early drollery of note occurred in the late 1930s, when he mailed several hundred engraved cards announcing that he would thereafter be known as D. D. Fontaine. Some time later he sent a second card to the same addresses, announcing that he was going right back to being D. D. Feldman. His mother, it was said, had advised him that her will made no mention of anybody named Fontaine.

In 1955, having won a measure of acclaim by sponsoring, at considerable cost, the D. D. Feldman Collection of Contemporary Texas Art, he employed one Ben Sonnenberg, a New York press agent, to stimulate interest in his new offices in New York. Sonnenberg described them as "the world's most beautiful business offices." *The New Yorker* sent a man to see the offices, on the twenty-first floor at 460 Park Avenue, and reported that they included a lavabo, as Sonnenberg chose to call the bathroom, with "panelling of Roman travertine, antique Italian rose marble floor, with trim of polished brass, towels and washrags marked 'D.D.F.'" An assistant press agent described the suite's black-and-white marble entrance-foyer floor as "identical with that created in 1675 by Sir Christopher Wren for the rebuilding of St. Paul's Cathedral in London." The magazine said the dining room was of "Carved Jacobean oak panelling; sixteenth-century stained-glass windows, one pane dating to 1572; Flemish baluster-leg table with red carnations; needlework chairs." There were other refinements to comfort the oilman, but thus, for all the world to see, was a Texas oil company at home in its New York "listening post"—Feldman's description.

Feldman's glory, or at any rate the occasion for penetrating the iron curtain of national indifference, was a New Year's Eve party on December 31, 1956. Tex, as Feldman is known, said the party cost $125,000, and wire-service reports described it as "the fanciest in Hollywood memory." Bing Crosby, Gary Cooper, Conrad Hilton, Fred Astaire, and other tissue celebrities were among the guests, for whom Feldman spent $75,000 to decorate one room of a Hollywood restaurant in the spirit of New York's Delmonico restaurant of the early 1900s. The entertainment starred the French singer Edith Piaf. The cause of the fete was Feldman's pique at a motion picture titled *Giant*. "I wanted to show the world that Texans can compete with the best in gentility," Feldman said to explain why he gave a party that cost more than a tenth of a million dollars. A wire-service story about the party ended: "The wealthy Texan objected to a scene in the movie which showed millionaire Texans as boisterous fun lovers. By 2 A.M. of Jan. 1, 1957, when the party started dwindling, the movie looked pretty authentic."

The day after Feldman's party it was announced in Texas

that Mr. and Mrs. John H. Blaffer had given the University
of Texas Press $20,000 to underwrite a series of art portfolios
by painters of the Southwest. Granted that Feldman spent
more in one evening's indulgence than the Blaffers would
spend in several years for art portfolios, the smallest of the
family's philanthropies, it was hard to find any public notice
of the Blaffers' gift except in Houston, where they live.

With the tabloid light on the few—sports, nincompoops,
popinjays, and die-hards of the look-at-me set—the world sees
Texas oil from the other side of the looking glass. Outsiders
marvel, their expectation on tiptoe to hear that the medieval
custom of *droit du seigneur* has been revived in Texas for the
convenience of oilmen. Chapters 6 and 7 consider complaints
of validity, but it is nonsense to set down Texas oil as a pea-
cock alley of egos, excesses, and eccentrics. The few's flair for
self-indulgence and exhibitionism inhibits the many, some of
whom have come to forego Cadillacs in favor of automobiles
of less pretension than those of their servants. The flamboy-
ants are causing wealth's trademarks to take cover.

The problem is further complicated by knaves in and out of
the state. The loony gas of oil riches has excited a host of
boomers. Flashing pretended wealth, they promise to return
riches for a small cash investment. In the wake of Texas
oil have come fortune hunters, confidence men, promoters,
swindlers, mountebanks, rainbow chasers—camp followers of
new wealth. They have no liaison with oil but contribute their
own weaknesses and part of the "Big Rich" curse. The lure
of Texas oil has gulled investors of millions of dollars, but in
the late 1940s a Texan is said to have promoted $25,000 with-
out fleecing a soul. Advertising for a thousand investors with
$100 each, he promised that all would get their money back
in ten years, possibly much sooner. He soon got his $100,000
—and was investigated by postal officers. They found no basis
for charges. The man sent each investor a $100 War Bond,
which would mature in ten years. Having spent $75,000 for

the bonds he had $25,000 left to drill a well. The thousand investors were his partners.

Living up to the legend has also deviled the state's oil. "Everybody in Dallas is an oilman as soon as he gets out of town," the manager of the Dallas Petroleum Club was quoted as saying in Paul Crume's column in the Dallas *News*. "Oilman—the Title Without Meaning," said a headline in the Houston *Post* in 1953. The word "oilman"—especially the phrase "Texas oilman"—connotes riches to many, but anyone can call himself an oilman. One does not have to pass a state board examination to become an oilman; there is no apprenticeship. One Houston oilman of wealth came to Texas in the late 1930s to sell washing machines, an illustration that can be multiplied by many hundreds.

Texas newspapers have found it impossible to trace Texas residences for some playboys who are identified in New York and West Coast newspapers as Texas oilmen. A widely publicized example was the sport who gave a $25,000 party in Hollywood in 1953. The title has allure for many who assume it. Jack Lait, a man who made human error and scandal a profession and was for years editor of the New York *Mirror*, once wrote that any claims to being a Texas oil millionaire "must be accompanied by certified bank statements" if he were expected to believe them. The test may have been an inconvenience, for Lait seems not to have made use of it. Even the reality of Texas oil is done in. D. D. Feldman *is* a Texas oilman of wealth, but his fortune is not notably large by such standards in the middle twentieth century. Yet a wire-service story about his New Year's Eve party described him as "reportedly one of the wealthiest independent oil operators in the world" and said Feldman's income "is estimated at $7,000,000 a year."

Hereford Ranch — Coast Country

6 A Prevalence of Oil

Oil's meaning to Texas is a paradox. It is thought to be the state's cornucopia, yet its pressures constrict the state and its meaning is braced by a number of myths. Oil's economy commands the state, yet oil and its allies reward few Texans on the whole. This dominant industry employs 8 per cent of the state's workers and pays 12 per cent of individual incomes in wages, royalties, and all other types of income. The percentages would wane, however, if they did not include more than forty thousand service-station employees whose jobs would be secure if Maine happened to produce the oil used in Texas. Oil's benefits do not affect the mass of Texans except as the industry is the state's chief taxpayer and through oil's enormous philanthropies, most of them spent only in Texas.

In 1950 the Texas Legislative Council, the research agency

of the state legislature, measured the importance of oil to the
state's welfare. "It appears that the petroleum industry is one
that utilizes capital to a much greater extent than labor," the
report said. "Therefore, although it is not of predominant importance [to Texans] in terms of number of employees and
income payments to individuals, it is of primary importance in
the State in terms of the value of its annual product." Agriculture and trade are more important as employers and
sources of income; manufacturing is equally important. Oil
does not sustain the mass of Texans.

A half-myth inspired by oil's critics is that oil commands
through the effectiveness of its propaganda. Oil commands
in several ways, but it does so as much through Texans' awe
of it—awe of its magic-wanding of fortunes, mainly—as from
its own effort. The degree of the state's approval of oil equals
the state's approval of itself. A few Texans scorn the state's
bark and brag; fewer criticize oil. No public official, no cleric,
no teacher measures oil's effects from all sides, unless privately. Criticism of the oil industry is unpatriotic in Texas. Except for the weekly *Texas Observer*, and before it the *Texas
Spectator* of 1945–48, there is no stage for oil criticism. Texans' view of oil is walled in by the state press. None of the
state's metropolitan papers evaluates oil's effects. An editorial in the Dallas *News*, in 1955, typifies Texas newspapers'
liaison with oil. "For all oilmen," the editorial concluded,
"this city's latchstring is always out."

The Texas Almanac, published by the Dallas *News*, is a
source book of value but is in no sense a book that evaluates.
Homer Price Rainey was president of the University of Texas
from 1939 to 1944, when he was discharged by a board of
regents in haste to evade the nuisance of mental processes.
Rainey's gift was the torment of evaluation. Oil's meaning to
Texas may be contrasted in two quotations from these unlike sources. Both quotations have validity.

The Texas Almanac, 1956–57: " 'Black gold' has contributed, directly and indirectly, most of the assets of Texas'

banks, insurance companies and other financial institutions, built most of its tall skyscrapers, and contributed most of the income to sustain the trade in its princely department stores. Oil and gas have enriched the farmer in rents and royalties . . . Oil and gas have borne much of the cost of the educational system of Texas . . . The greatness of the oil resources of Texas and the production therefrom constitute an outstanding phenomenon in the history of the world's mineral industries."

Rainey, 1946, in the opening speech of his campaign for governor: "We have in Texas the greatest storehouse of natural resources in the world. Yet we are still a poor state. That means that the people of Texas are not keeping in Texas, for their own benefit, a fair share of these resources in the form of tax revenues. We produce one thousand million dollars' worth of oil each year. We produce two hundred million dollars' worth of gas each year. We produce almost 90 per cent of the nation's sulphur. We produce about 80 per cent of the nation's carbon black. The vast majority of these resources go to other states and other countries to be consumed. . . . Texas is a sleeping giant. I propose that we wake up. I propose that we get from these resources and other sources enough tax revenue to give us a decent school system, a first-class health program, a good system of farm-to-market roads, an adequate welfare program." Rainey, a native Texan, was defeated and left the state.

It is not true that Texas oil is *never* criticized. Every other year, during the Democratic primary elections, Texans may hear criticism of the oil industry if there is a liberal candidate for governor. These challenges fleet through Texans' consciousness, and such criticism bears a resemblance to the funerary rites of certain primitive tribes. Stones are placed on the grave to weigh down the ghost and make sure it stays put until it loses its power to harm the living. Texas has such a funeral every other year because modern Texans have never elected as governor any but a friend of the oil industry.

There are many sides to oil. Oil has not given Texas the dedication to luxury and grandeur of California and Florida. More important, few Texas fortunes—none in oil—are based on the sweat of the little man. Oil has no thousands of mill and factory hands. It has fewer bent backs than industries in the North and South. Indeed, oil and one of its dependents, petrochemicals, have led to the paradox of burgeoning industries but comparatively few workers, many of whom are technical men. Without oil the Texas economy would be little superior to that of states in the Deep South. Without oil Texas would not signify, except in size and legend, among the states. Oil and the industries attracted to it have given Texas use of one of its important assets—space. But oil has also had steel-banding effects on minds which might otherwise have been free. And oil's regard for the state's welfare has been measured in terms of its own welfare, and thus has been astigmatic at best.

Not so long ago the oil companies ran a state-wide campaign which emphasized the dependence of Texas on oil. The principal advertisements in this campaign showed a picture of Uncle Sam in a Stetson hat, and beneath the picture was the caption, "If you are a Texan you are in the oil business." J. A. Burkhart, 1949, *Antioch Review.*

Some complaints against Texas oil could not be altered by the state even if it hoped to do so. The state's oil resources are, to a large extent, owned outside of Texas; profits and dividends of unknown proportion are paid and spent elsewhere. The only way the state can get a crack at absentee owners is through taxes. The oil industry pays nearly a third of the state's tax revenues; critics feel the industry should pay more. Another complaint that is partly outside of state action is that oil's clutch on Texas has endangered the state with a one-product economy. The abundance of oil and gas has caused Texans to neglect, or overlook, other resources of promise.

Of more importance, however, is the character of the oil hunt itself. Independent oilmen have never had to learn the maturing lessons of most other American businessmen—management of masses of men, dovetailing with labor unions, responsibilities of public relations and liaison. The root of the oil business—the independent oil operator—has the smallest ratio of employees to capital investment of any large American business. No American business has more influence on the public or more lethargy in its public responsibility. The influence is won through formidable lobbies in state and national capitals. The indifference to public responsibility is not owing to a public-be-damned attitude but to the independent oilman's remoteness from the public. He sells his oil not to the public but to a refinery, which does deal with the public. The public has little opportunity to prompt the independent oilman, being vaguely aware of him, as he is of it.

Transient journalists, often men of missionary fervor, and Texas liberals charge the oil industry with the state's binges of reaction. Calling Texas oil Republican and conservative does not set oil apart; the mind of Texas is Republican and conservative. Charges that Texas oil is trying to control primary elections in other states are a subject of Chapter 3—the guilty are a trio of oilmen; most oilmen have shunned this fascist helling. Charges that Texas oilmen were among the chief supporters of Senator Joseph W. McCarthy, when he was testing democracy's sinews, are conceived in ignorance. H. L. Hunt, H. R. Cullen, and Clint W. Murchison were the state's ringleaders of McCarthyism; few of their followers were in oil. Hunt, Cullen, and Murchison, being front-page figures, dilated McCarthy's appeal to Texas. The dimension of the Wisconsin senator's popularity in the state was shown by an event in Houston in 1954.

April 21, the anniversary of Sam Houston's defeat of Santa Anna, is San Jacinto Day. It is a holiday; one observance is at the San Jacinto Monument, near Houston. The Sons of the Republic of Texas invited President Eisenhower to be the San Jacinto Day speaker in 1954; Senator McCarthy was invited when the President declined. A spokesman for the Sons estimated beforehand that a crowd of forty thousand would hear the senator's talk. A million people live in the metropolitan area. School was out, businesses were closed, the weather was choice. Senator McCarthy's audience, newspapers said, was between six and ten thousand, but a census, made with precision by the Houston *Post*, came to only forty-two hundred. The senator had a smaller Houston audience than did a performer named Liberace a few months earlier.

Senator McCarthy's audience at the San Jacinto Monument included few oilmen. Few wives of oilmen are members of the Minute Women chapters in Houston and Dallas. Though oilmen are rarely identified with liberal causes in Texas, neither are they identified with conservative factions in Houston's school-board disputes or Dallas's communism-in-art controversies, subjects of Chapter 9. The Texas oilman's conservatism is an instinct aroused by elections—local elections are an exception—and by any legislative matter affecting oil and taxes. He is a pragmatist. He does not excite much at conflicts in education, art, society. He dreams of oil sands, not new horizons. He fears the mystery of government, state and national, not the mystery of abstractions.

In some ways the voice of the oilman comes out weak. He is favored by the state legislature, but not more so than some other groups and not as much as a few. He is comforted by governors, but most state appointive posts go to men who are not in oil. He is nursed by the press, but the press is quick to make a buffoon of him with its news of oil's exhibitionists. Few oilmen are elected to state or local offices—only one was ever governor—and it is not worth an oilman's trouble to be a candidate. Even his lobbies and his philanthropies have not made the Texas oilman a notably honored man in his own state. He is a prophet with riches' honor, thanks to every Texan's hope of getting a piece of an oil deal, but the honor is strained because most Texans suspect that they, too, could have an oil fortune with a little luck.

You have a situation down here [in Texas] comparable to pre-Bolshevik Russia. You have conditions of chaos and extremes which make for fertile writing materials. Gorham B. Munson, New York editor, 1945, in a speech at the Southwest Book Fair in Dallas.

Oil has another meaning to Texas, one camouflaged by the state's routine of oil. The stresses, excitements, and eruptions created by oil in the lives of the people have altered the collective behavior of Texans. The monotony of Texas oil—its everywhereness—inflates reality, or what strikes the people of other states as reality. Texans have become conditioned to a gold-rush philosophy. Extremes have been devalued to commonplaces. Martial law, lawsuits of stunning dimension and hope, and pitfalls of the path of least resistance are among the havocs of oil.

Martial law was called during the Mexia boom, in 1922, to curb "open and flagrant violation of the law, highway robberies, open gambling and selling liquor"—the usual causes of calling out the militia in oil's behalf. Martial law was declared in East Texas, in 1931, to control production and fortify conservation and prices. One oil lawsuit, contested for more than half a century, is for the recovery of $500,000,000. A lawsuit in the courts since 1940 is for the recovery of $100,000,000. The path of least resistance—fraud, skulduggery—is illumined in the Shell Oil Company's eleven-year fight to recover oil properties worth millions of dollars. They were lost through the secret deals of a senior Shell geologist in Houston. A Houston federal court held that the geologist duped his employer out of royalty and mineral interests by selling Shell's secret data on potential oil bonanzas. "We agree that [the defendants] should disgorge their ill-gotten gains," the Fifth United

States Court of Appeals said, in upholding the decision of the Houston court. Pirated oil holdings rarely come to the public's attention.

Now diminish oil's focus to the county-seat towns of Sherman and Littlefield. Sherman, population twenty-one thousand, near Lake Texoma and the Red River, got its first oil production the day after Christmas, 1951. The discovery well and others that followed are in the city limits—in a residential area. City ordinances limit wells to one a block. Each homeowner shares in the earnings of his block's well in proportion to the square footage of his property. No one gets on Easy Street with such a share—the average pay is around thirty dollars a month—but it is easy money. People in other neighborhoods gain indirectly. Three of the first wells were on lots owned by the city of Sherman; oil pay eases city taxes. In 1952 Sherman's oil-well inspector told a reporter, "The city has fourteen parks and we hope to have a well someday on every one of those parks."

Littlefield, population seven thousand, is the county seat of Lamb County, on the South Plains. The discovery of oil in Littlefield's city limits, in 1953, put several hundred homeowners in the oil business. Swiftly passing oil-well ordinances patterned on those of other Texas cities, the city of Littlefield set a $500 fee for each drilling permit and passed a two-cent-a-barrel city tax on production. Littlefield's economy was wholly agricultural until oil was discovered, profiting some of the people and the city government.

To abandon for the moment material advantages, oil has meanings of social consequence to Sherman, Littlefield, and many other Texas cities. The eyesore and earsore of drilling rigs in a residential area were worth a royalty of thirty dollars a month to people in Sherman's oil belt at the penalty of aesthetics and the shock of oil wells in places for woolgathering and recreation—city parks. Few cities have been so rewarded as Kilgore for the contradiction of oil wells in the city limits. Kilgore's taxes are low, the city government is free of debt, and public buildings have been built without the expense of municipal bonds. Yet the splurge of Kilgore's city-limits rigs is an extravagance of surrealism. Carthage, county seat of Panola County, on the Texas-Louisiana border, was in despair for water. The city—population six thousand—spent five thousand dollars to complete surveys for a reservoir. In 1952 oil was discovered at the heart of the proposed reservoir's site. The site was abandoned, the cost of the survey wasted, the value of other land needed for another reservoir rose, and there was the question of the new oil field's pollution of whatever water resource was finally developed. Oil's urgency often subdues man's.

The city of Houston gets oil royalties from wells in its city garbage dump. In 1955 the story of the Shamrock Hilton Hotel was given what one presumes was its last conceivable Cinderella touch when oil was discovered on a 447-acre tract owned by the hotel near the Houston city limits. Oil wells edge a score of Texas Main Streets. Not cities and towns alone but universities, churches, even a nudist colony—all Texas, save cemeteries—make way for oil's insistence and reward. Trinity University, at San Antonio, moved to a new million-dollar campus in 1952; three days later the Presbyterian school learned that oil was discovered on land it owned in Kaufman County. The Merriman Community Baptist Church, near Ranger, is on a two-and-a-half-acre lot. Some of its members drilled wells on the property during the Ranger boom. The church became rich, giving 85 per cent of the oil money to the Baptist General Convention of Texas. Later the church won celebrity when it was said to have refused an offer of a million dollars for drilling rights in its cemetery. Oil's urgency may have exhausted its possibilities in 1954 when a well was drilled seventeen miles southeast of San Antonio. The land was host to a colony of nudists, some of whom watched the drilling in that costume which is nature's gift to everyone. The spell of oil abridged even the nudist tenet that visitors must do as the Romans do: drillers were permitted to work in clothes.

The fact that it [a New Jersey man's collection of Texas lore] has been allowed to leave the state brought the comment from one Texas scholar that the state government did not have the funds to purchase the items and that the state's oil millionaires were less interested in history than in "making more money." John C. Devlin, 1957, New York *Times*.

The cliché that Texas is inhabited by but two classes of people, serfs and oil millionaires, who have not yet coped with the complexes of reading and writing, is owing in part to the state's prevalence of oil and to peculiarities of journalism which transform clichés into dogma. The bite of the quotation above, run of the mill in its disdain, is influenced by the greeds of oil itself and by antipathies and envies arising in states where oil is a commodity rather than a resource. Texas will shed this aggravation when it exhausts its oil, but some of the bother may be tempered by oil's remaining meaning to Texas—philanthropy. So much oil creates a scatter of individual wealth. More and more of the wealth is merging into philanthropy.

The motives for philanthropy—humanity's benefit, vanity, penitence, and escape from taxes—are not a concern here. Such motives are uniform everywhere. Texas, however, exempts from taxes only such foundation spending as is kept within its borders, which Dwight Macdonald, writing in *The New Yorker*, took to be "less a matter of economics than of simple disbelief in the reality of the extra-Texan world." However that may be, the 1955 edition of *American Foundations and Their Fields* lists Texas foundations fifth in assets of $113,000,000 after New York ($2,500,000,000), Pennsylvania ($362,000,000), Michigan ($309,000,000), and Ohio ($125,-000,000). Texas foundations were seventh in expenditures and seventh in grants. But the state's rank in philanthropy, now comparable to its rank in population, will climb with vim.

Texas wealth is new. No Texas fortune is a century old; few date from 1900. Some Texas fortunes—the families are known as "old" oil—were started before the First World War, during Texas oil's early bloom, but the majority have their roots in the wildcatting successes of the 1930s and the Second World War. Most of the founders of the state's great fortunes still live. The majority of its major foundations—$10,000,000 or more—have been created since 1950. Assets of the state's foundations, more than four fifths of them enlivened by oil, are a whisper compared with what they will be in a decade. Provision for many major foundations will not be disclosed until their founders' deaths. The size of other foundations of consequence, though they are now functioning, will not be known until their founders' deaths. By 1970 Texas will have a richness of foundation resources that may be exceeded only by New York, where the Ford and Duke foundations create a partial illusion of geographical origin. Texas's Moody Foundation, though not based primarily in oil, may be the third or fourth largest in the world: its assets are estimated at $400,000,000. Public disclosure of the Moody Foundation's assets has been temporarily voided by an heir's lawsuit brought shortly after the death, in 1954, of the founder, W. L. Moody, Jr. The suit was settled, out of court, in July 1957.

Education, religion, medicine, and agriculture have been the chief beneficiaries of Texas philanthropy. Some Texas foundations, notably the Hogg Foundation for Mental Hygiene and the Fondren Foundation, are motivated entirely by the will to benefit humanity. Many have a distinctly personal flavor. The Le Tourneau Foundation has been described by its founder and president, R. G. Le Tourneau, as "the Lord's treasury." Le Tourneau, who moved to Texas in 1946, is a manufacturer of earth-moving equipment. The foundation's goal is Christian uplift in the tradition of Southern evangelism, an ambition which has included a private Point Four program on a scale unknown to any but the Rockefeller and Ford Foundations. The Le Tourneau Foundation's work abroad has included projects whose magnitude would dismay some governments. Le Tourneau leased half a million acres in Liberia and is clearing and developing the land for natives with a task force of engineer-missionaries and boatloads of equipment and supplies. Le Tourneau is also resurrecting nearly a million jungle acres in Peru's Amazon basin. The foundation, whose assets are estimated at $20,000,000, is a mirror of its founder's hopes for man and what he calls his "partnership with God." "Send your money on to heaven and have it waiting when you get there," he urged a Houston audience in 1956. The quotation epitomizes the motivation for Le Tourneau's reversal of tithing's custom —not 10 per cent for God and 90 per cent for self but 90 per cent for God. Le Tourneau's foundation, however, is Texan only by residence. His fortune, independent of oil, was made before he came to Texas, and his foundation was established eleven years before.

The notoriety and aims of two Texas foundations made oil the subject of lingering resentment. In 1949 George W. Armstrong, Sr., of Fort Worth, offered oil properties valued at $5,000,000 to the Jefferson Military College, near Natchez, Mississippi, if the college would champion white supremacy and anti-Semitism. To get the oil land the college had to agree to "teach and disseminate through every medium possible the true principles of . . . Christianity, and the superiority of the Anglo-Saxon and Latin-American races." The college first accepted and then rejected the offer, after which its financial pinch was relieved in part by a $5000 gift from a Houston manufacturer for its "stand on freedom of education." In 1952 a federal court ruled that the purposes of the Judge George W. Armstrong Foundation were not charitable, religious, and educational, as Armstrong claimed, but were to influence legislation and spew propaganda. Contributions to the foundation, the court ruled, were not exempt from income taxes.

Armstrong's foundation dealt in bigotry publishing—pamphlets titled *Traitors* ("President Truman Is a Communist Traitor") and *Zionist Wall Street* ("The Rothschilds Run the World")—and nourished disunity. But Armstrong, who died in 1954 at age eighty-eight, failed to arouse controversy as did a Texan whose foundation worked with more subtlety. H. L. Hunt, through his Facts Forum, may have injured Texas and its oilmen more than any other individual. "Facts Forum," Hunt wrote on the editorial page of the Dallas *News,* in 1953, "is a nonprofit national educational organization devoted to the study of political science, soil and water conservation, and the art of living." Hunt's soapbox—*Time* magazine later called it "the most expensive personal propaganda mill in the U.S."—coaxed free time from radio and television stations throughout America with the pretension of discussing two sides of controversial issues. Hunt estimated that the free time would have cost $3,000,000 a year. Facts Forum sent public-opinion polls of questionable validity to fifteen hundred newspapers and five hundred radio and television stations. The forum won many of its devotees with thousands of dollars' worth of cash prizes. It published *Facts Forum News,* a monthly journal with a reported circulation of a hundred thousand. By 1954 Hunt and Facts Forum were subjects of a nationwide hue and cry, and in November 1956 Hunt surprised by suddenly suspending Facts Forum, without explanation, after five tax-free years of promoting his own art of living, the essence of which was fascism multiplied by McCarthyism. Hunt was repudiated by the public's indifference.

The Armstrong and Hunt foundations won more support outside of Texas than in. Both foundations had to contend with the aloofness of their neighbors during their heydays. The two foundations by no means represent Texas philanthropy, which is one of the state's lusters. Most of the two hundred or so Texas foundations are small and have modest intentions, but the proportion of major foundations is unusually high, a circumstance not owing entirely to oil's copious rewards. Few Texans of wealth have spent their money for yachts and other splendors of royalty. Floyd L. Karsten, a Houston oilman who is not yet involved in philanthropy on the foundation scale, was thought to be a spendthrift when he bought a 112-foot subchaser in 1952. He spent a reported $200,000 to refit the 88-ton vessel, built for Russia under the Lend-Lease plan, and make it a luxury yacht for deep-sea fishing. The result of Texas wealth's comparative frugality—airplanes, the one extravagance of note, are charged off to business expense—leaves resources of consequence for foundation spending. Robert A. Welch, the most seasoned Texas pinchpenny of his day, was the only Houston millionaire who refused to give a cent to charity, even to the city's United Fund. Yet his death, in 1954, disclosed the creation of the Welch Foundation, with assets of more than $20,000,000, to benefit chemical research in Texas. It was Welch's observation that Texas foundations had shown ample concern for churches, and he specifically excluded religious organizations from his foundation's benefits.

A windfall to the East Texas Boy Scout Foundation illustrates oil's philanthropy in miniature. In 1948 John E. Wrather, John C. Robbins, and three other East Texas oilmen owned a five-acre lease in Gregg County. As new trustees of the foundation, Wrather and Robbins wanted to get something done. What they did was give the Gregg County lease to the foundation and raise $16,000 in cash and several thousand dollars' worth of tools and equipment to drill a well. The well produced oil. The lease has paid the Boy Scouts a total of $75,105 through 1956, but the average pay of more than $8000 a year is expected to increase. The result is a "90 per cent increase in boys served," JC Underwood, the Scout executive, said in 1957.

No Texas philanthropy exists to pad or maintain the Texas myth or, surprisingly, to research what has been called the

state's principal industry, Texas history. The history of Texas
oil itself despairs for attention while some of its early leaders
still live, yet the main source of the state's foundations is
served by only one philanthropy. The project was established
in 1952 by Mrs. Walter B. Sharp, widow of a pioneer wildcatter, and her son Dudley C. Sharp, later Assistant Secretary
of the Air Force in the Eisenhower administration. Walter B.
Sharp, developer of the mud system of drilling, was a man of
ingenuity and brilliance who died, in 1912, at age forty-two.
Part of his fortune now pays for a tape-recorded oral history
of Texas oil pioneers, produced by the University of Texas.

Of the larger Texas philanthropies, cotton is responsible
for the M. D. Anderson Foundation, with assets of nearly
$30,000,000, but cattle, the other source of the state's early
wealth, has created no foundation of magnitude. The $20,-
000,000 in assets of Jesse H. Jones's Houston Endowment, Inc.,
come largely from the financier's success in real estate. But
few of the state's foundations exist without oil's help. The
Amon G. Carter Foundation's assets of $13,000,000 appear to
be a fruit of publishing, radio, and television profits, but the
foundation is the result of Carter's oil successes between 1935
and the middle 1940s. In 1947 he sold part of his oil holdings
for $16,500,000 and used the money to start his foundation.
In 1957, when he sold his American Liberty Oil Company
for $35,000,000, Toddie Lee Wynne, of Dallas, tithed $2,000,-
000—10 per cent of the net—to the Texas Presbyterian Foundation.

The range of the state's philanthropy escapes the novelty
that might be expected from the eccentricities of some of the
founders. Unorthodoxy of foundation intentions is rare in
America, and Texas conforms in this respect. The purpose of
the million-dollar Texas Educational Foundation, one medium of George W. Armstrong's bigotry, was "the support of
educational undertakings . . . advocating the perpetuation
of constitutional government"—a novelty mainly in the light
of Armstrong's interpretation of constitutional government.

The purpose of the Harding Foundation, of Raymondville, is "to further Christian education in schools and churches through the use of films depicting Bible history." One of the foundation's chief interests—its assets were half a million dollars in 1955—has been distribution of a book, *The Bible in Pictures*. The Caesar Kleberg Foundation (assets reported as $8796, total expenditures as $44 through 1951) is concerned with the state's natural resources. A foundation established by W. J. McDonald, a millionaire who lived in what was once a jail, who would make a journey of hundreds of miles to see a rare flower in bloom, resulted in the University of Texas's McDonald Observatory in the Davis Mountains. But religion and education are the main recipients of Texas philanthropy, with aesthetics growing in importance since the Second World War.

The state is becoming in some ways a reflection of its oil philanthropies. "It happens that SMU's annual budget [$4,000,000] is about the same as the school's oil royalties," said a story in the Dallas *News* in 1952; the royalties began in philanthropy. Though John H. Blaffer is in his early forties, he has built a wing of the Houston Museum of Fine Arts, an auditorium for Houston's Kinkaid School, and underwritten the publication of a series of art portfolios for the University of Texas Press, among other philanthropies. When the museum was soon in need of another wing, Nina Cullinan paid for it with the request that an architect of distinction design the building; Ludwig Mies van der Rohe was employed. In 1952 Mrs. Harry C. Wiess, widow of a noted oilman who was chairman of the board of the Humble Oil and Refining Company, gave Rice Institute $1,570,000 to establish a chair in geology. Two years later her three daughters gave the institute $1,000,000 to construct a geology building.

Blaffer, Miss Cullinan, and the Wiess daughters are second-generation oil heirs. Robert Lee Blaffer, J. S. Cullinan, and Harry C. Wiess were among early Texas oil leaders of intelligence and importance, men who helped start a tradition of giving for the public good. The tradition is influencing Texas in a way that hides from the state's critics. The character of such men—the intellect and integrity of E. L. De Golyer, whose distinguished library and home were given to the people of Dallas—may come at last to subdue the effects of oil's exhibitionists.

The Lower Rio Grande Valley —
The Cabbage Pickers

7 Crude Descending a Staircase

American oil has become the captive of its influence. Its comfort of inconspicuousness went by the board in the decade after the Second World War, when its influence on American politics could no longer be hidden. Its comparative obscurity to the public vanished in the storms, and in one case the notoriety, of four congressional issues: the tidelands dispute, the Kerr bill, the Harris-Fulbright bill, and production of oil for Europe following Egypt's seizure of the Suez Canal. Threading these nettles, sifting through every aspect of oil, is the depletion allowance, an issue of fear, revenge, and threat. Writing of Texas oil as a thing apart, an impression given by the two preceding chapters, ignores the facts of civilization. Two aspects of Texas oil—the Texas Railroad Commission and the magnitude of the state's production and reserves—affect domestic and international oil, but oil is not a state story.

Oil is a concern of nations. It is vital to world politics and will continue to be until a better source of power—nuclear, probably—is perfected. "It is now clear that no nation which lacks a sure supply of liquid fuel can hope to maintain a position of leadership among the peoples of the world," said a report published in 1947 by a United States Senate committee investigating petroleum resources. Countering this advantage is American oil's character. Oil's susceptibility to criticism is burdened by naïveté, piety, and outrage, even when it can make a substantial case for itself. The nuisance of adjustment is cowed. Oil pines to be a hermit in a crowd. A pamphlet published in 1956 by the Gulf Oil Corporation illustrates these attitudes and hopes in the plaint of its title: *The Industry Nobody Really Knows*.

As Picasso once said of his friend Braque, however, oil is one of those incomprehensible things that is easy to understand. The depletion allowance, oil's main concern, is a tax benefit to adjust for the exhaustion of mineral resources. An ounce of gold, a ton of coal, a barrel of oil taken from the earth can never be taken again; the asset is reduced, permanently, by one ounce or one ton or one barrel. A man who grows wheat or makes shoes does not get a depletion allowance. Wheat can be grown again on the same land and making a pair of shoes does not deplete the supply of leather permanently. The depletion allowance permits a man to deduct a percentage of his gross income, not to exceed 50 per cent of the net, in figuring his income tax. The allowance is 15 per cent for gold, 10 per cent for coal, and 15 per cent for most other minerals, whether produced in the United States or abroad. It is 23 per cent for thirty-six minerals if produced in the United States and 23 per cent for sulphur and uranium wherever they are found. The highest allowance, 27½ per cent, is for oil and gas.[1]

[1] Throughout this book the word "oil" and the words "oil industry" mean oil *and* gas.

As a rule the bone of contention is the amount of oil's allowance, not the theory of the allowance itself. Bills proposing the reduction of oil's allowance, usually to 15 per cent, have been proposed in every session of Congress since the end of the Second World War. The industry's hopes snag mainly on four barbs of its own: the Hunt-Murchison-Cullen political lust; the Superior Oil Company's attempt to corner the vote of Senator Francis Case, of South Dakota, on the Harris-Fulbright bill in 1956; the industry's penchant for coping with complexes following the Second World War as though it were dealing with those that followed the First World War; and the monkeyshines and buffooneries of oil's exhibitionists. These pitfalls have triggered a hue and cry that was distilled in an article by Richard H. Rovere, in 1956, in *The New Yorker*.

"For many years now, it has been plain to everyone here [in Washington] that the oil industry wields the most spectacular political power in the country," Rovere wrote. "Its activities may be less elaborately organized than those of the labor unions or the farm bloc, but they are numerous, daring, and regally financed. . . . The point is not that the oil interests exercise control by the purchase of votes, or even by heavy campaign contributions. They may now and then buy votes, and they certainly contribute heavily to campaigns, but what gives them their power is not what they do for the politician of whom they approve but what they are capable of doing against him. . . . It is axiomatic among members of Congress from the oil states—apart from California, where the diversity of economic interests permits diversity of opinions—that political survival is impossible in the face of oil hostility."

Rovere supported his views by showing, for one thing, the vote of congressmen from five leading oil states—Arkansas, Kansas, Louisiana, Oklahoma, and Texas—on the Harris-Fulbright bill. The bill, which would have exempted natural gas from federal price control, was passed by the House and Senate and vetoed by President Eisenhower in the light of the Case incident. "These five states send fifty-eight men to Congress," Rovere wrote. "On the Harris-Fulbright bill, these men—ranging in outlook from Senator Schoeppel, of Kansas, on the Right, to Senator Monroney, of Oklahoma, on the Left —voted as a monolithic unit: fifty-seven for and none against, with Speaker Rayburn not voting but supporting the bill from the floor. It is doubtful whether anything of this sort has ever before happened in connection with a piece of legislation involving any sizable conflict of economic interests."

Appearing before the congressional Douglas Joint Committee on the Economic Report, in 1955, two economics professors attacked the oil depletion allowance. Horace M. Gray, of the University of Illinois, argued that the 27½ per cent depletion allowance did not seem high when it was instituted in 1926 but was made so by the rise in taxes in thirty years. "In short," he said, "the depletion allowance has become primarily a private tax-escape device. . . . This lucrative privilege constitutes a powerful vested interest, the capitalized value of which amounts to billions of dollars." James R. Nelson, of Amherst University, said that while discovery risk is high for an individual wildcat oil well, "it may be quite low on the average for a large concern drilling many wildcat wells a year."

The industry rebuts that the depletion allowance accounts for America's wealth of oil reserves and thus is a factor in our world leadership. Without the allowance, oilmen say, the incentive to risk the cost of drilling an oil well would be endangered. The industry's claim that drilling an oil well is a formidable risk is no fiction. The average cost of Texas wells drilled in 1953 was $55,000 a well; 18,383 wells were completed, of which 37 per cent—one in three—were failures. The total cost of the 6813 dry holes that year was more than $375,-000,000. The industry's evidence of the risk is the proportion of dry holes. Statistics vary, but a ratio of one producer to eight dry holes is fair for wildcat wells. That estimate is not contradicted by the two-to-one ratio for Texas wells in 1953;

many of the wells were not wildcats but were drilled in areas where production was proved by a successful wildcat.

In a letter published in the *Christian Science Monitor,* in 1956, H. E. McKinstry, chairman of the Laboratory of Mining Geology at Harvard University, put the industry's case in another way. "When a haberdasher sells a necktie for $1, his profit is not $1," McKinstry wrote. "Even if he deducts a cost for running his shop, he still must deduct what he paid the wholesaler for the necktie before he can state what his profit is. Oil companies don't buy their oil from wholesalers, though. They have to find it by spending money on geology, geophysics, and drilling, including drilling hundreds of dry holes. . . . To find a barrel of oil costs some companies more than others, but to avoid elaborate accounting and keep things simple and uniform the law assumes with good reason that on the average the cost of finding oil is 27½ per cent of the sales value."

No matter the prejudices, it may be doubted that oil will lose any substantial part of its 27½ per cent depletion allowance, if any of it, unless it is replaced as a universal source of power. Necessity is apt to be a larger influence than political and economic debate in the long run. Oil's vitalness is the oilman's ally: America's need for more and more oil. The Panel on Peaceful Uses of Atomic Energy estimated that the domestic demand for oil will be 13,800,000 barrels a day by 1975, compared with 8,459,000 barrels in 1955. Thus more than seventy billion barrels of new oil must be found in twenty years. The estimate was for peacetime, however; America's need for oil is measured by the expectation of wartime maximums.

Two other factors favor oil's chances to keep the depletion allowance. Dividing drilling's risks into producing wells and dry holes takes no account of the considerable number of wells that produce little oil—a type Amos and Andy, the radio and television comedians, once compared with gushers by calling them oozers. Finally, the proportion of dry holes to wells drilled is increasing; it was 27 per cent in 1926, 37 per cent in 1955. Unless it is shown that reducing the depletion allowance would not materially affect the finding of oil, the 27½ per cent allowance would seem to be safe if the oil industry can impound its aggravations.

One of the most deplorable incidents in the economic progress of the United States is that "oil" should have become a bad word which politicians need only to utter to arouse prejudice against useful legislation and good citizens. Arthur Krock, 1957, New York *Times.*

The grim question is raised here [Washington] whether the State Department or the Texas Railroad Commission is making United States foreign policy. Richard L. Strout, 1957, *Christian Science Monitor.*

The most influential state regulatory body in America is the Texas Railroad Commission. The commission, through its principal function of conserving—controlling—the production of nearly half the nation's oil, has on occasion had the effect on domestic and world affairs of a federal agency of the highest importance. The conservation of oil, at first thought to be the goal of busybodies, now signifies as one of the chief factors in national defense and in any planning for war. This circumstance is influenced in part by man's inability to say just how much oil there is.

The history of man's attempts to guess the nation's oil resources has been a melancholy one. Government officials have been taking a crack at this puzzle since the First World War showed that the answer was worth knowing. In 1919 the director of the United States Geological Survey warned that "the position of the United States in regard to oil can be described as precarious." A survey that year showed that the United States would run out of oil by 1929, if not sooner, unless something was done to reduce consumption. A committee of President Coolidge's Cabinet made a similar forecast in 1926, as did other Jeremiahs through the 1930s, each putting off the date of our oil's exhaustion by a few more years. During the Second World War a number of government officials planned a government-owned corporation to refine and transport Middle Eastern oil in the event that Texas and Oklahoma oil fields should dry up, a setback the officials thought was imminent. On January 6, 1948, James V. Forrestal, then Secretary of Defense, wrote in his diary that within five years Americans might be forced to go back to four-cylinder automobiles if they had to depend on oil from this hemisphere. "Other men actually recommended that we step up bicycle production against the day when we would have no oil," Richard Rovere wrote in a *New Yorker* article that is the source of this paragraph.

As it has turned out through the middle 1950s, at least, these pessimisms were no match for new discoveries of oil, and some experts now feel that America has enough oil to last a century. In 1952 the President's Materials Policy Commission made an inventory of world resources available to the United States. "For years some people have been predicting that the nation's crude oil supply was going to be exhausted within ten to twenty years," said the commission's report. "Yet discoveries and output have continued to rise. In 1951, two barrels of oil were found for every one extracted and two cubic feet of gas found for every one extracted." One may presume, however, that oil is not inexhaustible, and the report of the Materials Policy Commission warned that domestic oil would have to be supplemented by increasing imports. The historic optimism of the oil industry itself has shown some signs of modulation. At the annual meeting of the American Petroleum Institute in 1952, two officials of the Standard Oil Company (Indiana) forecast that the industry might not be able to keep up with the government's requirements for reserve capacity. Reserve capacity is the amount production could be increased in case of war.

The industry sees no reason to give up the ghost, however,

even if the future's demand for oil should equal or surpass
the supply. Production of synthetic oil from shale and coal
is thought to be the answer, a belief shared by the United
States Bureau of Mines. The nation has shale and coal in quantity, and synthetic oil has been produced from both. The goal
is to find a way to produce such oil economically. The Materials Policy Commission found that "synthetic oil, probably
first from shale and later from coal, will come into commercial production within a decade or so—perhaps sooner."
A report by the Senate Small Business Committee, in 1949,
took into account synthetic production in making its estimate
of oil's longevity. Our reserve supply of oil, gas, shale, and
coal, the report said, "is sufficient to last for well over a thousand years."

Larger concerns aside, Texas has its own stake in oil conservation. The United States Bureau of Reclamation has forecast that by 1975 Texas will get a majority of its power from
Northern coal. Predicting that the state's need for power will
quadruple by then, the report said Texas's oil and gas will
then be too dear to be used for generating energy; it added
that the state's lignite resources are insufficient to fuel the
power stations. The report, covering seventeen Western
states, proposed a 500,000-volt power system generated by
coal in the North. By 1975, the report said, the seventeen
states would get 54 per cent of their power from coal, 38 per
cent from falling water, and 8 per cent from oil. The feeling
in Texas is that the bureau's report will prove to be another
note in the history of oil-reserve pessimism, but the story of
conservation in Texas has its roots in realities and conflicts.

The Texas Railroad Commission was organized in 1891 to
prevent rate discrimination and other abuses by the railroads.
In 1919, when Texas enacted an oil and gas conservation
law, its administration was given to the railroad commission.
The law has been amended with strength from time to time
and the commission now grants or withholds permission to
drill a well and fixes the maximum amount of oil that may

be produced from every well in the state. The theory is that over the long run such controls assure the maximum possible recovery of oil from each well. Critics say the purpose of controlling production is to protect the price by curbing the supply.

The three-man commission meets once a month, in open hearings, to decide how much oil may be produced the following month. Its engineers determine what is called the maximum efficient rate of daily production. But the commission is also charged with preventing "economic waste," with keeping production in line with demand to prevent the accumulation of large inventories—the source of the price-fixing charge. Each month the major companies advise the commission how much oil they plan to buy from producers the following month. The two factors, efficiency of production and market demand, determine the next month's allowable production. As a rule the commission's decisions are followed by the twenty-one other states of the Interstate Oil Compact Commission, and in effect the Texas Railroad Commission determines how much oil the United States produces.

Since 1932, when he was appointed to a vacancy, the dominant figure on the Texas Railroad Commission, and in American oil-conservation practices, has been Ernest O. Thompson. The youngest lieutenant colonel in the American Expeditionary Force of the First World War and a crusading mayor of Amarillo, in the Texas Panhandle, early in the Depression, Thompson was twice a candidate for governor, running second both times to W. Lee O'Daniel's carnivals. His elections to six-year terms as a railroad commissioner have been a monotony of success and an evidence that Texas voters, on occasion, are willing to indulge competence. Thompson has been a stranger to tranquillity since becoming a railroad commissioner. He has been a quarry of congressional investigations; he has been deplored, at different times, by one or the other divisions of Texas oil—independent producers and major companies; and he has always been viewed with alarm by Texas liberals, who suspect the railroad commission of evils beyond imagination. For a quarter of a century, however, Thompson has held the office, which now pays $17,500 a year, without becoming involved in oil's rewards. He owns two hotels in Amarillo but has never owned anything in the oil business. A lawyer who is estranged from the color and pungence of many Texas politicians, Thompson has managed to elude the title of politician. He created the administration of Texas oil and much of its sparse decorum without bending his integrity and—no mean achievement in Texas since the First World War—without scandal.

Oil bookkeeping is extremely flexible—with the depletion allowance, and with the intangible charge-off privilege, the oil company is in an unusually favorable position to meet and handle higher taxes.   From a weekly bulletin, 1951, published by Rotan, Mosle and Company, a Houston investments firm.

One of oil's substantial tax advantages is largely unknown outside the industry because critics harp almost exclusively on the depletion allowance. This other tax edge is the charge-off of intangible drilling costs—the driller's right to charge off in one year several types of costs which most businesses must depreciate for a period of years. These advantages cause wildcatting investments to be favored by film stars and others whose earnings give them an allergy to higher income-tax brackets. Thus Texas has been discovered by Hollywood as a source of something besides movie themes, and in the process, alas, a number of Texas oilmen have discovered Hollywood. Oil's reward to film stars may be measured by a sale in 1954 involving more than twenty million dollars. The property, in Scurry County, was sold to the Ponies Oil Company —operated for the profit of Southern Methodist University— by W. A. Moncrief, a Fort Worth oilman. Associated with Moncrief were Bob Hope and Bing Crosby, each of whom

owned 16 per cent of the property. The movie stars' share of
the sale was to be $3,368,360.30 each.

Nearly a hundred Hollywood figures, including Gene Au-
try, Lana Turner, Randolph Scott, Don Ameche, and Dean
Martin, have been identified in Texas oil, always in partner-
ship with a wildcatter. Texas oil is also a magnet for celebri-
ties in other fields. Risë Stevens, the mezzo-soprano of the
Metropolitan opera, and William Zeckendorf, the Munchau-
sen of American real estate, possibly represent the extremes
of oil's disciples. Artur Rubinstein, the Polish pianist, is not
known to have taken a fling in oil, but in 1953 he proved to
be subject to oil's attraction. Before performing in Midland,
a newer Texas oil city of importance, he was quoted as saying
he would "rather be a Glenn McCarthy, the Texas oil millionaire, than a famous pianist." McCarthy, infected with Hollywood fever more than most Texas oilmen who are prone to
this weakness, may have led more film people into the oil
business than anyone else. Early in his affair with the Shamrock Hotel, which he sold to Conrad Hilton in 1955, McCarthy
brought a succession of Hollywood stars to perform in the
hotel's night club. Part of the performers' pay was an interest
in McCarthy's New Ulm Field, a deal involving Dorothy Lamour, Edgar Bergen, Tony Martin, Dinah Shore, Frank Sinatra, Harpo Marx, and several others.

The tidelands controversy, at one time a flamboyant issue
in Texas, Louisiana, and California, was mooted in 1953 when
offshore oil lands were returned to the states by congressional
action. At stake in the states' rights scrap was whether the
landowner's one eighth royalty on oil produced from submerged coastal land would be paid to state or federal governments. Some idea of the stake, in Texas's case, is that the
state's Permanent School Fund was enriched by $48,124,585
from offshore oil benefits through June 1, 1955. What are
called tidelands are not that at all; the land is under water
at high or low tide, and in Texas it is a strip ten and a half

miles wide running from the mouth of the Sabine to the mouth of the Rio Grande.

The dispute backgrounds in the New Deal's beginning. In 1933 Harold L. Ickes, Secretary of the Interior, concluded that the federal government had no right to issue drilling permits or leases for submerged coastal lands. Such authority, Ickes said, belonged to the states "and the land may not be appropriated except by authority of the state." In 1937, after discovery of the Wilmington-Long Beach oil field off the coast of California, the federal government claimed this offshore land for a naval oil reserve. Secretary Ickes had changed his mind. Eight years later the government brought suit to stop a California oil company from using a state lease to produce offshore oil. In 1946, while the California case was before the Supreme Court, a Democratic Congress passed a resolution giving title to the submerged land to the states. President Truman vetoed the resolution and Congress's attempt to nullify the veto fell short of a two-thirds majority. The following year the Supreme Court ruled that California's offshore land belonged to the federal government and implied that the decision included all other submerged coastal land with the possible exception of Texas's. In 1950 the court ruled against Texas and Louisiana, and two years later President Truman vetoed a second quitclaim resolution, calling it "a free gift of immensely valuable resources . . . to the states which happen to be located nearest to them."

Adlai Stevenson, the Democrats' presidential candidate in 1952, favored federal ownership of the offshore lands; Dwight Eisenhower, the Republican candidate, favored state ownership. That was the principal cause—it may have been the excuse, for anti-Trumanism was virulent in Texas and the South generally—of Texas's defection from the Democratic party that year. When President Eisenhower signed the bill returning the submerged lands to the states, Texas regained title to more than three million acres. The bill restored state titles to their "historic limits"—three miles for all states but

Texas and the west coast of Florida, where the Spanish law of three leagues (a little more than ten miles) was approved.

Though the author's prejudice destroys objectivity, Texas especially would seem to have been plundered by the Supreme Court decision of 1950. The Texas case, thanks to the peculiarity of the state's admission to the Union, was unique, as President Truman said. Texas is the only state to own its public lands, a provision of the treaty between the Republic of Texas and the United States by which the republic became a state. "The court now decides that when Texas entered the Union she lost what she had and the United States acquired it. How that shift came to pass remains for me a puzzle," Associate Justice Felix Frankfurter wrote in a dissenting opinion when the Supreme Court ruled that the state's submerged lands were the property of the federal government.

This three-chapter evaluation of Texas oil scants the specifics of natural gas—the one industry that talks always in terms of trillions (of cubic feet)—and the interstate transmission of gas and the petrochemicals industry. Each is allied with oil; each is of significance to Texas; each has an influence on the nation, especially the gas transmission industry; each burgeons with an energy that bewilders. The Tennessee Gas Transmission Company, of Houston, was organized in 1944; twelve years later its assets passed a billion dollars, a speed of growth that may never have been equaled in American business. Natural gas is a subject of continuing discord in Texas: should Texas gas be exported to other states or kept in Texas? By 1957 Texas was the nation's third state in chemical production and first in construction of new chemical projects— more than half a billion dollars' worth.

Texas oil's future is misted by the future of synthetic oil and nuclear energy. The reality of foreign competition is already being faced. "Texas can expect the oil reserves . . . in the Middle East to have a direct bearing on Texas crude production in the future," the Texas Legislative Council reported in 1950. America's share of world oil production greatly exceeds its share of the world's reserves; the Middle East's share of reserves greatly exceeds its share of production. Texas, with 17 per cent of the world's reserves, cannot provide 22 per cent of the world's production indefinitely.

III METAMORPHOSIS:
URBAN ILIAD

SOUTHWEST TEXAS - ANY COUNTY SEAT

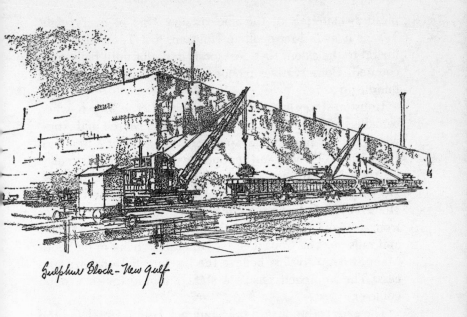

Sulphur Block - New Gulf

8 Great Expectations

I

Largest city in Texas, largest in the South if Baltimore is not South, largest in America with racial segregation, Houston sprawls on the Gulf plain, coaxing the future. Oil producer, oil refiner, oil bookkeeper, gas sender to the nation, deepwater port fifty miles inland, anthill of huge law firms, it takes traditions from the present. Roy Rogers and ten thousand at the fat stock show parted by a wall from Leopold Stokowski and three thousand at the symphony. Church town, medical center, university city; air conditioned, stewing in education conflicts, breathing assurance, it skipped half a century in fifteen years. War did it. The Second World War cohered with a good geology. Geology cohered with industries needing natural gas and crude's leftovers to make chemicals and plastics—materials of the nuclear age. One of every eight Texans lives in Metropolitan Houston, first Texas city to go liberal to the extent that decision is in doubt until ballots are counted. Conservatives monopolized the outcome until the middle 1950s.

Houston stores up vitality from December to March, when camellias season the air with color, and in March and April, when azaleas nourish the spirit. Roses bloom at Christmas. Huisache, dogwood, and redbuds open in March, magnolias in April. Winter shades under live oak, juniper, and pines. December to April is a benediction; the rest is hot and humid. Houston has been new for fifty years. Most strangers enter from the west, north, or east, the city's side doors as highways and rails go. The front door faces south. Driving in on South Main Street, travelers believe the legends of Houston's success. The approach recalls a state fair midway—a neoned come-on.

The eyes cotton first to the Shamrock Hilton Hotel and the Prudential Building, hub of a spread of skyscrapers covering what were open fields at the end of the war. Past the hotel, as the neon fades, past towers of apartments and offices on the near and far right, is the Texas Medical Center, the superlative of Houston exuberance. Excepting one hospital, the area was a forest within the city in 1946. Six more hospitals, including one of the world's leading cancer-research centers, and a medical college, a dental college, and a medical library were built in a few years. Most of the cost of more than fifty million dollars was paid by oil and cotton wealth. The medical center is too dispersed for the traveler to take in, as is the beauty of Rice Institute—also the result of philanthropy—across the street. Continuing north, on the right, is the vast green of Hermann Park—another millionaire's gift—and on the left are the only mansions near the downtown flanks. Farther north, past Warwick Circle, is a funnel of churches and shops leading to the sky line.

"What one misses most in Houston are old things," Paul

Rothenhausler, a Swiss reporter, wrote in 1951. "After a few days [in Houston] one sings the praise of the past—just for contrast's sake." Preserved in an alfresco museum are two ante bellum houses—the only visibles of Houston's age. The city is not concerned with the past. Not till 1954 did the Harris County Heritage and Conservation Society organize to rescue remaining evidence of the old. Not till the same year did another group start collecting photographs and mementos of the city's history. Spanish moss, gentling from oaks and sweet gums, and royal palms image the Old South and the tropics, but the city deserted the ease and siesta of Southern and tropical moods in the 1920s. Motion keys Houston's character, subduing reflection. The character is expressed in oil and an annual fat stock show, in religion and sports, flower growing and outdoor living.

"M" Day, as July 3, 1954, was called, epitomized the city's gusto. When the chamber of commerce divined that metropolitan Houston's population would then reach a million, a festival was planned to welcome the millionth citizen. Houston Bucks were printed in a denomination of $1,000,000. A huge thermometer, its peak registering 1,000,000, was put at a downtown corner and the reading raised a notch a day. Thousands of auto-bumper signs said "I'm One in a Million—Houston." Firms changed their postage-meter messages to read "Houston's a Million Strong." At a town meeting, held in Hermann Park on July 3, Mr. Million was identified as B. C. McCasland, Jr., who moved to the city the day before from Clinton, Mississippi. Aged thirty-six, a geologist, and father of five children, he typified the city. Receiving gifts said to be worth $10,000, he was flown to the eleven larger American cities to talk about Houston. Two years later, when the Bureau of the Census estimated the populations of Houston, Milwaukee, St. Louis, and Washington, it was found that "M" Day may not have been premature. The population of metropolitan Houston was put at 1,077,000 as of January 1, 1956—an increase of 35 per cent since the 1950 census.

A query by a New York matron, visiting Houston for the first time in 1950, shows America's credulity in the city's "Big Rich" myth. Passing the Rice Institute campus—three hundred acres of lawn, hedges, and trees; buildings in Byzantine, Moorish, Italian, and Spanish designs—she said, "Tell me, who lives there?" The myth fringes the city's character more from America's belief in it than from fact. It flowered mainly in the derring-do of Glenn H. McCarthy, an oilman whose pungence intrigued the nation for a while; in the extravagance of the opening, in 1949, of what was then McCarthy's Shamrock Hotel; and in the manner of H. R. Cullen's philanthropy. In 1949 Cullen disclosed, as an afterthought to a speech, that he was going to give away an estimated eighty million dollars' worth of future oil production. He doubled the sum when Houston leaders called to thank him a day or so later.

The city responds to the myth by making millionaires its heroes, their lore its legends: a country club's membership fee is more than ten thousand dollars; women's rest-room fixtures are gold-plated at the Petroleum Club; the Tejas Club—limit sixty members—uses gold-plated paper clips. The Petroleum Club is atop the Rice Hotel, beneath which is thought to be an oil structure of promise. As nearby property was sold for two thousand dollars a front inch in 1947, it is doubted that oil wells will be drilled on downtown Main Street, though derricks edge the street seven miles south of the hotel. Millionairing lures, but the people's character is illumined by a Main Street sign on the First Baptist Church. Near the center of the business district, the sign spells "Jesus Saves" in electric lights. Contradicting the evangelist Billy Graham, religion pervades the city's life. To forty thousand in Rice Stadium on the last day of his revival, in 1952, Graham said Houston was a "more wicked city than Hollywood." At an earlier service he said the majority of Houstonians would spend eternity in hell. The evangelist also said that the month-long revival was "the greatest campaign I have ever conducted."

Though it legends in wealth, Houston is a city of working people. They came in mass during the Second World War—forty thousand to the shipyards alone—and most remained. Unlike the state, whose population has grown largely from the excess of births over deaths, Houston grows more from people moving in from the rest of Texas and other states. The board of directors of the Houston Chamber of Commerce, where natives might be expected to dominate, reflects the newness of the population. Of the board's twenty-nine members in 1956, eleven moved to the city after 1945, seven of them in 1951 or later. Only one of the twenty-nine was born in Houston, only eleven more were born elsewhere in Texas.

After you have listened to the talk of one of these pioneer veterans [of Houston] for some time, you begin to feel that the creation of the world, the arrangement of the solar system, and all subsequent events, including the discovery of America, were provisions of an all-wise Providence, arranged with a direct view to the advancement of the commercial interests of Houston. Alexander E. Sweet and J. Armoy Knox, 1883, *On a Mexican Mustang Through Texas.*

Houston, where Franklin Roosevelt nominated Al Smith for the presidency in 1928, has been excelled in American urban growth only by Los Angeles since the Second World War. It was the twenty-first city in population in 1940, fourteenth in 1950, twelfth in 1955. The New York *Times* has quoted Lloyd's of London, an underwriters' association, as predicting a population of three million for Houston by 1980. Estimates of more validity prophesy a population of two million by 1975. The city's growth, however, is not everywhere a subject of awe. In 1956 Harry A. Keep, owner of a Houston electronics firm, sent two classified ads to the New York *Times*. Before printing them the *Times* wrote to Keep: "Also to comply with our advertising regulations, we shall appreciate your changing the phrase '. . . in the nation's fastest growing city' to read '. . . in one of the nation's fastest growing cities.'"

Although hundreds of miles from the state's chief cattle-raising area, Harris County has more cattle than any other in the state. Irrigated land has made the county a rice producer of importance. Houston signifies in cotton, not as a grower but as a spot cotton market and for its Anderson, Clayton & Company, largest cotton firm in the world. In oil, natural gas—especially in the nationwide distribution of gas —and in manufacturing oil-field equipment Houston leads. Forty-eight oil fields in the county produce more than eighty thousand barrels of oil daily, the area has twelve refineries, the city is headquarters for the Humble Oil and Refining Company and the Continental Oil Company. Houston trails in but one phase of oil—finance, dominated by Dallas, Chicago, and New York. By 1957 the city of Houston was receiving around seventy-five thousand dollars a year from royalties on wells at the city garbage dump; other wells were to be drilled at the city prison farm. Oil rigs are within a few yards of businesses on South Main Street. Paul Kayser, president of the El Paso Natural Gas Company, was asked at a press conference in El Paso why his firm, which owns El Paso's tallest building and supplies West Texas gas to western states, has its headquarters in Houston. He answered that the only place in America to keep in touch with the oil business is Houston.

The fantasy of the city's growth recalls its beginning. Houston was planned by A. C. and John K. Allen, brothers from upstate New York, as a real-estate venture. Santa Anna had just burned Harrisburg, a few miles down Buffalo Bayou, before the Battle of San Jacinto. Its site in several ways superior to Houston's, Harrisburg was rebuilt after Santa Anna's pillage but lacked promoters of the Allens' gifts. In October 1836, when Houston was but a plat surveyed by two brothers—one, Gail Borden, later invented a process for condensing milk—John Allen made a proposition to the Texas Congress, then meeting at Columbia. Move the government to Houston, he said, and the Allens would build it a capitol. "Capitalists are interested in this town," the Allens said in their petition to Congress. Earlier, even before the Bordens had surveyed the townsite, the Allens had advertised the proposed city in the New York *Herald* and the Washington *Globe*. The phrase "ONE MILLION DOLLARS," in capital letters, was used in ads about Houston before there was a Houston.

The Allens, having made their city the republic's capital before the city existed, began building in fact what had succeeded in fancy. The government moved to Houston, in May 1837, before the town was finished. The two brothers were as vitamins to the place. Travelers were hard put to find food and lodging in Texas, but the Allens opened their home, without charge, to all who needed it. Their bookkeeper later said that although their hospitality cost them more than three thousand dollars a year, the Allens thought it was an expense that would bring riches to the city.

Modern Houston needs the Allens' talent for producing small miracles. The city's superlatives are jeopardized by troubles common to swift growth. The individualism of its people, however, has given the city an extra complication, one that cannot be altered without building the city anew in some other place. Houston is the largest city in the United States without a zoning ordinance. This concession to a pirate's regard for the aesthetics of living areas weakens city planning, holding beauty and homeowners' confidence to a minimum in the older residential areas. Used-car lots, laundries, drive-ins, service stations, in some cases small industrial plants, are found in residential neighborhoods from which they would be banned elsewhere. "Houston is of interest," said O'Neil Ford, a San Antonio architect distinguished for the merit of his work and the poverty of his diplomacy. "Other cities have their slums in one place; Houston spreads them all over." The city needs more parks, and its bayous—a local disgust—could be beautified as San Antonio has improved its river. The nation's twelfth largest city was in fifty-seventh place in support of public libraries in 1955. Houston has more than three thousand railroad grade crossings; the five railroads serving the city enter on thirteen separate rights of way.

. . . why Houston should be sensitive about anything is beyond me, for it has a strength and power and rude majesty all its own. In time, perhaps, it will achieve greatness. Ralph Coghlan, 1950, Saint Louis *Post-Dispatch.*

II

It seemed to me that [in Dallas] I was at the heart of an empire ruled by a youthful, energetic people who were unafraid and had never tasted the bitterness of disillusion. David L. Cohn, 1940, *Atlantic Monthly.*

Daily in the 1920s the Chicago *Tribune* printed on its editorial page a "Program for Chicagoland," of which Article 1 was "Make Chicago the First City of the World." The Dallas *News* does not encourage civic stimulation on that scale; its goal is to make Dallas the first city of the United States. An obsession with being Dallas pervades the city and the *News.* "This is the most interesting man-made city in the United States," John Rosenfield, amusements editor of the *News,* wrote in 1953. The quotation, implying that some cities were made by other than man, typifies the Dallas conviction that Dallas is singular. Excerpts from Lynn Landrum's column on the editorial page of the *News* illumine this spirit. In 1954: "God has favored Dallas." The same year: "By taking thought and by taking courage, we can make Dallas the brightest, cleanest, most thriving city in the whole land." In 1955: "Greater Dallas is to come in a greatness that staggers comprehension." Later that year: "In all that the eye can see and statistics can compass, Dallas is blessed and even envied."

With Dallas in a fever of prosperity and growth, Mayor Robert L. Thornton chided the people because "Dallas is riding a Shetland pony when it ought to be riding a big white horse." The mayor, a bank president whose East Texas picturesqueness relieves the urbanity of the city he leads, goaded Dallas in his 1955 Christmas card. A caricature of himself at the controls of a steam shovel in front of the sky line, it said: "Full steam ahead for '56. Let's keep the dirt flying in and for Big D to assure all of us many Happy Holiday Seasons down the road." Dallas is characterized by arch-conservatism, by concerns for commerce and the State Fair of Texas, for religion, football, and fashion. Above all these except conservatism it is also characterized by civic ardor. "As long as I live I will do everything in my power for the city I love," Mayor Thornton said in 1955. Decades of such striving have rewarded Dallas with its significance.

The personality of Dallas and the *News* in the 1950s and that of Chicago and the *Tribune* in the 1940s resemble each other. Like the second pair, Dallas and the *News* insulate themselves from the shock of world affairs, and both are to Texas what Chicago and the *Tribune* are to the Midwest—leaders of conservatism. In the late 1930s Dallas boasted that it was the largest open-shop city in the United States. In 1942, when the Fair Labor Standards Act was an issue, Dallas held a "giant We Want Action mass meeting," as the *News* called it, to oppose the bill's provision that workers be paid overtime rates for work in excess of forty hours a week. In a full-page announcement of the meeting, which was attended by several thousand people, the *News* represented the forty-hour provision as "a law which says a man should work only 40 hours per week! . . . Is there a law which says our sons must fight only 40 hours a week or die only 40 hours a week?" The question was in italics. Nowhere did the announcement

say it was possible to work more than forty hours if given
overtime pay.

What Dallas and the *News* would destroy in the 1950s is
called "left wing." From a *News* editorial in March 1952: "Yet
the expanding role which the left-wing Department of Labor
is taking in this field [seasonal labor from Mexico] is open to
question." From an editorial in August 1954: "The simple
decision, come Aug. 28 [the date of the gubernatorial runoff
primary between Ralph Yarborough and Governor Allan Shiv-
ers], is this: If you are a leftist, vote Yarborough . . . if you
vote right, vote Shivers." April 1952: "In that year [1932], the
Roosevelt forces began deliberately to destroy the basic constitutional theory of state sovereignty upon which the republic is founded." December 1954: "This is a happy day for Communists and their fellow travelers in America. Senate censure
of the one man [Senator Joseph W. McCarthy] who has done
most to expose their web of treason within our government
gives them the green light." May 1956, when the Supreme
Court annulled a Pennsylvania sedition law: "The Supreme
Court thus becomes a threat to state sovereignty second only
to Communism itself."

"In the North you can now look for a rash of strikes led by
labor leaders of the Lewis-Petrillo type," Landrum wrote in
1954. "Any industry so paralyzed has nothing to lose by leaving—and everything to gain by coming here." The *News*
often represents the North as a foreign and undesirable place
from which industrial leaders will retreat when they learn
about Dallas. It is true, however, that the Dallas area's union
labor has not congealed as a political force; it does not act
with much unity. The *News,* on the other hand, maintains
that a lack of unity hounds the conservatives.

In 1956, when Price Daniel won the governor's Democratic
primary by three thousand votes out of more than a million
and a quarter cast, Dick West wrote on the *News* editorial
page: "Price Daniel can thank Dallas, as Allan Shivers did in
1954. Dallas remains the most dependable producer of con-

servative votes in Texas. . . . The 21,000 lead Daniel received here . . . saved his neck, because there were almost disastrous shifts in other big counties in favor of [liberal candidate Ralph] Yarborough." Writing on the editorial page the same year, Sam Acheson said: "Dallas is thought of today as the stronghold of the Conservatives in Texas politics. . . . Even [in 1896] the majority of local voters were stanchly conservative."

The *News* represents Dallas conservatism to perfection. The paper's success is no mystery. It and Dallas agree as do no other newspaper and city in the state. The *News* reflects every facet of the city's personality. When it appeared that the Cotton Bowl might not be filled for the New Year's Day football game of 1957, the *News* ran front-page editorials headed "Let's Fill the Bowl, Dallas" and "It's More Than a Game." The editorials called the game "an irreplaceable civic asset" and said that "if this game isn't a sellout every year, it isn't good for Dallas." The city strains to money's welfare, as does the *News*, which measured the community benefits of Christianity in terms of economic rewards in its lead editorial of June 8, 1952. "God's Business Is Big Business," the editorial was headlined.

Its people seem encased in correct clothes, right ideas, sense of class. Dallas represents something the United States has made with money. Erna Fergusson, 1940, *Our Southwest.*

Some cities, like Dallas, get vehement, almost impertinent, in demanding that I predict a great future for them. Roy V. Peel, director of the Bureau of the Census, 1952, in an interview published in the Houston *Post.*

In 1871 the United States Congress chartered the Texas and Pacific Railroad, authorizing it to build part of a transcontinental line along the thirty-second parallel. The track would run fifty miles south of Dallas, too distant to benefit the town of four thousand people. The Texas legislature could not be expected to divert the railroad's course to help Dallas, so the city's leaders conceived a ruse. Just south of Dallas was Browder Springs, a landmark unknown outside the area. When a bill giving the railroad a subsidy of public lands passed the legislature, it included a rider, added by the Dallas legislator, specifying that the track must come "within one mile of Browder Springs." The rider did not mention Dallas, but thus the city got its second railroad and the first of importance.

Such adroitness has typified the city's rise for nearly a century. It showed eighty years later when Dallas wanted a new downtown hotel. The Statler chain hoped to build the hotel but was unwilling to finance the total cost alone. Members of the Dallas Chamber of Commerce formed a corporation—the Cosmopolitan Hotel Company—to sell $1,500,000 worth of debentures and lend the money to the Statler firm. The sale was oversubscribed when Dallas businessmen were asked to buy the debentures. The new 1001-room hotel, by then named the Statler Hilton, was opened early in 1956.

In 1948, when the Chance-Vought Aircraft Company planned to move from Connecticut to Dallas, the plan was threatened when company officials learned that runways at the Dallas airport were too short for the company's use. Rex B. Beisel, head of Chance-Vought, called Dechard A. Hulcy, a Dallas leader who helped persuade the firm to move. "About that move to Dallas—" *Fortune* quoted Beisel as saying. "It all hinges on whether those runways can be extended." Hulcy asked how long they should be and said he and his friends would see about it. "Three hours and forty minutes later Beisel's phone rang," *Fortune* said. "It was Hulcy. He just wanted to let Beisel know that the City Council had been persuaded to call an emergency meeting. Two hundred and fifty-six thousand dollars had been voted for runways. Work would begin Monday morning." A new industry and fifteen hundred employees, plus their families, moved from the North to Dallas.

More than any other city in Texas, more than Houston by far, Dallas has been a planning city. It began measuring its present in terms of the future in 1910, when George B. Dealey, publisher of the Dallas *News* for twenty years, persuaded city officials to hire George E. Kessler, a city planner of note. One result of Dealey's instinct for humanity, and his intelligence, could not be comprehended by Dallas people—or any other large body of Americans—of his time or since. In a study of city planning he made in 1916, Dealey advocated Kessler's conclusion that cities should limit their size —"the greater the population of a city, the less it can meet reasonable demands for comfort and happy living conditions." The Kessler Plan was followed in 1927 by the Ulrickson Plan, resulting in a $23,900,000 bond issue for improvements. The Bartholomew Plan, made during the Second World War to prepare for postwar growth, led to more than fifty million dollars' worth of improvements. In 1955, still thinking ahead, Dallas set up another group to plan for metropolitan area populations of 928,000 in 1960; 1,336,000 in 1964; and 2,440,000 in 2000.

A Dallas Chamber of Commerce report in 1956 estimated that more than 400,000 people—about 50 per cent of the population—moved into the metropolitan area in the previous ten years. In the early 1950s manufacturing overtook merchandising as leader of the city's economy, but it will be slow to overtake merchandising in the city's character. Deciding early what a city ought to be and fulfilling the requirements when it could, Dallas is the most cosmopolitan of Texas cities. It "is in the springtime of its career as a big city," Jack B. Krueger, city editor of the *News*, wrote in 1954. The speed of the city's onward-and-upward spirit often seems to elude its shadow, but its self-esteem escapes the ego's penalties through a history of performance. "How much better if we devoted our time, energy and thought to making Dallas the best town in Texas rather than the largest," George Dealey wrote in 1916. Dallas tries to do both.

gulf Coast Rice Field with Rice Dryers

9 All Mimsy Were the People

A mural was hung in the Dallas Public Library three months before the new building was opened in 1955. Made by Harry Bertoia, a Pennsylvania sculptor, the mural weighed three thousand pounds, was twenty-four feet long and ten feet high. Its many pieces of metal of variant shapes were welded to eleven vertical rods, suggesting political signs tacked at random to a row of telephone poles. "It is very modern and contemporary, of course," Bertoia said. "It is a mirror to the person who looks at it. Those who find nothing have evidently not prepared their lives and probably are very happy about it."

The city that thinks of itself as the Athens of the Southwest seems not to have prepared its life for the Bertoia mural, and it proved to be very happy about it. As the mural's cost of $8700 was to be paid with tax money, Mayor R. L. Thornton

and members of the city council went to see it. They did not
care for it. "It looks to me just like a bunch of junk," the
mayor said. "Besides, it looks like a cheap welding job." Even
so, the mayor found a silver lining: "I'll say one thing—it'll
attract attention. It has good advertising possibilities." Such
was indeed the case. No one did more to advertise the mural
than Lynn Landrum, of the Dallas *News*, a columnist who
has incited readers' anger and joy for two decades. Once,
deploring churchmen who hope to make the United States
a part of one world, he wrote: "The Columntator is a nationalist. He is a narrow nationalist. He is a narrow, reactionary
nationalist." At another time he described himself as "South-
ern-born and old-fashioned and narrow-minded in a lot of his
notions." Never dealing in craftiness or slick talk, Landrum
blunts his conservatism. Liberals angered away by his views
miss the most flavored writing in Texas newspapers.

Landrum wrote of the mural: "The soul-stuff of steel bed-
slats, with junk-yard gussets and timbre de goulash ought
never to be submitted to naked eyeball appraisal. It calls for
that je-ne-sais-quoi, that leichglaubbigzeit, that hornswoggle-
mazooleum without which soarings of jam-session genius is
inadequately appreciated." That was in line with Landrum's
theory that to actually see the mural would prejudice a man.
Deciding that the mural should have a name, he offered a
prize—"a notable work of art, namely, a hand-rusted piece
of junk overlaid with mayonnaise"—to the winner of his contest to name what he called "Bertoia's Bust" and "Welder's
Saturday Night." Entries included "Cancan at the Crema-
torium," "Carnegie Metal," "Staircase Descending a Nude,"
and "Tribute to Dallas—by Fort Worth." At one point Landrum concluded from the mural's weight, dimensions, and
cost "that art is worth $2.90 a pound in Dallas and $18.12½
per cubic foot." The city's Bonehead Club competed with
Landrum, announcing that it had employed a French mu-
ralist to design a replacement for Bertoia's work. The French-
man's sketch was described as "a mule's skull with tin cans

hanging off each side, topped by an umbrella. It is entitled 'Gee Haw!'"

In spite of the nonsense, however, the Bertoia mural was an issue of consequence. Guilt for employing the sculptor fell on George L. Dahl, the library's architect, who finally bought the mural in self-defense and had it delivered to his home. Mayor Thornton and two city councilmen made a statement at the time, saying, "We think that to buy more books and things of that character for the benefit of the most people would be a much wiser investment for the taxpayers than a mural which only a limited number would understand and enjoy, and we are deeply grateful to George Dahl for his fine contribution [by taking the mural off the city's hands]." Paul Crume, a *News* columnist, printed an anonymous verse the next day:

> The mural of Bertoia
> Will no longer annoia.

"The basic issue was not whether the Bertoia screen was good or bad," wrote Rual Askew, art critic of the *News*. "It was . . . whether a ranking artist should suffer the indignity of a line of reasoning which says that what is unfamiliar is suspect, that what is not 'liked' by some is unacceptable to all." A *News* editorial disagreed, saying, "It is apparent now that the metal decoration recently placed in the new library did not belong there. The place for experimental forms of art and for art fads and novelties is in the art gallery, not in the public library." A group of art's defenders raised the money to buy the mural and gave it to the library; being innocent of tax money made it acceptable. Approving the gift, the city council had the last word, lecturing art, artists, and architects with annoyance.

The mural's adventure means little compared with two other demonstrations of the mind of Dallas. One lasting for months was led at its showdown by Alvin M. Owsley, former national commander of the American Legion, former United

States minister to Rumania, to the Irish Free State, and to
Denmark. Owsley has a history of eagerness to protect America from excesses of democracy. Described in the *Atlantic
Monthly*, in 1956, as "the Legion's ranking orator," he was
quoted as telling a Legion group that he would "throw the
United Nations into the sea." The group was investigating
the demerits of the United Nations Educational, Scientific,
and Cultural Organization. The *Atlantic* continued: "In a
burst of indignation he cried that a UNESCO scientist had
reported that there is no difference between the blood of the
white man and the blood of the black man." "The Reds are
moving in on us," he said during the Dallas communism-in-art
dispute. "Let us hold together . . . Let those who would plant
a red picture supplant it with the red, white, and blue. White
for purity, blue for fidelity, as blue as our Texas bluebonnets."
And later: "Shall we not establish a policy of patriotism,
Americanism and Christianity for Dallas?"

Patrioteers hounded the city in 1955. Picasso's paintings
were censored. An American Legion post frightened the
board of trustees of the Dallas Museum of Fine Arts into
banning paintings by communists or suspected communists.
The "Family of Man," a photographic exhibit shown elsewhere without trouble, was condemned as communistic.
Against that background the museum's board acted again late
in 1955. It reversed its earlier stand by resolving to "acquire
works of art only on the basis of their merit as works of art."
The Communism in Art Committee of the Dallas County Patriotic Council reacted by asking the board to do two things:
remove the paintings of artists Leon Kroll, William Zorach,
Ben Shahn, and Yasuo Kuniyoshi from a forthcoming "Sport
in Art" show and "redeclare your policy to not buy or show
any works of persons who have communist or communist
front records."

When the board reaffirmed its stand—Owsley said this decision "hit me like an atomic bomb"—the patriotic council
called an open meeting. A small auditorium was more than

filled for the two-hour meeting. Speakers said the motives for
wanting to overcome the board's resolution were that exhibit-
ing works of communist artists enriched the Soviet treasury
and disgraced America's war dead. It was decided to ask the
Dallas Park Board, which approves city funds for maintenance of the museum, to enforce the council's requests.

Speaking at a Rotary Club meeting, Eugene McElvaney,
a vice-president of the First National Bank in Dallas, scorned
the "brand of patriotism associated solely with an obsessive
fear of communism. . . . Certain patriotic groups, almost in
desertion of the fundamental defenses of our freedoms . . .
devote their major energies toward banning or censoring, and
imagine they are fulfilling their highest devotion to home and
country." He suggested that such patriots concern themselves
with scandals in the state government and other problems
that would not compromise the principles of democracy. The
Rotarians gave McElvaney a standing ovation, indicating
that Dallas is not typed by the democracy cramps of the patriotic council or the spasms of its minority pressures. John
Rosenfield wrote essays of brilliance in the *News* and the
Southwest Review, especially in the last, supporting the museum and rebuking the city's "aesthetic vigilantes." Gerald
C. Mann, a former attorney general of Texas and a member
of the museum's board, was a leader of courage for the trustees. The park board and the city council, to which the park
board is responsible, upheld the trustees. No proof showed
that the four painters were communists or sympathizers; some
evidence contradicted such claims. "There is a lot of difference in being on some list as a communist and being one,"
Mayor Thornton said.

The other controversy of importance, in the 1950s, was
fomented by John O. Beaty, firebrand, Phi Beta Kappa, and
professor of English at Southern Methodist University. Professor Beaty is the author of *The Iron Curtain Over America*,
a book described by *Zions Herald*, Methodism's oldest publication, as "the most extensive piece of racist propaganda in

the history of the anti-Semitic movement in America," and
in Ralph Lord Roy's *Apostles of Discord* as "a dangerous
threat to democracy and a new embarrassment to sensitive
Christians." Published in 1951, the book enlarges the prejudices of Gerald L. K. Smith, who called it "the most sensa-
tional book of this generation" and "the greatest . . . of its
kind ever to appear in print." Another who praised the book
was Alvin Owsley. *The Iron Curtain Over America*, Owsley
said, is "one of the great documents of our times" and "should
become the first reading of every patriot in the land." Steeped
in bigotry, accusing the Roosevelt and Truman administrations of being pro-Semitic, Beaty and his book were repudiated by S.M.U., one of the most liberal-minded church
universities in the United States—by the administration, the
faculty, and the student body.

The controversy bloomed when the *Southwest Review*
published its autumn 1953 issue, titled "Freedom in America." A literary quarterly sponsored by S.M.U., the *Review*
leads Texas publications—often without followers—in lighting
up darknesses of custom and prejudice. "The Protestant Un-
derworld," an article written by Margaret L. Hartley, an
editor of the *Review*, discussed Beaty's book with aversion.
The professor replied in a pamphlet titled *How to Capture
a University*, saying the *Review's* article was one "of many
manifestations of the effort of a certain powerful non-Christian element in our population to dominate Southern Methodist University." After condemning the B'nai B'rith and the
National Conference of Christians and Jews, Beaty deplored
that the *Review* had permitted "a locally prominent non-
Christian" to be spokesman for the sponsoring committee of
the Institute on American Freedom. The institute was a series
of talks at S.M.U. by Paul G. Hoffman, Gerald W. Johnson,
Kenneth C. Royall, and Henry M. Wriston; its purpose was
to "rediscover and examine the basic principles of freedom
as written into the Constitution so that the perpetuation of
these freedoms may be assured."

The "non-Christian" whom Beaty did not name is Stanley Marcus, president of the Neiman-Marcus stores and a man of courage. The committee itself included Mayor Thornton and some others whose integrity and fair-mindedness more than checked Beaty's anti-Semitism. Beaty was comforted in Dallas by Owsley and a few more of like mind while the Dallas *News* covered itself with neutrality. In two editorials, the paper resolved the witches' brew into a dispute between liberals and conservatives and suggested that S.M.U. make up its mind between the two. Dallas papers feel that the less said the better in such disputes. Heckling and censoring activities of Dallas Minute Women virtually escapes notice in the papers, whose indifference keeps contention going.

Patrioteers won an easy victory late in 1956. "Another row over Communist art has been nipped in the bud by removal from a Dallas Public Library exhibit of two works by Communist-leaning Spanish Artist Pablo Picasso," began a story in the *News*. It was nipped in the bud by surrendering to anonymous callers. "This group—I don't know just who it was, but people who were against it—began calling to protest [the showing of a Picasso rug and painting]," James D. Meeks, the librarian, was quoted as saying. The library board supported his decision to ban the works, calling the display "a mistake." John Rosenfield later wrote in the *News*: "This would be as good a time as any for our fair city to arrive at a clear and simple code to govern the exhibition of paintings, the performance of music and drama, the circulation of books or any other expression of mankind's creative spirit or mental processes. This should be: If anybody objects yank it down or ban it from the halls, or burn it up." The library took its stand on exhibitions in February 1957, opening "an exhibit on nutrition of milk and milk products."

What matters is that enlightenment and democratic principles usually prevail. The mural was returned to the library, the patriotic council censored the art museum in vain, and Beaty was unable to corner S.M.U. The university is the city's light. In 1955 it was beset by criticism because books about communism were in its library, because it invited a psychology professor to speak on ministerial counseling, because it permitted a labor seminar to meet on its campus, and because it offered a short course for adults called Freedom Agenda. Willis M. Tate, a former S.M.U. football star, was installed as the university's youngest president in 1954, when he was forty-three. He succeeded Dr. Umphrey Lee, who is one reason for the university's character and importance. Talking to a Kiwanis Club in 1955 Tate told of the four criticisms listed above, and he told what the university was going to do about them:

"We at S.M.U. are here to teach young adults how to think and how to cope with the real world around them. . . . Part of the young adult's process of maturing is this grappling with all ideas. This is not a dangerous conception of teaching. It has been used by colleges and universities since the beginning of their existence, and has produced the most stalwart leadership in our American life. . . . This is the real power and strength of a university. Maintaining this atmosphere [of freedom] is most difficult since many people . . . do not believe in the American tradition of open discussion. . . . There are risks involved in freedom of education and discussion, but we'll accept those risks."

Tate, McElvaney, Mann—the president of a Methodist university, a banker, and a corporation lawyer, and so not weakened, as would be the case in Dallas, by the liberal label —and other leaders of their type have rescued the city from dead ends of the closed mind. As a rule they lead without the editorial support, or at best with the qualified support, of Dallas newspapers.

What would Dallas be without those few institutions we all think we jointly own? Answer: just another Houston.
Lon Tinkle, 1954, Dallas *News*.

Being just another Houston is not something a city falls into by lacking some institutions. Houston is beset by the source of Dallas trouble: a minority of fanatical nationalists. Dallas leads the state's conservatism and Houston leads in turning away from conservatism, yet the cities are one in provoking ideological conflict. Houston shines in terms of Dallas controversies: anti-Semitism is not an issue, nor was the "Family of Man" show; exhibitions of work by Picasso, Rivera, and the like are shown without incident at two museums. Contradicting its liberal trend, Houston boils in education conflict. Industrial suburbs, a main source of liberal votes, have their own school districts; their residents neither live nor vote in the Houston Independent School District.

The Houston School Board champions dissension. The people have come to accept its contentions as though such were the natural state of the academic world. The board is the city's main forum for debating larger issues: the welfare state vs. free enterprise, the United Nations, federal aid to education, racial segregation. Its principal rows in the decade after the Second World War involved George W. Ebey, UNESCO, the content of textbooks, and segregation.

A textbook in civics was banned in 1949 because it spoke of "strong socialistic and even communistic trends" in the United States—the words were not capitalized—without troubling to denounce them. Though banned in Houston, the text was used in many parts of the country, including more than a hundred Texas schools, several of them in Harris County but outside the Houston school district. Five years later the text was reapproved for use in Houston schools when "criticized areas" of the book were deleted. Book banning erupted again in 1957, when the board's Mrs. Earl Maughmer condemned a geography text because the United Nations was praised in its foreword, another text because a chapter was titled "It's All One World," and a third because it said the government is obligated "to promote the welfare of all the people." Out went all three books.

In 1953 the ninth-grade history course was pruned of debate on the "strengths and weaknesses" of the United Nations. The move was made on the theory that teen-agers could not be expected to comprehend a matter on which adults had not agreed. Study of the United Nations is limited to how and why it was organized and what nations are members. An anti-UNESCO slate of candidates was nominated for the 1952 school-board election by a group called the Houston Committee for Sound American Education. "Save the schools from socialism" was its slogan; "Citizens of Houston, save your schools from the dangerous influence of UNESCO," said a sign at its headquarters. Two of four anti-UNESCO candidates were elected. The annual United Nations essay contest, banned by the board that year, continues outside the school system through the city's United Nations Council.

The Ebey dispute, matching extreme nationalism against the constitutional freedoms, became a national spectacle. George Ebey came to Houston in 1952 from the Portland, Oregon, schools. A year later he was discharged as deputy superintendent—technically his contract was not renewed—following charges of doubtful validity and concealed origin. He was investigated for two months by former FBI men. He was attacked before the school board by John P. Rogge, a lawyer who neither lived in the school district nor would name his sponsors. Ebey was charged with being a communist sympathizer because he failed to oppose with vigor a communist faction in the American Veterans Committee of California when he was state chairman of the A.V.C. An undercurrent of racial prejudice based other charges against Ebey.

At a crowded meeting charged with drama, the school board dismissed Ebey by a four-to-three vote. Garrett R. Tucker, a member of an influential law firm, voted with the minority. Thought of as a conservative when he was elected, Tucker defied a label. Before voting to keep Ebey he reduced the dispute to its essence: "More is at stake here than George

Ebey. A vote against Dr. Ebey, under the present circumstances, is a vote for John Rogge and for the anonymous
forces behind him—forces which would not be content with
Dr. Ebey's scalp, but would be encouraged . . . to attack as
'disloyal' or 'controversial' other school administrators and
teachers with whose . . . views they disagreed."

George Ebey left Houston, but the dispute lingered. When
the National Education Association, acting on requests from
teachers, sent a committee to investigate the troubles, conflict
flared again. The committee's conclusions, announced in
December 1954, included: "On certain issues . . . [school]
board meeting discussions are often conspicuous for bitterness and rancor. . . . The manner . . . by which some [board
members'] points of view are presented has damaged the es-
prit de corps of the Houston school system and tends to lessen
public confidence in the whole school program. . . . The
committee encountered sharp division, deep-seated suspicion, animosity, and fear among groups in the . . . school
system." James M. Delmar, the retiring president of the board,
said of the report: "The school board doesn't need any suggestions from the National Education Association—whether
they are good or bad."

Dissension continued when liberals won a four-to-three
board majority in the election following these events. Applied
to the school board, however, the word "liberal" does not have
its accustomed meaning. "Anywhere else . . . these school
board 'liberals' would be [considered] 'conservatives,'" Ellen
Middlebrook, of the Houston *Post*, wrote in 1955. Miss Middlebrook concluded that the effects of one board meeting that
year would be "powerfully manifest for the next three or four
years."

In 1953 the principal of an elementary school—she was de-
moted two years later—removed the word "democracy" from
the American's Creed, though the text was approved by the
United States House of Representatives in 1918. She said she
altered the creed to "clarify" it for her pupils, telling a parent

who protested that Russia had caused "democracy" to become a "dirty word." For the words "a democracy in a republic" she substituted "a constitutional representative government; a republic." Protesting vigorously, parents got the
original version of the creed restored. Three months earlier
the same principal wrote a pamphlet, *Americanism Versus All
Other Isms*, saying that the "Roosevelt-Truman administrations invited, even aided and abetted, the destruction of our
American republic."

The school district of the nation's twelfth largest city has
the nation's sixth largest enrollment. Houston is near the bottom of larger American school districts in the proportion of
community resources spent for public schools. Some classes
have been held in school cafeterias, auditoriums, in one case
in a teachers' lounge, because the erection of even temporary
structures has not always kept up with the growing enrollment. All that saves the system from the fascist mentality is
the opposition's tenacity and the fact that the public is informed. The Houston *Chronicle* sides with reaction, the *Post*
and sometimes the *Press* oppose, and school dissension often
dominates the papers' front pages. School-board meetings are
broadcast and televised. The issues get a wide public hearing.

School-board rows have not monopolized activities of the
city's vigilantes of the mind. Starring in this role are the Minute Women of the U.S.A., supported at times by the American
Legion. In 1950 a Houston Committee for the Preservation
of Methodism got attention for its attacks on Bishop G. Brom-
ley Oxnam and for its pamphlet, *Is There a Pink Fringe in the
Methodist Church?* The Minute Women, however, lead the
search for darkness. Adopting the methods of totalitarian
states, especially thought control, the Minute Women were
unchecked until 1953, when the Houston *Post* published a
series of eleven articles by Ralph O'Leary. Though the *Post*
led the Republican movement in Texas in 1952 and 1956, and
though the president of the paper, Oveta Culp Hobby, became a member of the Eisenhower Cabinet, the Minute

Women charged that the paper gave in to communist pressure. The majority of letters to the editor during and after the series—the *Post* printed pages of letters—condemned the Minute Women.

The series, for which O'Leary and the *Post* got five awards, subdued the Minute Women for the time. Their method of thought control consisted, for one thing, of putting observers in classes at the University of Houston to find out if instruction measured up to what they call Americanism. O'Leary described the results of such spying by saying: "There exists a reign of terror among patriotic clergymen, editors and school teachers here, particularly those in the slightest interested in social improvements. It is reported widely among churchmen that there is a shadowy list of five or six Protestant clergymen due to get the 'Ebey treatment.' There is similar fear among the faculties of Houston's institutions of higher learning. . . . Teachers in the public schools have been fearful this fall, too, since a local [radio] commentator urged parents to have their children observe and report what teachers said in their classrooms on 'controversial' subjects."

In 1952, when the Houston Central Council of the American Legion felt that one vigilance committee was incapable of coping with the city's communist and socialist trends, a second committee was appointed. The chairman was John P. Rogge, spokesman for George Ebey's invisible assailants and a veteran of many campaigns to test the sinews of those rights the Constitution tries to ensure. A newspaper story said the purpose of Rogge's committee was "to watch for any subversive groups or organizations which might come to Houston to hold meetings under the auspices of churches, schools or other organizations." The committee was appointed the day before the opening of the Quakers' annual Institute on International Relations. Heckling and other oppression by Minute Women and members of Rogge's group caused the Quakers to regard Houston as one of the most reactionary cities in America. The Quakers, opposing racial and religious prejudices, were charged with being subversive by the groups that tried to void their free speech. Several speakers of importance were heckled by these claques at other times, and pressure brought by the patriots caused some talks to be canceled. Censorship attempts continue, but their effect has been blunted by the public's growing suspicion, largely a result of the *Post's* Minute Women series.

Now the fight over school segregation stirs the city. Houston's population includes a larger proportion of Negroes than any other Texas city. The 1950 census showed Negro populations to be 150,452 (19 per cent) in Houston, 83,352 (13 per cent) in Dallas, 39,898 (11 per cent) in Fort Worth, and 33,551 (7 per cent) in San Antonio. Houston's large Negro population and its Southern tradition combine to make the city's opposition to integration more virulent than in any other Texas city. San Antonio, with the state's smallest big-city Negro population, was integrated without much opposition.

Hubert Mewhinney, reviewing the school-board dissension in a story in the *Post,* in 1954, concluded that members of the board were under a compulsion to follow the example of the Puritans, as described by Samuel Butler:

> And prove their doctrine orthodox
> By apostolic blows and knocks.

Attempts to prove the orthodoxy of reaction, to maintain yesterday's attitudes and customs of thought, to impose censorship in the face of America's freedoms, define the mind of articulate minorities in Houston and Dallas.

Central Texas. Gin Yard

10 Pride's Sweet Compare

AJAX: What is he more than another?

AGAMEMNON: No more than what he thinks he is.

AJAX: Is he so much? Do you not think he thinks himself a better man than I am?

AGAMEMNON: No question.

AJAX: Will you subscribe his thought, and say he is?

AGAMEMNON: No, noble Ajax; you are as strong, as valiant, as wise, no less noble, much more gentle, and altogether more tractable.

Troilus and Cressida, Shakespeare

As Ajax marveled at the pride of Ulysses, seeking a comparison of favor to himself, so Houston and Dallas contemplate each other. Two hundred and forty-three miles apart, with more than a fifth of all Texans in their metropolitan areas, they compete for power and glory. Dallas, oddly fenced in on the blackland prairies of north central Texas, is Metropolis surrounded on four sides by Texas. Houston, unconfined on the Gulf plain, is Texas with the gusto of Fielding's *Tom Jones* added. Hubert Mewhinney, a Houston *Post* writer who devils the city at times, defines it differently.[1] "It is partly an unconscious romanticism and it is partly a conscious cult that one still thinks of Houston as pre-eminently a Texas city," he wrote in 1952. "But it is not. Houston since the war, and to a large extent even before the war, has not been so much Texas as . . . standard American." As much can be said for some aspects of both Houston and Dallas. Texas sees the two cities as un-Texan; visitors see Texas in Houston's character.

The two cities pivot urban life in a rural-minded state. Houston and Dallas are as different as Los Angeles and San Francisco but not similar to them. You lose Texas on the main streets of Dallas, in restaurants and hotel lobbies, in the society. People move hurriedly, dress with conscious purpose, clip their speech a little. Dallas has a manner, suave, and everybody runs to stay in the same place. It is Yankeefied to a high degree. Houston is more casual. The pace is slower, the eagerness not so eager. What strikes the stranger is Houston's physical ruggedness—a skyscraper reared up beside a barbecue stand, disorder with Southern trimmings. Houston seldom bothers to prove that it has made good; Dallas has to prove it all the time. Houston looks to be new; Dallas, a few years younger, seems older. Houston wildcats and refines oil, Dallas finances it. Houston has its sleeves rolled up, Dallas wears a coat.

Dallas got its importance from determination, Houston from advantage more than determination. Dallas has no port,

[1] Walter Prescott Webb, the historian, described Mewhinney as "that most delightful survival of the intellectuals of the late medieval period." One motive for Webb's description may have been that Mewhinney, who reads Herodotus in English only if the Greek text is hard to find, is apt to think of any literature written more recently than the seventeenth century as *avant-garde*.

no oil resources, no rice fields, no wealth of cattle—no comparable assets to equal Houston's. Dallas has no Gulf of Mexico, no Intracoastal Canal, and no ship channel. It envies the channel more than any other Houston advantage. "Probably the greatest, most farseeing project ever consummated in Texas was the deepwater channel to Houston," the Dallas *News* editorialized in 1955. Being the largest American city not on a water route, Dallas dreams of making the Trinity River navigable for 294 miles to the Gulf of Mexico.

It has but one edge on Houston aside from the unity and dedication of its leaders: it centers a trade area covering parts of four states. It had to contend even for that advantage because Fort Worth and Wichita Falls are central to the same region. Yet the city's location is often pitied. Sir Alfred Bossom, designer of an early Dallas skyscraper, said upon revisiting the city in 1953: "There is no natural reason for this great city." The *News* often writes to the same effect, but in 1956 Sam Acheson wrote on the editorial page: "Often it has been said that Dallas came into being without rhyme or reason, with no natural advantages that would head it toward the rank of metropolis. Such a view is . . . contrary to what happened . . . Any map . . . brings out the dominating fact instantly. It is the Trinity River. And here in its upper reaches . . . it branches out into [three] almost parallel fingers . . ."

The go-getter spirit characterized both cities until the late 1930s, when it vanished from Houston. Dallas is managed by an institution that improves on unity, but the unity of Houston's leaders depends on circumstances. Nothing more concerns each city's future save the longevity of the state's oil and gas resources, whose absence would affect Dallas less. Houston has enterprise, but its leaders' unity often gives in to individualism and competing egos.

Commanding Dallas is the Citizens Council, a junta of the city's bosses—men who can make decisions without awaiting anyone's approval. Chartered in 1937 as "charitable" and "educational," its 175 members join for life; professional men are barred and few oilmen have been invited to join. Dallas has a city manager, it elects a mayor and a city council, but the Citizens Council runs the city. Not responsible to the public, the council rarely announces its decisions; only the effect of decisions becomes known. The council's control has been watered since 1949, when *Fortune* wrote about it, but public awareness was not followed by criticism because the council benefits Dallas.

The council has impelled construction of Negro housing projects and a medical center; it instigated a $22,000,000 program to help solve the city's water problem. It sees to it that what it thinks is good for Dallas is accomplished. In spite of its achievements, however, Dallas pays a price for the oligarchy. Large issues are settled without public participation. Because of the council, and the fact that the *News* and the Dallas *Times-Herald* shrink from local contention, Dallas has no stage for public debate, no medium through which issues of public concern can be argued. The hurly-burly of such argument in Houston is unheard of in Dallas, where controversy in public is thought to be unseemly. No issue concerning the public—not even a triviality—is decided in Houston until the people have a say-so.

The two men who dominated Houston's rise in the first half of the twentieth century came to the city because of lumber. Jesse H. Jones came from Dallas, in 1898, to manage a lumber firm when an uncle died; Oscar F. Holcombe came from San Antonio, in 1905, to work in a sawmill. Other men—personalities of more pungence but less effectiveness—have helped shape and command twentieth-century Houston, but Jones and Holcombe commanded the others, or rode them down. A third man, the most gifted and altruistic of the city's leaders, tried to make Houston a utopia for its people. Will C. Hogg, son of Governor James Stephen Hogg, died too soon to fulfill his dreams.

Jones—he was called "Mr. Houston," and there was never any argument about it—was the giant among Houstonians. He

became, at the same time, Secretary of Commerce and head
of the Reconstruction Finance Corporation under Franklin
D. Roosevelt. Holcombe—he is called "The Old Gray Fox,"
and there is no argument about that, either—has been Houston's mayor through all of the city's important growth. He
was elected to eleven two-year terms between 1920 and 1956,
meanwhile making a fortune as builder, real-estate developer,
and aide to Houston's expatriate Howard Hughes. Except for
Jones and Holcombe, Houston's leaders have a tradition of
quarrelsomeness. Publicly and with the tact of monkeys at a
cathedral wedding, they have sometimes made a fete of ag-
gravating each other. "Jones has been away from here for the
last twenty-five to thirty years and has come back to Houston
and decided, with the influence of a bunch of New York Jews,
to run our city," H. R. Cullen said of Jesse Jones during a
zoning election fight of the 1940s. Jones favored zoning; it
was one of the few fights he lost.

The main cause of Dallas-Houston rivalry is as old as Texas:
compared with the coast, the state's interior is poor in natural
resources, especially water. Another gall to the interior is that
freight rates favor the coast cities. In effect, Dallas and Houston are competing for their industrial futures—the state's
water resources. Dallas has improved its position by combin-
ing its statistics with those of Fort Worth, its neighbor. The
combination is more than a convenience to compete with
Houston arguments. The thirty-three miles between Dallas
and Fort Worth have become an industrial entity whose
significance grows. William Zeckendorf, of New York, and the
Rockefeller family joined in the middle 1950s to plan a
$300,000,000 industrial center midway between the cities.
Necessities of economy are causing accord between two cities
whose rivalry has equaled that of Minneapolis and St. Paul.
Fort Worth, holding the flavor of the state's tradition and
character, was shaped in the image of Amon Carter, who
managed to shade even Dallas's civic pride. Publishing the
Fort Worth *Star-Telegram*, indulging in careers of extrover-

sion and intimacy with the great, investing his life in playing up to the public's notion of the Texan, Carter was the foremost civic booster of his time. Leading Fort Worth to its importance, he linked its economy with that of Dallas, the city he despised. The two metropolitan areas together have the largest concentration of Texans though their combined area is but a fraction larger than Harris County's alone.

Aside from dilemmas common to all cities whose growth has made a juggle of municipal funds and dreams, Dallas must overcome two obstacles and one attitude, Houston the same, if they are to hold their magnetism. Dallas needs water —it needs water more than it needs to solve all its other problems together; it needs *Lebensraum,* or living space, because it is almost completely hemmed in by incorporated suburbs; and it needs to trim its first-or-nothing philosophy. Houston needs to become less dependent on petroleum, it needs to nourish the port of Houston with more zeal, and it needs to abandon its quantitative thinking in favor of the goals of Will C. Hogg. In 1926, at a cost to himself of more than fifty thousand dollars, Hogg organized the Forum of Civics with these words from Pericles as its motto: "No Athenian should ever confess that he neglected public service for the sake of his private fortune." Describing the Forum, Hogg once said, ". . . underlying the stated purposes of such an organization there must be the basic desire to make this city more enjoyable, more adequately equipped, more beautiful—and consequently more useful for everyone who lives and works therein."

The need for water haunts Dallas life. In 1956 the Dallas City Council renewed, at a cost of $35,000, its cloud-seeding contract with a Colorado firm, though the contract was soon canceled. Water was rationed for the second summer in a row in 1956, when lawns could be watered only on alternate days. That summer the water's salt content rose to nearly a thousand parts of salt to a million parts of water; by comparison, Houston's water was seventy-two parts salt. The salt got into the water system when the city had to supplement its supply with fifty million gallons of water daily from the Red River. For days thousands of people drove to four municipal wells, waiting in line to fill jugs with salt-free drinking water; grocery stores sold fresh water for twenty cents a gallon; the sale of distilled water boomed.

Dallas is meeting its water problem with aggressiveness, but the only thing it can do about its problem of living space is make the city of Dallas and Dallas County one governmental unit. The city is confined by twenty-eight incorporated communities. "The City of Dallas has been almost completely encircled by the incorporation and annexation actions of other municipalities in Dallas County," said a report made in 1956 by the city's planning department. The problem has led to bitterness and reprisal. "The American flag should be taken away from the Dallas City Hall and be replaced by the biggest dollar mark that can be erected there," C. R. Sargent, mayor of the neighboring industrial city of Grand Prairie, said in 1955. The remark was triggered by the Dallas City Council's refusal to relinquish its annexation of two aircraft plants. The plants add $229,000 a year to Dallas tax revenues, but Grand Prairie's mayor claimed they are served by his city rather than Dallas.

Houston needs to ask itself a question: What happens when oil resources diminish? The city has industrial initiative—natural gas, chemical plants, and other rewards of petroleum primacy—but cannot hold its prosperity with petroleum alone. The city lacks local cash to attract other kinds of industry. Dallas banks are run by bankers, Houston's by lawyers who have been slow to change policies existing before they dominated the banks. Not only did Houston banks lose the chance to finance the Texas oil hunt but they have had far less dare than their city. James A. Elkins, Sr., a lawyer and an influence on Texas politics for three decades, is an exception. He aroused Houston bankers by practicing a liberalized Giannini-type of banking. His City National Bank was one of the smallest in Houston in 1928. Twenty-seven years later, even before he merged it with the First National Bank —the city's oldest—the Elkins bank became first in Houston.

The decline of the port of Houston's position owes to the city's belief in its destiny of success. Complacency and a want of imagination, especially a want of public support, caused the port to fall behind those of Philadelphia and New Orleans in the tonnage figures by which ports are ranked. "Houston's claim [to being the second port in the United States] has been rather tenuous, based largely on the vast movement of petroleum and its products through the port, but the tonnage figures were there. Next to New York, Houston had the largest port tonnage," editorialized the Houston *Post* in 1956, when the port fell to fourth place. The port's decline awakened the city's leaders, who had the job of awakening the people. Voters rejected bonds for port improvements in 1955 but approved them in 1957 for the first time in ten years. Houston could learn from New Orleans about running a port but is not much inclined to heed example.

The main centre of pilgrimage [at the opening of a Houston bank's new building] was a glass case . . . Within it was a tower, some ten feet high, composed of a million dollars in notes. . . . At other times, other tables—the counters of the fabled Fifty and Hundred Dollar Store of Neiman-Marcus, in Dallas. Here a vitrine similar to that in the Bank contains a million dollars' worth of diamonds. Lord Kinross, 1956, *Punch.*

The architecture of the two cities, as expressed in their sky lines, may be called Elbert Hubbard-Modern. Larger buildings are functional in the word's euphemistic sense—design providing a maximum of revenue, or space to be rented, and a minimum of aesthetics. The Dallas sky line has more character, variety, and appeal than Houston's—a monotony of type causing it to seem that most of the higher buildings were

designed by one man with but one idea. Houston's plan has
an edge on Dallas, which was planned as a river-front town
before railroads changed its destiny. The cities' business districts characterize their plans, that of Dallas being a hodge-
podge of comparative antiquity and streamlining. Alistair
Cooke, the British journalist whose work is evaluating America, described Dallas as "a ramshackle town" in 1953. A Dallas *News* editorial the next year said the downtown area was
"dingy from overhanging signs, garbage cans, overhead wires
and trolley poles." Trolleys disappeared from the city's streets
early in 1956 and Dallas has since spruced its downtown
area. Layers of seediness and shine give its business district
the look of older cities in the North, one reason Northerners
attune to Dallas more swiftly than to Houston. Houston's
business district is new without relief; its streets are wider
and the result of plan rather than chance, as in Dallas.

Houston dominates the state's heavy industry; the Dallas-
Fort Worth area dominates light industry. Prolonged summer
heat makes air conditioning more commonplace than television in both Dallas and Houston. Air conditioning's prevalence in Houston gives rise to an aristocracy known as the
Never-Sweat Set. Its members are said to live in air-conditioned houses, work in air-conditioned offices, and drive between the two in air-conditioned cars. Dallas had forty-four
days of 100-degree temperatures, or higher, in the summer
of 1956 and fifty days of the same in 1954, setting a summer
heat record. Though Houston's temperatures are lower, its
higher humidities crease the spirit. Dallas has little of the
flavor of Texas and none of the history except its own. Houston
has shared the state's history since just after the Battle of San
Jacinto. It was the capital of Texas in the first years of the
Republic, it was a lair for Civil War blockade runners, and
it mounted a sea attack down Buffalo Bayou that recaptured
Galveston from Union forces.

Of the two newspapers in Dallas and the three in Houston,
the Dallas *News* and the Houston *Post* have had more effect

on the character of each city. The main difference in the papers is their opposite editorial positions on some issues of consequence. The *News* has no sympathy for UNESCO but has favored "the poor, floundering" United Nations with reservations. "No, let's keep U.N. It has its uses. But in heaven's name, let's quit counting on it to preserve either peace or security," the *News* said in 1954. The same year Lynn Landrum described UNESCO as a "magpie nest for every crackpot cowbird and cuckoo in ideology . . ." The *Post* approves both the United Nations and UNESCO. The *News*, opposing federal aid to education, suspicioned the passage of the federal highway program of 1956. "A far better solution for our undoubted highway needs . . . would have been to relinquish user taxes to the states and permit them to formulate their own programs," the *News* said. [The *Post* favors federal aid to education and to highways.] The *News* aggressively supported Senator Joseph W. McCarthy; the *Post* opposed him.

The *News's* position on the censorship activities of Dallas patriots is hard to pin down, but it seems to have a split personality in this respect. Its critics—drama, art, and literature—oppose the vigilantes with vim and often contradict the paper's editorial page. Editorials sometimes resolve these issues with a potluck offering—some of one view and some of the other in the same editorial. The *Post* has had more courage than any other Texas newspaper in guarding the American freedoms. Its series about the Minute Women and its notable coverage of dissension in Houston schools take precedence, but an incident in 1953 also showed its opposition to patrioteers' censorship. The American Legion asked a theater not to show a Charles Chaplin film, *Limelight*, because of Chaplin's failure to become an American citizen and what was said to be his taste for communism. The Houston *Chronicle* supported the Legion; the *Post* opposed the Legion and the film was shown.

The *News* leads the state's opposition to mixing the races

in schools but opposes white-supremacy groups, warning that they may reproduce the Ku Klux Klan's evils. The paper has called the National Association for the Advancement of Colored People "the National Association for the Agitation of Colored People" in a lead editorial. In February 1956, in an editorial titled "Majorities Have Basic Rights, Too," the *News* approved this solution to the dilemma: "The 'pepper-and-salt' plan would set up all-white, all-black and mixed schools to be attended by voluntary registration." The *News* has bitterly assailed the Supreme Court, calling the court's integration decision a violation of states' rights. "It has been noteworthy, perhaps, that Britons have gotten along for more than a thousand years without a supreme court," concluded an editorial in October 1956. The *Post*, though stating its position infrequently, urges compliance with the Supreme Court integration decisions. "The decision [of May 17, 1954] is now, in effect, the law of the land and must be faced and accepted," the paper said two days after the court announced the decision. The two papers' positions on this issue were contrasted in their editorials on the Southern Manifesto of March 1956.

The *News:* "The Southern bloc that spoke out boldly in Sunday's manifesto clearly made the U. S. Supreme Court's arrogation of lawmaking power the principal issue. In the comparatively brief but virile declaration, that was stressed three times . . . the News suggests again that the most practicable means [to avoid integration] is to force submission of a clarifying amendment to the Constitution. Surely no proponent of integration can object to ascertaining the desires of the American people."

The *Post:* "Precisely what Southern members of Congress think they will accomplish constructively by their attack on the United States Supreme Court other than win votes in their respective bids for reelection this year in their home states is as vague as their manifesto itself. Do they honestly think that by denunciation and dissent they can intimidate a majority of the present members of the court into reversing their position on racial segregation? Or, do they think that they can win enough support from the rest of the country to change the Constitution in such a way that the 14th amendment, in effect, would be repealed? . . . Texans can hold up their heads with pride that only four of their 24 members of Congress have become parties to the instrument."

The editorial page of the *News* has more flavor than the *Post's*, whose subjects often want for meat. The *News's* flavor is epitomized by the conclusion of an editorial of May 4, 1952: "Texas is tired of being run over, outraged and robbed. It is getting monotonous." The *Post's* flavor is sometimes that of its lead editorial of July 6, 1956, titled "Little League Baseball Fosters Sportsmanship and Enterprise." Both papers call themselves Democratic and both are Republican in essence. The *News* is Old Guard Republican—"Ike [Eisenhower] is looking more and more like a New Dealer miraculously put on a cash basis," it editorialized early in 1957—and the *Post* is Eisenhower Republican. Both papers recall the New Deal with aversion, the *News* more than the *Post*, and both condemned Harry S. Truman. Indeed, the *News* made an impression on the former President. In 1956, when Margaret Truman was to be married, Thomas Turner, of the *News* staff, sent the former President a clipping of a *News* editorial praising Miss Truman. Truman thanked Turner by letter, scribbling an afterthought at the bottom: "That paper [the *News*] has treated me like a pickpocket."

Dallas gives one the impression of being in a world detached from the continental land mass of the United States. David L. Cohn, 1940, *Atlantic Monthly.*

Houston is obsessed by the future. Just as they have annexed everything else down there in sight, they have annexed tomorrow. Houstonians co-exist in the present and the future. Lon Tinkle, 1954, Dallas *News.*

The philosophies of Dallas and Houston began drawing

apart in the years after the Second World War. In the general
election of 1952 Dwight Eisenhower got 58 per cent of the
votes in Harris County and 63 per cent in Dallas—a difference
of 5 per cent in the cities' conservatism. Allan Shivers, a conservative, opposed Ralph Yarborough, a liberal, in 1954's second Democratic primary, Shivers getting 53 per cent of Harris
County's votes and 60 per cent of Dallas County's. The difference increased to 7 per cent. Houston completed the first
phase of its merge with liberalism in the 1956 runoff primary,
when conservative United States Senator Price Daniel opposed Yarborough. Daniel carried Dallas with 59 per cent of
the votes while Yarborough carried Houston with 51 per cent.
The difference increased to 10 per cent.

Two of six candidates for governor in the first 1956 primary
were W. Lee O'Daniel and J. Evetts Haley, a writer. Both
based their campaigns on white supremacy, promising to
maintain that condition by force of arms. Dallas cast 17,000
fewer votes than Houston, but O'Daniel and Haley each got
more votes in Dallas, Haley nearly twice as many. President
Eisenhower got 61 per cent of the votes in Houston and 65
per cent in Dallas in the 1956 general election. In April 1957,
when Texas had a special election to fill Governor Price Daniel's unexpired term in the United States Senate, Ralph Yarborough, the winner, carried Houston. Congressman Martin
Dies, an extreme conservative, led in Dallas, Republican
Thad Hutcheson was second, and Yarborough ran third.

Houston's withdrawal from its conservative tradition will
shake the city's balance for years. The elections from 1952 to
1957 indicate a trend, not an accomplishment, but the city is
moving toward the liberalism that became a tradition of
larger American cities in the 1930s. Dallas shows few signs of
changing its political mood. Only one American metropolitan
area gave President Eisenhower a larger percentage of its
vote than Dallas in the 1952 election. It is the only Texas congressional district to be represented by a Republican congressman. Bruce Alger won the office in 1954 and again in

1956, when he defeated a popular Democrat, District Attorney Henry Wade. Their campaign, Lynn Landrum wrote before election day, "has boiled down to a competition . . . to see which one of them is in more complete disagreement with Democratic Presidential Nominee Adlai Stevenson's views. . . . Wade contends that he is as conservative as Alger is." Alger got 55 per cent of the votes.

Nursed by merchants and bankers, Dallas has grown—the Columbia Encyclopedia's words—"soberly and ambitiously." Stimulated by wildcatters and lone wolves, Houston has grown with gusto. One might, with exaggeration, compare Dallas to Richardson's *Pamela: or Virtue Rewarded,* and Houston to *Tom Jones,* by Henry Fielding, who began writing his lusty novels to protest the smug piousness of *Pamela.* As Texas inches from the county mind to city attitudes, Houston and Dallas dominate the state's urban life and thus are the only cities interpreted in this book. When J. B. Priestley, a Briton talented in opinion, dogmatism, and provocation, wanted to see what "represents the newest, the most prosperous, the most 'progressive' America," he came to Dallas and Houston. Traces of Pangloss's optimism shadow the cities' outlooks. The fancy that one city or the other is the best of all possible worlds has been buoyed by prosperity, confidence, and jubilation. The grimness of ideological fighting keeps optimism from running over. Conservatism has been champion in both cities. In Houston it is fighting for its life.

Panhandle Sky Line
Wheat Elevators and Combines

11 Rejoice of the Cuckoo

Texas is governed by a minority whose bonds are fear of the city and suspicion of university learning. The undemocratic process resulting from suppression of the cities by rural Texas is the state's chief internal problem next to its need for water. Suddenly and with more effect than in many states, Texas became urban with rural-mindedness prearranged by law. Urban Texas has had the majority of votes since 1950, but rural Texas has the majority where it counts—in the legislature. Legislative fear, or pretended fear, of city-slicking has subdued duty, responsibility, and necessity.

In 1954 the Texas House of Representatives was asked to appoint a committee to study the state's criminal laws. The committee was to have no power to do anything; it would only make a report. The proposal was made by Representative Tom King, of Dallas County, population 700,000. The population of De Witt County is 23,000; Tom Cheatham, its representative, came to his feet.

"This is a particular whim of Dallas," he told the House. "My experience has been that when Dallas wants to do something, you'd better watch out! . . . This is just an attempt of Dallas men to make life miserable and unhappy for the little man. Let's deprive Dallas of this opportunity to wreck and to ruin our criminal code. . . . The first thing you know they'll be coming down here [to Austin] from Dallas trying to rewrite the Bible to fit their whims and desires."

The country lawyer's oratory prompted the legislators. Palming the issue, Cheatham attacked on the ground that the inquiry was wanted by cityfolk. The proposal was defeated, though the FBI had recently reported that the nation's crime rate was at its peak. Minutes later, in another show of the legislature's capacity for comprehension, the House refused to consider an anti-arson bill introduced in the Senate by a Dallas man. Three Senate bills to improve the state's arson laws died in the House that day. A legislator from Denton, a small town north of Dallas, said he opposed the bills because penalizing people for starting fires would be "a great departure from our criminal law."

Such a departure is a necessity, yet more than twenty years of attempted reform have been in vain. Twenty-seven reform bills were introduced at one session of the legislature; twenty-five were killed, provisions of the other two sided with the defendant. Texas criminal laws favor defendants with a partiality that is notable even in the South. Reform would have the effect, in many cases a novelty, of making guilt an antonym for innocence. The conviction of a man for drowning his wife was reversed in the Texas Court of Criminal Appeals because it was not shown in what kind of liquid she was drowned. The conviction of a man who had stomped a woman to death was reversed because the charge did not specify what he had stomped her with. The state's criminal judges do little more than referee debate between prosecutors and defense lawyers. But rural Texas opposes reform as being urban meddlesomeness.

Unequal representation in the House of Representatives shadowed the state, in 1936, when the Texas Constitution was amended to disfranchise Texans of the future—beginning in 1950, it developed. The amendment was "intended specifically to restrict representation of the rapidly growing cities," Stuart McGregor, editor of the Texas Almanac, wrote in the Dallas *News*. It provides that no county may have more than seven representatives unless its population exceeds 700,000, when it may have one representative for each additional 100,-000 of population.

No county was affected until the reapportionment of 1951, based on the 1950 census. Equal representation would have been one representative for every 51,000 Texans, or sixteen rather than eight for Harris County (Houston) and twelve rather than seven for Dallas County. The amendment, however, gave Harris County a population ratio of 100,000 to each representative and Dallas County a ratio of 87,000 to 1; the average for the state was less than 50,000. Though the Texas Constitution provides for reapportionment after each federal census, none was made from 1921 to 1951, and then only because a constitutional amendment of 1947 made it expedient for the legislature to do so. The extremes have increased since 1950—one reason Texas is typified by what J. Frank Dobie has called "the county mind," meaning the closed mind.

Rural Texas forces cities to pay the taxes while cities despair for money to bridge their growth. Rural Texas sneaks lawmaking equity away from labor unions and masses of white-collar workers, preventing effective political organization in industrial areas. The imbalance spews more poisons, solidifying powerful lobbies, nursing other special interests, and rusting the majority's concern for government. Only patience will reward the cities. The 1936 amendment provides that equal representation will be restored when the state's population reaches 15,000,000, a figure that may be reached in the 1980s. Rural Texas not only denies cities equal representation in the state but in the nation, having prevented congressional redistricting from 1933 to May 1957, when it was less than half done. Speaker of the House Sam Rayburn's Fourth Congressional District has a population of around 250,000, one of the smallest in the nation, while that of the Eighth Congressional District—Houston—is more than a million. The partial redistricting of 1957 gave Houston a second congressman, but from 1950 to 1957 the city was the most populous congressional district in the nation; its people had the least representation in Congress.

The state's chief urban crushes—the Gulf coast and the Dallas-Fort Worth area—might profit from a threat vexing California: secession. Unlike California, however, such an extremity is theoretically possible for Texas, with its right to divide itself into as many as five states. Northern California is trying to protect its water resources from the drier, more populous southern region. In 1941 the north proclaimed the new state of Jefferson and inaugurated a governor, but the farce was devastated in the crisis of Pearl Harbor. No longer a farce, the plan was revived in 1956 when the Provisional State of Shasta was formed.

One can imagine a state with a wealth of resources, shaped something like a smaller California, on the Texas shores of the Gulf of Mexico. Nueces County (Corpus Christi) would be the southwestern flank, Jefferson and Orange counties (Beaumont, Port Arthur, and Orange) the northeastern flank, and Harris and Galveston counties (Houston and Galveston) the center of the new state, which could be called Gulf. Including sixteen counties,[1] most of them on the Gulf of Mexico, it

[1] Aransas, Brazoria, Calhoun, Chambers, Fort Bend, Galveston, Harris, Jackson, Jefferson, Matagorda, Nueces, Orange, Refugio, San Patricio, Victoria, and Wharton counties. A few of these are rural in character, but their economy is shifting because of their nearness to cities.

would have a land area roughly equal to the combined area of Massachusetts, Rhode Island, and Connecticut and a population a little larger than Oregon's. Secession, though seeming an absurdity, may be the only self-defense for urban Texas. Harris County has 14 per cent of the state's eligible voters, but elects only 5 per cent of the state's legislators. Something like the state of Gulf, a writer's lark munchausenized for illustration, could become a threat unless the state government manages to get in sight of the cities' dilemma.

A formidable obstacle to a secession threat, paradoxically, would be opposition by some urban groups—city men whose fortunes are abetted by rural dominance. Dean E. McHenry, writing in 1946 of California's rural-urban hostility, said "privately owned utilities, banks, insurance companies, and others . . . have discovered some 'cow country' legislators more responsive to their demands . . . than are urban representatives. The urban legislator is more likely to be influenced by organized labor." Rural dominance in Texas assures that even urban legislators have little cause to heed union members, no matter their number.

Meanwhile, the lopsidedness of minority rule speeds far ahead of population growth—"a strange development," the Dallas *News* said in wonder. People moving to Texas are filling the cities, which is to be expected. What multiplies the jeopardy is that people from the state's rural areas are also moving to the cities. The result is farce layered with troubles: while population gushers into the cities, rural Texas is being drained. The exodus from rural areas is a national phenomenon with common causes, but in Texas it has also been impulsed in other ways. The drought and the decline in cotton cultivation caused by the loss of foreign markets have been large influences in forcing the state's farm tenants into the cities.

Eighty-seven per cent of the state's surface was farm and ranch land with a population of 950,000 by 1956. The remaining 13 per cent of the surface was urban, with a population of 7,707,000. The state's fifteen metropolitan areas—more than any other state, but by no means all of urban Texas—alone contained a majority of Texans by 1957, yet the nearly eight million urban Texans are commanded by the less than a million rural Texans.

The speed of the state's population shift has concealed some of its dangers in the more gradual national trend. Forty per cent of the state's population was on the farm in 1934; twenty years later the figure had shrunk to 13 per cent. From 1930 to 1954 the state's farm population declined by 52 per cent—nearly twice as much as the national decline of 28 per cent. Since 1945 Texas has lost farm population more than twice as fast as the nation—28 per cent compared with 12 per cent. Between the censuses of 1940 and 1950, 108 Texas counties gained population, but 146 counties lost. In that decade the population of urban Texas jumped 66 per cent, and by 1950 Texas was 63 per cent urban compared with 64 per cent for the United States. There is no question that Texas exceeded the national proportion of urban population by 1957, though it is second to Florida as the most urban of southern states.

The constitutional amendment of 1936 extends the principle and injustice of England's rotten boroughs of the nineteenth century. Prosperous cities such as Birmingham and Manchester had no representation, while a hamlet favored by the Crown might have two representatives. More than a century later Houston and Dallas have roughly 50 per cent representation—the percentage is rapidly declining—while rural Texas, favored by the state constitution, fills the legislature with its will. The cities' dilemma is so hopeless of remedy that in 1955 the Dallas *News* recommended statesmanship as the only way out. "In Dallas, as in Houston and the other larger centers, our problem is to provide in our legislative delegation an order of statesmanship so able that it can make friends [with] and influence rural Representatives," Lynn Landrum wrote. "Above all, we need men of a personality to persuade our country neighbors to look with some kindliness upon the problems of rapidly growing counties where resources and methods of 50 years ago no longer suffice."

The rural-urban conflict is as old as the first city. It nettled the Roman Empire as it galls America fifteen centuries after. It has evaded compromise and ignored justice from the beginning, and yet few issues have been so free of clutter; equity of representation—a grievance leading to the American Revolution—is the essence of the dispute. The United States ails with partly disfranchised cities, but there are some special agonies in Texas: the suddenness of urban populations, the alum effect of cities on the rural population, and the misfortune that Texas cities have had a tendency—or necessity—to cluster.

The wide spaces of Texas are widening. When the Spanish conquistadores first explored Texas, it was one great wide space. Later, as population increased, the wide spaces contracted. . . . Then, paradoxically, the wide spaces began growing wider again, although the population continued to increase.   Stuart McGregor, 1956, Dallas *News.*

Texas is fancied to be filling with newcomers from the North, tempting outsiders to scorn that population growth will tranquilize the state as soon as the Texans are outnumbered. The mockery snags on two characteristics of the state's population. One, detailed in Chapter 16, is newcomers' low resistance to the state, their censure dozing in the infection of becoming Texan. Outsiders' hope of casting Texas in the image of other states is no more likely to materialize now than when Edward Everett Hale begged "the North [to] pour down its hordes" upon Texas in 1845. The other characteristic—it may be fading—is that the surge in the state's population has not come from outside Texas.

Texas has always been three-quarters full of Texans. The

state's increasing population owes to a high proportion of births over deaths, but far more to Texans' reluctance to leave Texas. The state's population increased by more than a million between 1940 and 1950, yet only twenty-seven thousand were added by migration—the excess of newcomers over people leaving the state. Seventy-five per cent of the state's population in 1950 was born in Texas, and the census also showed that of all living Americans born in Texas, 81 per cent still lived in the state. Only three states—California, Michigan, and New York—have higher percentages of stay-at-homes.

The state came to be thought of as a mecca for the North when oil and industry overwhelmed agriculture's economic lead. Such thinking has some substance in the cities, but it was still a delusion as of the 1950 census, when most newcomers were from next-door states, and it still is. The 1950 census showed that more newcomers came from Oklahoma than any other state, followed by Louisiana and Arkansas. Fourth, but distant from those three, was Missouri, then three more Southern states and Illinois. No Northern state was close enough to signify. The 1960 census, however, may show an important shift in the regional source of the state's newcomers. For nearly a century the mutual concern for cotton lured Southerners to the state; it was the South that poured its hordes into Texas. But the 1950 census showed that natives of all Northern states nearly equaled those of the South in Texas, and by 1960 Northerners will possibly outnumber Southerners for the first time.

In 1956 the American Institute of Public Opinion—the Gallup Poll—inquired of the few, "Have you ever thought you might like to move to another state?" and, "To which state?" Those who had thought of moving favored California more than any other state; Florida, Arizona, and Colorado were next; Texas was fifth. The poll also gauged other aspects of state desirability in what is imagined to be the public mind. Most beautiful? Texas was seventh. Best job opportunities? Seventh again. Healthiest climate? Texas was sixth. The validity and mystics of hocus-pocusing with the daydreams of 170,000,000 people may be questioned in view of the demerits of nearly all of the several Texas climates, but it is a pity the poll omitted the query, "Why?" Thirty-one of the forty-eight states were ignored in the four categories, but Texas was not first in any and as high as fifth in but one. Why then *do* people move to Texas?

Most come to succeed, an ambition that has added to the state's vitality, if not the approval of others, since the Great Depression. They are merchants walled in by older competitors in the North, lawyers and doctors dodging the dismalness of sniping away at clients and patients in matured areas, anyone hoping to grow with newer populations, anyone hypnotized by the gold of modern Texas myths. People come to Houston and Dallas, say, not for the climate or scenery—chief attractions of California, Florida, Arizona, and Colorado— but to follow the rainbow. All the seats are not taken. Other causes of the state's magnetism include: Texas has no income or sales taxes, though neither may be remote; it has some corporation-tax advantages; alimony is banned. But such chamber-of-commerce inducements have not lured newcomers as effectively as a mist: hope. "The cowards never started and the weaklings died along the way" was a saying of the forty-niners and the Oregon Trail to explain the grit of those who got through. The spirit of the frontier, hardly noticed as such since the rush to the Cherokee Strip, has drawn many Texas newcomers. The frontier, neoned and superhighwayed, still moves west and southwest.

The moving population that vexes the state, however, is its own. Texans moving from the country to the city have not surrendered their rural thinking, a mentality based largely on old-time religion—prejudice, prohibition, and fixed ideas. Dreading adjustment, they tend to anchor the cities' future to their own childhood nostalgia. Writing in *The Saturday Evening Post* in 1956, Sam Rayburn symbolized this ruralness: "I was raised on a poor, back-country Texas farm. As a young boy, on Sundays I'd sit on the fence and just wish to God that somebody would ride by on a horse or drive past in a buggy—anything that would relieve my loneliness. . . . That's why, when I go home to my little town of Bonham and see farmers' cars parked in the square, while the men visit with their friends and the women shop, my heart is gladdened."

IV PRIDE AND
PREJUDICE

GRIMES COUNTY COURTHOUSE - ANDERSON

Sunday Morning in Warrenton

12 Thy Kingdom Come

"There are no churches in Texas, no ministers of the gospel, no religious associations. Mother, I am afraid the way from Texas to Heaven has never been blazed out," William H. Jack wrote to his mother in 1836. The way has been blazed since then, smoothed with religiosity that touches all life. Church and stadium are joined through prayer, amplified to standing thousands, at the start of football games. In 1956 Governor Price Daniel's inauguration was preceded by a "prayer breakfast" attended by seven hundred who were exhorted by the evangelist Billy Graham. Since 1951 the Texas State Fair has ended with a mass religious meeting—a "Transcendent Wonder of Worship"—in the Dallas Cotton Bowl. "No other such exposition closes its annual show with a public, reverent acknowledgement of the blessings of God which have made it possible," editorialized the Dallas *News*.

"Everything in Texas seems to open with prayer. Meetings of bankers' associations, conventions of insurance salesmen, public gatherings of every kind—all open with prayer. . . . One minister . . . told of being invited to open the selection of a bathing beauty queen with prayer," the *Christian Century* said in 1952. A political ad in a Tyler newspaper, in 1954, pleaded: "A man who does what this man does for the cause of Christ and His Kingdom will surely do better for the cause of the people and his precinct." For years the Houston *Post* printed a daily Bible verse on page 1, replacing it with a daily prayer in 1957. In 1952 the Dallas *News's* front-page story—not an editorial—on the death of a local jeweler said he was "an outstanding example of his belief that full happiness can be obtained only in adhering strictly to the teachings of Jesus Christ. . . . Though an idealist, he was practical in business and, as in all things else, turned to the Scriptures for guidance in winning his daily bread."

"The churches in Texas are as out of the ordinary as everything else in that state. . . . Texas churches, one comes to believe, are felt in this fabulous state more than any other institution. . . . The very atmosphere of Texas seems to favor churches," the *Christian Century* said. The state's religion "is militant and emphatic," John Gunther wrote in *Inside U. S. A.* "The Texas atmosphere is filled day and night with the howlings of primitive preachers who make sinners jump through hoops of fire as they sit before their radios. More perhaps than Georgia or Mississippi . . . Texas is given to religious orgiasticism, hydrophobic fervor, Sodom-and-Gomorrah sermons. Hosts of holy men working frenetically in around-the-clock shifts beat off the hosts of Satan," David L. Cohn said in the *Atlantic Monthly* in 1940.

Cohn wrote before the surge to cities, yet the state's new urban mass has not turned from but to the churches. Five of the nation's twelve largest Methodist churches, including the first two, are in Texas; the largest Baptist congregation in the United States is in Dallas; threescore churches have more than five thousand members each. Houston had 335 churches in 1936; twenty years later it had more than twelve hundred. The *Christian Century's* reporter, writing of the Highland Park Methodist Church in Dallas, told how it had helped start four more churches in its own area. The reporter was taken to the site of the fourth, to be built that year: "It looked like any other pasture . . . and it faced open fields. 'Why here?' was the natural question. 'Where's the congregation to come from?' 'You see that wheat field? [the guide asked.] The contractor promises to have 450 houses completed there by January 1, and every one of them will be sold before it is finished.'"

Religiosity, evangelism, and conservatism band the state's church life: *organized* Christianity and *orthodox* Protestantism. Religion is not personal so much as group. The governor of Texas was an exhorter at a Dallas revival in 1952, causing no special notice. A year later the governor asked Texans to pray and fast for rain. In Waco, in 1952, when a cloud-seeding firm worked in vain, church people demanded prayer and no more airplanes. In 1956 the Dallas City Council renewed, temporarily, its contract with a cloud-seeding firm. The action, condemned by many on the ground that rain is God's work, resulted in a remarkable public statement to come from the mayor of a city of more than half a million people. "Our council believes in God and in prayer," Mayor R. L. Thornton said. "We also believe that God expects us to use our talents of every kind to help ourselves and our fellow man; that failing to do so we are derelict in our obligation to God."

Religion helps account for the state's poverty of communism and other radical doctrines, but the spell of religion's fervor helped the rise of two demagogues—James E. Ferguson and W. Lee O'Daniel. Religion has tied the state to its crust of blue laws and given Texas the mores of the South's most powerful legislative body, the Southern Baptist Convention. The Baptist General Convention of Texas has more influence on the state than oil, which it resembles in its reluc-

tance to yield. Roman Catholics and Methodists are next to
Baptists in numbers; Methodists and Roman Catholics are next
in religion's influence.

*Religion in the [nineteen-] fifties, perhaps to a greater de-
gree than in previous decades, was a potent conservator of
the Southern way of life. . . . The most powerful demonstration in the middle of the twentieth century of Southern religious ambitions was the conduct of the Southern Baptist
church.*   Francis Butler Simkins, 1953, A *History of the
South.*

Texas is on the western flank of what the North calls the
Bible Belt, or the Uplift Belt, or the Bourbon Belt. Whether
the state's dominating idiom is Western, Southwestern, or
Southern, that of its religion is Southern without relief. To
say that the state's frequent withdrawal from world and
even national realities is owing to oil wealth ignores history,
emotion, and religion, notably the religion of the Southern
Baptist Church. Southern Baptists broke from American Baptism, in 1845, when the Church's board of foreign missions, its
office in abolitionist Boston, would not accept slaveowners as
missionaries. The South broke away at the North's suggestion.
Northern Baptists may have since marveled at the Southern
Baptist Convention. Its eight and a half million members, all
whites, outnumber the group it left by nearly five to one. Of
all American Baptists in twenty-three denominations, more
than a third belong to the one Southern denomination—Baptism's conservative, Calvinistic wing. Through its reflection,
the Baptist General Convention of Texas, it may be the main
influence on the mind of Texas in the twentieth century. The
twelve thousand delegates to Southern Baptism's ninety-sixth
annual meeting, in 1953, reacted only once to their president's
opening talk. That was when the Reverend J. D. Grey, of
New Orleans, scorned the notion that Southern Baptists would
merge with any other group of Baptists or join any association

of churches. Reflecting an attitude that flourishes in Texas, a portion of Dr. Grey's talk follows:

"We are pressured by two conflicting forces. On one side is the ecumenicalism of United Protestantism; on the other is the anythingism of non-denominationalism. We are like a healthy, wealthy, attractive young lady. These ambitious Lotharios are making eyes at us. But we have not, can not, and will not even drop our handkerchief to invite or encourage their attention. . . . One would-be suitor [apparently the National Council of Churches of Christ in the United States, of which a Texan, Methodist Bishop William C. Martin, was then president] has made bold to announce that a chair is being reserved for us. But this young lady, in all graciousness, would suggest that before she occupies that chair it will have become an antique. No doubt this suitor means well in thinking of that chair as a love seat, but this young lady realizes that for her it would become a hot seat. And, too, she feels that this chair would be for her virtually an electric chair. Personally, I think the young lady is correct. For the moment she sits down in that chair she signs her own death warrant and sets the date for her execution."

Baptists excel other faiths in Texas in efficiency of organization. Congregations include few occasional worshipers. Sunday school is a cradle-to-the-grave plan. Church lights burn every night for meetings, dinners, discussion groups. The faith is based on primitive Christianity. Infant baptism is renounced. Each church is an autonomy, each member the arbiter of his soul. There are no bishops; no member has any spiritual authority over another. Aloneness—aloofness to mingling with anything foreign—is dogma. Dr. Grey's repudiation of religion's one world, the ecumenical plan, reflects the wide berth Southern Baptists give to secular ambitions of such scope. Nearly one in four Texans is a Baptist of one group or another, including Negroes, trained from the cradle to shy from alliance. The state's fear of the United Nations and its opposition to federal rights arise in part from Baptist convictions.

"I used to be against the Baptists, in a way," Lynn Landrum wrote in the Dallas *News*, in 1953. "I thought of them as a sort of prairie-dog, ant-hill church group. But I have come to respect them. . . . The Baptists are a giving people. . . . When they put a brother under the water [in baptism], his hip pocket goes under, too. . . . If that were not true, one of our Dallas congregations couldn't take its annual big collection with a washtub as the collection plate." Giving is not monopolized by the rich among Texas Baptists. Abernathy, a farming community in West Texas, has a population of seventeen hundred, of which five hundred are members of the First Baptist Church. In the spring of 1952 the church's pastor, the Reverend G. A. Kennedy, asked each member to give a tenth of his land to God. The following December the church had a "Consecration of the Plow" service to receive the tithes. The farmers filled two washtubs with $14,132.65, though 1952 was a drought year. San Antonio's Trinity Baptist Church, less than four years old in March 1953, had 1228 members. "The majority give 10 per cent of their income to the Lord's work," the Reverend William Stuart McBirnie, pastor, said at the time.

Texas Baptists have mocked a President to fortify their faith. In 1945 President Truman, a Baptist, was to be given an honorary degree by Baylor University, largest of the state's Baptist colleges. The President declined when the Baptist General Convention of Texas opposed honoring a man who drank bourbon and played poker. Two years later, when Baylor renewed the offer, Truman came to Waco to receive the degree. Baylor had already given degrees to John Nance Garner, former vice-president of the United States, and H. R. Cullen, an oilman who gave a million dollars to the Baylor University College of Medicine in Houston—two Texans whose taste for bourbon is believed to exceed President Truman's.

Earlier, Baptists were given the twelve-story Nixon Building in Corpus Christi. When it developed that a tenant sold beer, and that he could not be removed out of hand, the Baptists sold the building to Sam E. Wilson, Jr., a Texas oil millionaire noted for his pungence and race horses. In 1925 H. L. Mencken, in his *Americana,* took up a different aspect of Texas Baptism's defense of principle: "Troubles of the learned in the Bible Belt, as reported in a dispatch from Waco: Because he did not believe that Noah's Ark, with the dimensions mentioned in the Bible, was capable of accommodating a pair of all the animals extant in the world at Noah's time and because he had been criticized for expressing that belief, C. S. Fothergill, instructor in history at Baylor University, resigned today."

The unyielding spirit of Texas Baptism is illumined in the apocrypha of a story about the head of a Baptist school who lost his job when he was caught in his secretary's arms. "God forgave me, my wife forgave me, my children forgave me, but not the Baptist Church," he said. Yet evangelism's severity has not sapped but increased the Church's numbers since the Second World War. The 1,463,293 members of the Baptist General Convention of Texas—by no means all of the state's Baptists, not including half a million Negro Baptists and a few minor groups of white Baptists—gave their church $71,-900,000 in 1955, an average of nearly fifty dollars each. The 3720 churches baptized 65,403 new members—"converts"— that year. The state's 1956 trend of two new Baptist churches a week is expected to continue for at least five years. Except for Dallas, a Methodist center, and San Antonio and the Mexican border, Roman Catholic centers, nearly all Texas is a Baptist stronghold.

Sixty Baptist Churches In Houston Laying Down A Mighty Barrage Against Devil & Cohorts Page 1 headline, March 20, 1952, *Gulf Coast Baptist* ("Christ All Over").

Water internally, externally, and eternally. The Reverend J. B. Cranfill, prohibitionist and a leader of Texas Baptism in the early 1900s.

Racial segregation, the concern of three later chapters, vexes Texas and Southern churches no more than those of the North. The Church is the most segregated institution in America. In 1946, when Frank S. Loescher surveyed the racial practices of 17,900 American churches in six Protestant groups, he found only 860 with mixed congregations—mostly white churches attended by one or two Negro families. General assemblies of most Protestant bodies have since urged their churches to forego race lines, but churches have been reluctant to do so in every region. The largest Protestant group in the South, prompted by the tradition and prejudices of its region, has more at stake and more to redeem than any other denomination, and the Southern Baptist Convention has voted to support the Supreme Court ruling of May 1954. Meeting in St. Louis a month after the court's decision was announced, most of the five thousand delegates were shocked when their Christian Life Commission proposed that they support the decision. The resolution did not compromise, and there was little question that it would be defeated. The Reverend Jesse Burton Weatherspoon, a professor at Louisville's Southern Baptist Theological Seminary, arose.

"Last night," he said, "we had a foreign mission program, and a lot was said about taking Christ to people around the world. I wonder what some of those people in China and Japan and India would think about our sending missionaries to them if they knew that right here in our own country we rejected a chance to go." He pointed to a huge banner bearing the convention's motto: "Forward in Christ." The resolution was approved.   ◆

Texas Baptists, at their annual meeting in November 1956, evaded the issue of color lines in churches, resolving instead to spurn "lawlessness, mob rule, and the resistance of constituted authority" and to accept "the Christian attitude of nonviolence." The Texas resolution continued: "We further call upon our people to remember that as Christians we are to speak and act in the spirit of brotherliness and Christian love, constantly reminding ourselves that in God's sight there are no inferior races of people. We urge our people to seek a true interpretation of the teachings of the Bible pertaining to race, rejecting those misinterpretations of certain Bible passages which are used to justify race prejudice. We further recommend that our people accept the biblical truth that man is his brother's brother, and that they subscribe to their theory and accept and practice the Christian principle that every man, regardless of race, color, creed or any of the superficial barriers that divide men, is of infinite worth before God."

Such words are thorns in many parts of Texas, notably in East Texas, where Negro and white Baptists dominate religion. But the resolution had no bearing on segregation in individual churches; it took no notice of the subject. Texas Baptism is black and white and no merging about it, a paradox of Christian faith: "The South-wide emphasis of Southern Baptists during the next year will be on Christian morality in daily living," the Houston *Post* said of the opening of the Baptist General Convention of Texas in 1955. Texas Baptists' considerable effect on the state makes them the main concern, yet what other Protestant faith in the state can throw the first stone?—a query that may be asked of the nation as well. Governing bodies of the state's larger denominations have resolved that segregation is contrary to Christianity, but no Methodist, Presbyterian, or Episcopal church, no Christian (Desciples of Christ) or Church of Christ congregation had withdrawn race lines by 1957. One Lutheran church, the Reverend Paul T. Seastrand's Augustana Evangelical Lutheran Church in Houston, did so with effect. A few other churches, notably Unitarian, withdrew race lines without being tested to any large extent.

The eagerness of some Texans to criticize the Baptist Church as the chief preserver of segregation in Texas illustrates ignorance's bliss. The notion plays hide and seek-very-little with realities of other faiths' practices. As a group, Baptists want for the intellectualism of, say, Episcopalians, and thus Baptists are burdened with men who bray aloud what many Episcopalians may well be thinking. Methodists, Presbyterians, and Episcopalians are more sophisticated groups than Baptists, more practiced in discretion. Many Texans—many Americans—are willing to worship with Negroes; their cross is the fear of social mingling. What of church suppers, of meetings and parties of children's and women's groups? they ask. Negroes shy from half integration as whites shy from complete integration. The dilemma is the same in Waco, Texas, and Bradford, Pennsylvania.

Texas, however, has produced Southern Baptism's leading spokesman for segregation: the Reverend W. A. Criswell, pastor of the First Baptist Church in Dallas, largest Baptist church in the nation. Dr. Criswell, born in Eldorado, Oklahoma, in 1909 and educated at Baylor University and the Southern Baptist Theological Seminary, heads a downtown church with nearly twelve thousand members. The church's $4,500,-000 plant includes, besides the main church, an eight-story parking and recreation building and a five-story activities building. Dr. Criswell got a measure of fame after speaking to a Baptist conference on evangelism in Columbia, South Carolina, early in 1956.

Newspapers quoted him as saying that opponents of racial segregation are a "bunch of infidels in dirty shirts who are dead from the neck up." Later, in an interview in Oklahoma City, Dr. Criswell said the quotation was taken out of context. "I was talking about Communists and racial agitators who don't share the spiritual aims of our people in the South," he said. But he added: "Segregation is just natural. Ducks live only with other ducks, geese with other geese, and so on. Any man who says he is desegregated is soft in the head." He was asked if he would object if a Negro family attended his church. "No, I wouldn't care," he said. "But we don't want to be in church with colored people, and they don't want to be in church with us. We see things differently and they don't preach the same way we do."

In Canada to speak at a meeting of Baptists the following October, he was asked how a Christian could support segregation. "You put the colored folks and white people together in one church and one hundred respond. Separate them and one thousand respond," he said. "Which do you think is better? . . . It doesn't mean we hate each other. We love each other." Two months later, speaking at a Bill of Rights Day dinner given by the Sons of the American Revolution in Houston, he attacked again: "If anyone wants his children to consort with colored people that's his business. But as for myself, I look upon that with contempt. . . . No governmental agency out of Washington is going to force anybody to go about with colored people in Clinton [Tennessee], Dallas, or Houston. Clinton decided it and in Houston you'll decide it. That's the way our forefathers conceived it."

In January 1957 Dr. Criswell began a series of sermons on evolution, bridging from 1925 and Tennessee the Fundamentalists' swan song, as it was prematurely thought to be, at the trial of John T. Scopes. Speaking from his Dallas pulpit to a capacity audience of three thousand, Dr. Criswell opened the series by saying that the theory of evolution "is a bunch of hypothetical guesswork" and "has not one single fact to substantiate it." He said he was preaching the series—the opening sermon was titled "The Creation of Man—God or Gorilla?"—because "evolution theories being kept before the general public confuse, distort, and discredit the Holy Bible." Speaking in Fort Worth a few days later, Dr. Criswell attacked the "social gospel," which he called "religious liberalism and a modernistic movement." Liberalism and modernism are the devil's work to hard-shell Baptists.

The other Texas minister to lead segregation forces is also Baptist and also a Dallas man—Carey Daniel, pastor of the First Baptist Church of West Dallas, vice-chairman of the

Texas Citizens Council for Continued Segregation, and cousin of Governor Price Daniel. In a letter to the Dallas *News,* in 1955, he offered the Bible as authority for segregation: "The Lord Himself was the original segregationist. When He separated the black race from the white, He did not even put them in different parts of town or even in different countries. The black race had a continent to themselves." Late in 1956 the Reverend Daniel offered to turn his church buildings into an all-white school if Dallas schools were forced to integrate. He said his school would teach condemnation of the United Nations and show up evolution as "a damnable heresy." Whether they represent the will of Texas Baptists, Criswell and Daniel do not represent the group's doctrine, as shown earlier. In 1957 Texas Baptists' Christian Life Commission published two forthright tracts spurning the claim that the Bible approves segregation and urging that "Christian principles" be applied to race problems.

In January 1957 C. Avery Mason, bishop of the Episcopal Diocese of Dallas, seemed to score Criswell and Daniel in a talk at the diocese's annual meeting. The bishop called no names but accused "segregation troublemakers" of trying to incite America to "suicidal diversion" instead of helping to solve race problems. "We did not create the racial tensions present today, but we are, under God, responsible for what may happen if we perpetuate them with willfulness," he said. Among Criswell's and Daniel's other opposites in Texas are a Roman Catholic and another Episcopalian: Robert E. Lucey, archbishop of San Antonio, and John E. Hines, bishop of the Episcopal Diocese of Texas. Bishop Hines is one of the few Texas clerics to condemn the citizens council groups—"groups of citizens banded together for the purpose of nullifying the effect of the Supreme Court ruling," he said in 1956. The following year he attacked segregation bills being considered by the legislature.

The state's one and a half million Roman Catholics are in seven dioceses and one archdiocese. In April 1954 Archbishop Lucey forbade segregation in the eighty parochial schools in the San Antonio archdiocese. Describing racial segregation as a sin, his order said "no Catholic child may be refused admittance to schools . . . purely for reasons of color, race, or poverty." Later he bitterly assailed the state's segregation bills as "hate legislation." Relief of the Catholics' problem, however, is aided in two ways: the authority of Catholic prelates over Church affairs is incomparably greater than that of Protestant officials, and few Texas Negroes are Catholics. The reverse of these circumstances applies to Texas Baptism —the faith of more than half of the state's Negroes and the faith whose leaders have no authority over Church affairs.

God is much more broadminded than most people give Him credit for being. Attributed to Will Rogers.

Religion and religiosity pervade Texas. The most widely printed religious cartoon feature is drawn by a Texan, Jack Hamm, who "draws for God" and sends the weekly cartoon without charge to more than seven hundred newspapers and magazines. Dallas has a gospel Tin Pan Alley providing the South with much of its religious music. In Dallas is the Little Church, 21 by 40 feet, its furnishings scaled to size, for children. Baylor University, Southern Methodist University, Texas Christian University, representing the dominant Protestant denominations in Texas, are three of the state's eight educational institutions of importance. T. Whitfield Davidson, a state district judge, once told columnist Lynn Landrum how he judged the law: "My friend, I suppose I ought not to claim more than a plain, cornfield knowledge of the law. But this I try always to do: I cock one eye toward the Constitution of the United States and then I cock the other eye toward the Ten Commandments, and I line up the law." Though Landrum himself is a Methodist, he has invented a church of his own for convenience in discussing religion in his column.

He is the Leading Elder, and the only member, of the Epis-
cobapterian Church, Reformed, Unigational Synod.

George W. Strake, the oil millionaire, is the state's leading
Roman Catholic layman. His philanthropies to Catholic institutions have rewarded him with the Knight of Malta decoration, highest papal award to a layman, and membership
on Notre Dame's board of lay trustees. Years after he discovered the Conroe oil field he described the source of that success: "I dedicated my adventure in Conroe to the honor and
glory of God. It was His will that I use every means at my
command to complete what I had started. It [his discovery
well] wasn't natural. It was something supernatural." Such
testimony to God's influence in business success is commonplace in Texas. Speaking to a Catholic group in Dallas, in
1951, Strake gave his theory of Christian economics. "Under
the old, monopolistic capitalism, the owner kept all his eggs
in his basket and gave the workers a few of them in the form
of low wages," he said. "Under communism and socialism
the state makes an omelet and gives the workers a piece of it.
. . . Under Christianity, we should divide the hens."

Some believe that Texans' daily familiarity with the language and manners of religion results in spiritual superficial-
ity. A Northern Church leader, not identified, who was in
Dallas when a reporter for the *Christian Century* was there,
was quoted as saying, "Never have I encountered so much
religion that meant so little." The *Century's* reporter did not
agree. "If their [Texans'] religion sometimes seems to lack in
sophistication, it does not lack in reality."

East Texas Sawmill

13 Pandora's Box

Spared by fortune, Grimes County lazes in bottom land's fertility and history's travail. At the merging of the post-oak and pine belts less than fifty miles northwest of Houston, the county wanes in the shadow of the state's rush. La Salle, returning to the Mississippi, was murdered and buried there in 1687. The land, settled more than a century later by members of Stephen Austin's colony, got the state's first cotton gin in 1828. Indian raids calloused the area until the 1840s. But the die was cast for Grimes County early in the 1830s, when the area was settled by cotton planters and their slaves. Reconstruction penalized the county for the success of its Confederate munitions plant: between 1871 and 1883 it was represented by eight Negro legislators. Negroes, carpetbagged

with illusion, outnumbering whites five to four, ruled the
county till 1899, when the whites erupted in a spasm of
revenge from which the county has never recovered. More
than fifty years later the White Man's Union started that year
is the most formidable white-supremacy group in America, a
refugee from court and law because the county is off time's
path.

Most of Grimes County is a backwash of modern Texas.
Twenty-six thousand people lived there in 1900, twenty-two
thousand in 1940, fifteen thousand in 1950. Cotton, water-
melons, honey—thousands of bee colonies—and history support the county. Its pivot is Navasota, population six thousand, but its heart is Anderson, county seat, population six
hundred. Still preserved at Anderson are ante bellum houses
and the Fanthorp Inn, a goal for stagecoaches when it was
built in 1834. The courthouse, built in the 1890s, is one of
the loveliest in Texas. Square, built of stone and red brick,
the two-story building's outside double stairway forms an in-
verted white V at the head of Main Street's melancholy.

The White Man's Union was hedged in caution long before
Supreme Court decisions of 1944 and 1953—both Texas cases
—affirmed the Negro's right to vote in primary elections. The
union arose from the evil it promotes. For thirty years after
Reconstruction the whites of Grimes County were voided at
the polls by Negroes egged on by carpetbaggers. For half a
century since then, whites have excluded Negroes from the
polls. Their method was described by Milton Turner, a reporter for the Beaumont *Enterprise,* after he attended a
White Man's Union campaign rally in 1952. His presence
caused no fuss or comment; he made notes and photographs
at will. No one said a reporter from the city was unwanted,
or wanted, for that matter. "Members take the White Man's
Union matter-of-factly," Turner said five years later. "They
don't crow about it and they aren't ashamed of it."

The White Man's Union votes every fourth year—four
months before alternate state Democratic primary elections.

The union elected county officials to four-year terms long before a constitutional amendment of 1954 changed the length of such terms from two to four years in all counties. Only members—whites—vote in the union's private primary. Winners become the union's candidates in the state primary four months later and again two years afterward. As there is no way for anyone outside the union to get on state ballots, the official elections are a bore to the union's candidates, who get every vote. It cannot be said that the county's six thousand Negroes—40 per cent of the population—are wholly disfranchised. Theoretically they are welcome to vote in the state primaries if they pay their poll taxes, in which case they would have the same choice of candidates for *state* offices that voters have in all 254 counties. To a Negro in Grimes County, however, the offices of governor, lieutenant governor, and attorney general are as remote as kings and judgment day. What concerns a Grimes County Negro are the sheriff, the county judge, the county attorney, the county school superintendent. Having no choice of such candidates but that of the White Man's Union, Negroes have no incentive to pay $1.50 for the right to vote. It may be questioned that they have the means, either: the median income of Negro families—not individuals—in Grimes County is less than seven hundred dollars a year.

The union further arrests democracy by curbing the rights of whites, too, through the novelty of its lottery. Every fourth year committeemen from each county precinct meet at the courthouse and draw offices from a hat. In 1952, when Turner's report was written, Navasota drew the county judge's office, Courtney the sheriff, Shiro the treasurer, and Iola the district clerk. Any member of the White Man's Union in the Navasota precinct could be a candidate for county judge but for nothing else. The Courtney precinct, with around 3 per cent of the county's population, filled the important office of sheriff. Any number of the precinct's union members could be a candidate for sheriff, but no member from any other precinct could run for the office. After the drawing, however, precincts may switch offices by agreement if the union's president and executive committee approve. No one may hold office for more than four years. Two offices, county attorney and county school superintendent, are exempt from the drawing and open to candidates from any precinct.

The quadrennial campaigns last a month. Turner described the climax, "Campaign Day," of 1952's electioneering: "All the office seekers formed a caravan [of autos and trucks]. Starting from Anderson, the group, under sponsorship of the Grimes County Chamber of Commerce, swung through Pleasantville [Turner apparently meant Plantersville] and on around the county, winding up that night in Navasota. . . . Old-fashioned, open-air stump speaking was the order of the day . . . as citizens of each community on the route gathered around for the speech-making. . . . As campaign speeches filled the afternoon air and politicos pledged to live by the law of the White Man's Union, an occasional negro drifted into the gathering to listen attentively." Grimes County, Baptist and dry, its roll of hills patched by prairie, is once a year a mecca for cityfolk who trail the bluebonnet. Only a stone's throw from Washington-on-the-Brazos, where Texans declared their independence from Mexicans, the county is content, assured that its Negroes are in their place, its whites in theirs. It is an intimate of calm; foment has been a stranger to Grimes County since 1900.

In Texas live some of America's richest Negroes, doubtlessly the largest concentration of Negro millionaires in the world. Chiefly oil and cattlemen, some have so much money they have no idea what their total wealth is . . . Houston is sometimes called the "Bagdad of Negro America." 1952, *Ebony* magazine.

Solution: Italy, a town of twelve hundred people in central Texas, has a white city hall and a Negro city hall, a white mayor and city council, a Negro mayor and council. The Negro council deals with Negro problems, suggesting solutions to the white council for approval. "This is an outstanding instance of practical interracial relations that might well be emulated throughout much of the Southland," the Dallas *News* said, in 1953, when Italy's Negro city hall was dedicated. *Solution:* Harry K. Johnson built interurban lines in Mississippi and Louisiana before coming to Texas in the early 1920s to build one between Houston and Baytown. Buying five thousand acres in Harris County, he laid out three townsites, calling them Highlands, Little Mexico, and McNair. He sold Highlands land only to whites, Little Mexico land only to Mexicans, and McNair land only to Negroes. McNair, down at the heels, is still an all-Negro town, population fourteen hundred. *Par:* Throughout Texas, in cities and villages, Negroes live to themselves, restricted by custom and economy to their own areas, as they are throughout most of America. In Houston, whose population is 19 per cent Negro, they gradually moved into a white area of consequence in the early 1950s; it soon became all Negro.

The census of 1870, the first after Negroes were freed, showed the state's population to be 30 per cent Negro. Since then their number has increased in every census, but their proportion declines. In 1940 one Texan in seven was a Negro, one in eight in 1950, one in nine in 1955. The state's prosperity keeps the total of Texas Negroes from falling but many are migrating, mostly to California. The white population of Texas increased 23 per cent between 1940 and 1950; the Negro population increased 6 per cent. Texas had 977,458 Negroes in 1950, 80 per cent of them in the state's replica of the Deep South—East Texas. A few slaves helped Texas win its independence at the Battle of San Jacinto; some free Negroes in Texas later owned slaves themselves. On June 19, 1865, now known as Juneteenth, or Negro Emancipation Day in Texas, the state's slaves were freed by order of a Union general sent to Galveston to take charge of the North's victory. The price of that freedom, caused in part by the Negroes' tyranny during Reconstruction, is still being paid.

Not till Supreme Court actions of 1944 and 1953 did the Negro win the right to vote in state Democratic primary elections. The rites of emotion, and of the judiciary process, were magnified in all their mystery by the long series of checks and suits. In 1923, believing that an earlier Supreme Court decision put party primaries beyond federal control, the Texas legislature passed a law: "In no event shall a negro be eligible to participate in a Democratic primary election held in the State of Texas, and should a negro vote . . . such ballot shall be void and election officials shall not count the same." Four years later the law got to the Supreme Court, which found it "hard to imagine a more direct and obvious infringement" of the Fourteenth Amendment, which was adopted "with a special intent to protect the blacks from discrimination." The state legislature then repealed the law and authorized "every political party in this State through its State Executive Committee . . . to prescribe the qualifications of its own members."

Soon afterward the executive committee of the Democratic party in Texas resolved "that all white Democrats . . . and none other" could vote in primary elections. The Supreme Court voided the resolution in 1932. The party had not exhausted its resources, however, and a white primary rule was adopted again—not by the legislature, not by the state executive committee, but by Democrats meeting in state convention. The Supreme Court got the issue again in 1935, and this time the court ruled against the Negro. It concluded that the Democratic party was a private association and thus might exclude Negroes from its primaries without violating the equal-protection clause, which applied only to the action of state governments.

In 1944, in a suit brought by Lonnie Smith, a Negro dentist in Houston, the court considered the issue for the fourth time. Reversing its position in the 1935 case, the court held that

Negroes' exclusion from Texas primaries was unconstitutional,
a violation of the Fifteenth Amendment's prohibition of discrimination in the right to vote because of color. The court
reasoned that the Texas primary was an integral part of
choosing public officials. On July 22, 1944, after more than
twenty years of lawsuits, Negroes voted in a Texas Democratic primary for the first time. The case broke the white
primary in Texas and in many parts of the South. Texas Negroes were quickly assimilated into the primary without incident. A few areas, however, managed to hold out a while
longer.

One of these was Fort Bend County, flanking Houston on
the southwest. The county's Jaybird Democratic Association
is an older version of the White Man's Union. Founded in
1889 at the climax of a notorious Texas feud, it lost the advantage of the White Man's Union—remoteness—after the
Second World War. Its undoing was the difference in Fort
Bend and Grimes counties. "Rich, populous," the 1956–57
edition of the Texas Almanac says of Fort Bend County,
adjectives that could not be applied to Grimes County even
by its chamber of commerce. Its nearness to Houston and
its resources put Fort Bend County in the main stream of
Texas success. In 1954 the county produced nearly twelve million barrels of oil; it is an important gas producer and produces sulphur in quantity; it is rich in rice and cotton production; it is the antithesis of Grimes County. And in 1953
its private white primary was voided by the Supreme Court.
The court's action was presumed to affect the White Man's
Union, but the union seems not to have heard.

His vote at last assured, the Texas Negro's citizenship continued on a first-come, second-served basis. But for the first
time Negroes are winning some ground by grant of their historic nemesis, the state Democratic party, as Texas liberals
become more effective.

Robert Cargill, an East Texas oilman, organized the Texas
Referendum Committee and quickly got 153,868 petitioners,

forcing submission to voters of three segregation issues in the first Democratic primary of 1956. The aim of the referendum, or public-opinion poll, was "to clear a path for the Democratic convention in September to give the Legislature a party mandate to exact specific legislation," Dawson Duncan, of the Dallas *News,* wrote in June. Some areas, notably Houston, San Antonio, and Beaumont-Port Arthur, rebelled and tried to keep the referendum questions off their ballots. Controlled by liberals, county Democratic executive committees in the three cities denounced the referendum. The Houston group said it was an "illegal effort to cover up the scandals and corruption of the Shivers administration by appealing to Ku Kluxism for a campaign of hate"; San Antonio's resolution was similar. The segregation issue "must necessarily be reconciled by each separate school district under the supervision of the courts," the Houston resolution said, adding that interposition—one of the referendum's subjects—"would be armed rebellion against the United States." Such words from whites indicate that white supremacy is by no means a universal of the mind of Texas.

The referendum questions, which finally got on the ballots in all three counties in the face of threatened suits by the Texas Referendum Committee, were:

"Number 1: For [or Against] specific legislation exempting any child from compulsory attendance at integrated schools attended by white persons and negroes.

"Number 2: For [or Against] specific legislation perfecting State Laws against intermarriage between white persons and negroes.

"Number 3: For [or Against] the use of Interposition to halt illegal Federal encroachment."

It was charged that the wording of the questions was slanted to favor prejudice. "The proponents [of the referendum] are morally obligated to explain precisely what 'specific legislation' they have in mind, to explain why they think a favorable vote on these propositions . . . is necessary or desirable . . .

and what use they would make of a favorable vote if it should
be given," Brian Spinks, of the Houston *Post,* wrote before
the July election. "As the propositions are phrased on the ballot, it is impossible for any voter to tell what they mean by
reading them or what he would be voting for or against. . . .
Certainly the voters are entitled to some clearcut definitions
rather than vague generalities so that they will know if they
are voting for anarchy or for orderly government."

On July 28 Texas Democrats voted more than three to one
for the first proposition, nearly four to one for the second,
and more than four to one for the third, but nearly half a
million who voted for governor skipped voting on the referendum questions. The aftermath of the election disappointed
the referendum's supporters. The resolutions committee of the
state Democratic convention, meeting in September, opposed a motion by a Dallas man to ask that Governor Shivers
"immediately order the convening of a special session of the
legislature . . . for the purpose of enacting legislation in ac-
cordance with . . . the three segregation referendums." The
committee also tabled the same man's motion to call the
N.A.A.C.P. subversive. The resolutions committee had a liberal majority; the convention had a thin conservative majority.

Most Texas congressmen and many state legislators have
shied from signing the various segregation manifestos, as
they are called. Five of twenty-two Texans in the national
House of Representatives were among the ninety-six signers
of the Southern Manifesto of March 1956. The document declared the South's defiance of the Supreme Court decision
forbidding segregation in public schools. Price Daniel, then
a United States Senator, was the sixth Texan to sign the document; Senate Majority Leader Lyndon Johnson and Speaker
of the House Sam Rayburn were not asked to sign it. However: "The important thing to remember . . . is that all Texans in Congress oppose school integration," Leslie Carpenter,
a Houston *Post* Washington reporter, wrote later that year.

He said seventeen Texas congressmen refused to sign the manifesto on the ground that it would harm more than help the South's stand against civil-rights bills.

Early in 1957 State Representative Joe N. Chapman, of East Texas, asked state legislators to sign what he called the Texas Manifesto. He announced pointedly that the names of those who did and did not sign would be made public. Referring to the segregation referendum, the manifesto said, "We hereby pledge our vote and influence and call on all other members of the Texas Legislature to join with us in faithfully discharging our duty to Texas by supporting approximate legislation designed to carry out the principles of states' rights and constitutional law . . ." It is not known how many signed the document, but probably it was fewer than Chapman hoped; he did not make good on his threat to publicize the names of signers and holdouts.

THE REPUBLIC OF TEXAS, SAN AUGUSTINE COUNTY, KNOW ALL MEN BY THESE PRESENTS: That I, Oran M. Roberts, for and in consideration of the sum of Ninety Dollars, do . . . sell unto Abner Parther a certain negro girl about fifteen years of age named Sarah of dark complexion, warranted to be a slave for life, the same to have and to hold to himself and legal representatives. Bill of Sale & Mortgage, recorded December 27, 1842.[1]

Texas Negroes have gained on some of their past without help from courts. As with most changes in modern Texas life, the shift began at the end of the Second World War. The dual citizenship of the Southern Negro still applies in strength to most of East Texas. In the rest of the state, and in all the larger cities, the Negro is halfway to the counterfeit equality of the North's passive segregation. Compared with Mississippi, "Texas is a kind of heaven" for Negro rights, Roy

[1]Later Roberts was twice chief justice of the supreme court of Texas and, from 1879 to 1883, governor of the state.

Wilkins, an officer of the N.A.A.C.P., said in 1956. That is not the kind of heaven men dream of, however. The Texas Negro is more fenced in by custom and attitude than state law.

The state has five Jim Crow laws. Three laws require segregation in schools, state parks, and intrastate public transportation; one forbids intermarriage of Negroes and whites and one requires separate showers in coal mines, the last a triviality in Texas. "Similarly," Margaret L. Hartley wrote in the *Southwest Review*, in 1952, "local ordinances do not go nearly as far in this direction as is popularly thought. The fact that city police have sometimes been used to enforce tradition rather than law has been to blame for misapprehensions on this point." The customs are those of the South, and they tear at man's prides. A Negro is not addressed as "Mr." or "Mrs." but usually only by first name. He must drink from fountains and use rest rooms marked "Colored"; if neither is provided on public premises he must wait till he finds one elsewhere. The Houston *Post* led the state's metropolitan newspapers in equalizing the Negro's name in the press, and by the 1950s many big dailies in Texas were reporting the Negro as a citizen more than a race.

The Negro's fight for equality seesaws between the relief of courts and the gristle of violence, between the good of the white race's conscience and sympathy and the bar of the white race's dread of familiarity and fear of economic loss. Negroes have played for the state's Texas League baseball teams since 1952 without causing concern, but in 1955 the Yoakum High School forfeited a football game to Robstown because eight Negroes were on the Robstown team. School segregation was abolished in Robstown that year, but not in Yoakum. Negroes have played on Houston's public golf links without incident since a Supreme Court decision affirmed the right in 1954, but two years later a jazz concert by one Fats Domino was stopped when Negroes and whites in the segregated audience disagreed as to which race was allowed to dance. Houston and Dallas medical societies began admitting Negro doctors in 1955, and two years earlier whites named Dr. James Lee Dickey, a Negro, the "most useful citizen" of the small central Texas town of Taylor, but violence jeopardized Houston in 1952 and Fort Worth in 1954 when Negroes bought houses in white residential areas.

The five thousand members of the state's Negro American Legion posts had but twenty-six votes in the Legion's state body until 1956, when they were given equal voting rights —nearly three hundred votes—with whites. In 1952 a Negro became foreman of a Houston jury for the first time since Reconstruction; possibly he was the first Negro foreman of any Texas jury since that time. Yet three bombs exploded in Beaumont one night early in 1957. A man's house was one of the targets because, he said, he had "taken a middle-of-the-road" stand on integration. A Greek Orthodox church was bombed in the mistaken belief that Beaumont's Mayor Jimmie P. Cokinos was a member; Cokinos had halted picketing at Lamar State College by men and women trying to prevent blacks from enrolling in the school. The third bomb exploded under a truck owned by State Representative Rufus Kilpatrick, who had voted to send to a committee a bill favored by the legislature's integration bloc.

The Supreme Court ruling banning segregation on city buses was complied with swiftly, though largely on a basis of "voluntary" segregation. Slowly but steadily Texas industries are abandoning segregation; an important change came in 1956, when oil workers ended job discriminations that severely penalized Negroes. The Negro's purse is meeting equality with little ado in the cities. "Economic equality is always a prelude to total equality," Henry A. Bullock, director of graduate research at Houston's all-Negro Texas Southern University, said in 1956. Dr. Bullock's evidence, a book titled *Pathways to the Houston Negro Market*, surprised both races. His report is based on a poll of 1028 Negro families and 127 stores where they trade. His findings included: the median income of the city's Negro families advanced from $2900 in

1940 to $4016 in 1955; the average of Negroes' savings is considerably higher than that for all Houstonians; Negroes, 21 per cent of the population by Dr. Bullock's estimate, make 15 per cent of the purchases—$168,000,000 worth in 1955. He found that Texas Negroes are getting better jobs, some as chemists and engineers for firms that once employed only whites.

The nature of racial violence draws attention to itself, but violence is not the theme or even the shirttail of coping with segregation in Texas. Evan Edward Worthing, a white man, made much of his fortune from real estate in Negro sections of Houston's Fourth and Fifth wards. There was no nonsense about Worthing; Negroes never mistook him for a crusader or dreamer. Born in Michigan, educated at Texas A. and M. College, he worked for the Southern Pacific until his side line of real estate paid more than his job. When he died, in 1951, he left $118,000 to distant relatives, employees, and friends and $1,350,000 in a trust fund to pay for college educations for graduates of Houston's Negro high schools. Each scholarship is for four years—$4000; 115—$460,000 worth—had been awarded from the trust's income through mid-1957.

View of Fort Worth

14 "Certain Unalienable Rights"

September 1956

Two years and four months after the United States Supreme Court ruled that "separate but equal" is not enough, the Mansfield Independent School District was the first in Texas ordered to put its white and Negro school children in the same classrooms. It was a poor choice of leadership for an experiment in emotion. Of the half million people in Tarrant County, all but twenty-five thousand or so live in the Fort Worth metropolitan area. The others include a thousand whites and nearly four hundred Negroes living in Mansfield, a farm town in the southeast corner of the county, fourteen miles from the center of Fort Worth. Mansfield's luck has been a pauper from the start, in 1844, though the date gives it a five-year edge on Fort Worth. The town is a museum of an urban area's past. A state highway is its main street. Its mayor is Bud Halbert, a part-time barber of veined antiquity. Some of its men work in Fort Worth, but Mansfield's cast is the small farm. The head of the school board is O. C. Rawdon, a farmer. The Ku Klux Klan and a lynching are in Mansfield's recent past, fitting the forlorn town for its day in the sun.

"If Dallas, Fort Worth, or [other] big cities had got it first, things might be different. But why should our little town be used as the guinea pig?" the Dallas *News* quoted a Mansfield merchant after the town erupted. One answer is that the want of equality in Mansfield's white and Negro schools invited action. The school for whites is a brick building. Though Negroes got a new four-room school in 1954, they have no indoor toilets and had no running water—teachers brought drinking water in milk cans—till a well was drilled on the grounds in 1955. Negroes have no school lunch program, few teaching materials, no flag and no flagpole on the school grounds, and their school is on a heavily traveled road with no fence to guard children at play. The school for white children has all these things.

Steeped in poverty, the school board tried to cope with the problems in the late 1940s. It appointed several Negro sub-trustees and asked them to all board meetings. The sub-trustees were not ignored; their opinions were encouraged, their suggestions for the Negro school's needs got action if the board thought the district could afford it, and they guided the board's hiring of Negro teachers. The sub-trustees got the new four-room school and the well, but the other lacks goaded the board and the advisers into a dead end and early in 1955 the board dismissed the Negroes. They hired a Negro lawyer in Fort Worth, saying later they had no plan at the time to sue for integration but hoped to force the board to put their school on a par with the white school. As the town's Negro school was for the first eight grades, another grievance concerned Negro high-school students, who rode a public bus to a segregated school in Fort Worth. The bus let them out twenty blocks from the school and did not start the return trip till two hours after school was out. Negroes asked for a school bus for high-school students. Meanwhile, a chapter of the N.A.A.C.P. had been organized in Mansfield five years earlier.

In September 1955 a few Negroes tried in vain to enroll in the white school, and that October they sued the board. Federal District Judge Joe E. Estes ruled in Fort Worth that the suit was "premature" and "precipitate," that the school board was acting in good faith. The United States Court of Appeals for the Fifth Circuit reversed the ruling and directed Judge Estes to order the Negro and white schools to merge forthwith. Thus in 1956 Mansfield became a partner in news with Clinton, Tennessee.

For a year the Mansfield *News,* a weekly paper, had printed letters from members of citizens councils, groups whose aim is to keep blacks out of white schools. The paper's editorials took the tone of the letters: the Supreme Court is dominated by Communists, the Bible opposes integration. Late in August 1956 crosses were burned two nights in a row in the town's Negro section. A Negro dummy, hanging on Main Street, bore two signs: "This negro tried to go to a white school" and "Wouldn't this be a horrible way to die." A Mansfield Citizens Council, organized at the last hour, made plans to keep Negroes out of the white school. August 30 was the first of three registration days.

A mob of more than two hundred men and boys bullied the schoolhouse that morning. Some carried signs—"Nigger stay out, we don't want niggers, this is a white school," "A dead nigger is the best nigger," "Coons ears $1.00 a dozen." A dummy threatened from the school's flagpole. Sheriff Harlon Wright came from Fort Worth with four deputies: "I'm here because an old man who [has] lived in the Mansfield colored section for fifty years tells me that he received telephone threats giving him twenty minutes to leave his house before it is bombed." Mob leaders warned Mansfield mer-

chants to close their stores and come to the school. Those who
objected were told there might be reprisals; all stores closed
for two hours. No Negroes came to enroll. A black man was
hard to find.

Its size doubled, the mob returned the morning of August
31—second day of registration, the day Negroes were expected. The mob boiled and threatened the air; it was meaner
than the day before, resenting sheriff and deputies. Vigilantes met all cars entering Mansfield. Anyone suspected of
sympathizing with Negroes was escorted out of town. The
Tarrant County district attorney, having warned against violence, sent Grady Hight, an assistant, to the school. Angering
at something he said, the mob closed in, cursed him, roughed
him until his nose bled, kicked him until deputies rescued
him. By now Mansfield was agitated by pamphlets sent by
citizens councils in Mississippi and Alabama, by racial propaganda postmarked New Jersey, California, and Missouri. No
Negroes came to enroll the second day.

The town simmered while the school was closed for the
Labor Day weekend. Governor Shivers sent two Texas Rangers to Mansfield and authorized the school board to transfer
out of the district any student whose presence might cause a
riot. The governor's act put an end to any remnant of black
hope. Did a Negro try to enroll, the board could now send
him on to a Fort Worth school. "I haven't been in contempt
of any court," the governor said. "As governor I have strong
responsibility to preserve peace and order. I did so in the
Mansfield case. I took action to insure absence of violence
and the protection of law-abiding citizens. I have not taken
any action in defiance of anyone. I acted to prevent trouble
and not to do what would cause further trouble." The Dallas
News, in an editorial, said the governor's act was an instance
of "interposition of the state . . . between the power of the
Federal Government and members of the Mansfield School
Board." The News editorial ended: "If interposition is to come
to a test in Texas, there appears to be developing at Mansfield

the classic and perfect occasion for its attempted operation. Texas voted for interposition, you remember."

A child could still enroll on September 4, first day of school, and the mob—smaller now—returned for the third time. An Episcopal minister came from Fort Worth to offer God's solution; he was harassed and left the place. The mob got its way. No blacks tried to go to the white school; none is apt to try for some time. "The people here just don't want a Negro to go to school here with the whites," the mayor said. That is still true, yet not everyone was set to revolt. A reporter asked a high-school girl if she would go to school with Negroes. "I don't know," she said. "We would have to accept it, I guess. There's a lot of other people in the world." The school-board president's daughter is a junior in high school. What would he do if Negroes were admitted? "I will let her go [to the school], of course," he said. "I've always tried to abide by the law. But I won't like it." The town's Roman Catholic priest condemned the mob. The Methodist minister preached against lawlessness, but later an editorial in the Mansfield *News* spoke of "pin headed, religious fanatical preachers."

The long-range lesson [of the Mansfield and Clinton strife] is that genuine community spirit . . . should be a major index of the "deliberate speed" with which the Supreme Court order should be enforced. Desegregation must come . . . But the strictness with which the law is applied . . . must depend to some degree at least upon actual conditions within each community affected. Editorial, 1956, New York *Herald Tribune.*

February 1957

John Howard Griffin, of Mansfield, has written two novels of consequence as a blind man: *The Devil Rides Outside*, resulting in a Supreme Court ruling against a Michigan law used to ban the book in Detroit, and *Nuni*. Early in 1957, while walking on his farm, his sight suddenly returned and he saw his wife and two children for the first time. Born in Dallas in 1920, Griffin went to France to study medicine at age sixteen, but for years he studied medieval music instead. He lived abroad until France fell to the Germans, when he returned to the States. His sight faded gradually after he was injured during the Second World War, much of which he spent in the Pacific area, and by 1947 he was blind. By then, living on a farm near his family's home, he was raising hogs to prove that a blind man could farm with success.

Stout, six feet as to height, an Episcopalian converted to Roman Catholicism, Griffin saw his town's peril with a mind tuned to the world, experienced in contrast. Theodore Freedman, of the B'nai B'rith Anti-Defamation League, and Griffin wrote a report, *What Happened at Mansfield,* published in 1957. What follows is from the league's report—the text of Griffin's impressions, written soon after the events:

"During this time no Negroes appeared on the scene and no word has been heard from them. They are keeping at home and quiet. The people have been rendered completely confused. The small group of fanatics more or less control the town and have the backing of the majority of the people who do not approve of them, but approve of their championing of 'the cause.' At this point a local resident, myself, begins to prepare an article on the situation. The news gets around. Both sides immediately assume that it will be against them; but the White Citizens Council side is the most alarmed. They tell me to stay out of it. Some express anxiety over my physical safety. I announce . . . that the large majority of the people are following, against their will and conscience, sub-human species.

"At this time I am contacted [by the Anti-Defamation League] about the study of crisis community situations. I agree to do the research locally, since we do not think the local people would co-operate with any outsiders. I begin to make extensive interviews. I let it be known that the findings whether good or bad will be published nationally.

"The steam has died in all except the small group of fanatics. I find great resentment, and after the interviews, attempt to explain the situation to each interviewee. The findings become obvious and there are many embarrassed and red-faced people here, some who think that what we lost is far greater than what we gained. Those who were the scapegoats—the ones who refused to fire their colored help—are looked upon now with a certain respect. The tide is beginning to turn. At the outset, it was very difficult to get interviews. But when the story got around, many people took courage and volunteered, among them some of the conservative leaders. If this were going to be published, it was a sobering thing to them—they wanted the record straight, wanted themselves cleared and written down as opposers of violence, and as regretting the whole thing.

"The fanatics, losing none of their ardor, gradually lost prestige. It began to play out. Still, no one spoke up. The preachers had been repudiated. The feeling of triumph was still strong. Mr. F. [one of the leaders, not identified by name in the report] was still distributing his pamphlets. On October 15th [1956], I sent a letter to the local newspaper, a very impersonal letter, listing the background of the distributors and publishers of these hate pamphlets. Nothing more. The editor came to see me, very contrite. She said she wanted to be on the right side and that if I thought she should, she would fire the people running the paper who had written such inflammatory editorials. I refused to express myself on this. She asked for permission to publish this information [about the hate pamphlets], and I gave it to her. The information appeared, as coming from me, and I expected severe repercussions. To my surprise, it was highly praised. People said they hadn't realized how they were being used by hate groups. They said it would have been better to go ahead and integrate than to get led astray like this.

"The local newspaper has ceased publishing editorials having anything to do with the situation, but this week they published a very long letter from the Methodist minister, who decided to speak out in public also. The fanatic opposition is temporarily quiet, and they have lost all prestige in the community; although the community is still torn with false statistics, propaganda, and residual beliefs aroused against the Negroes and Jews. Perhaps it might be more exact to say that there are a number of individual fanatics left in town—men and women who still think they acted gloriously and who think it would have been even more glorious if a Negro or two had been killed—'just to show them.' But these have no respect for the radical leaders, and not much for each other.

"The subsidiary effects arising from the crisis situation were horrifying to most of the people who now view them in retrospect. These effects would appear to be: the pattern of a fanatical group taking over, forming a dictatorship as oppressive to the white race as to the colored; the pattern of working on the young, teaching the hatreds; the pattern of the destruction of reverence for values which most people consider of prime importance—namely, destruction of reverence for law, for religion, for human persons, for privacy of conscience.

"Most people think it will take a long time to overcome the great harms of these crisis-weeks in this community."

Griffin's conclusion, shown in a series of questions and answers at the end of his report, was that the people of Mansfield were still opposed to mixing whites and blacks in their schools. "Is this true of the Negro population?" he was asked. "Yes, at least compulsory desegregation," he said. Eight more of the questions and Griffin's answers follow:

QUESTION: Do you think that most people [in Mansfield] favor the use of force, if necessary, to maintain school segregation? ANSWER: Certainly they did at the time. It is touch and go now. Another test might prove that most still do, out of stubbornness rather than deep conviction. It might also, if there were enough people willing to express their true feelings, show that most people do not.

QUESTION: Do most people [now] believe that desegregation is inevitable? ANSWER: Most do now.

QUESTION: Does the Negro populace favor the use of force for desegregation? ANSWER: Not the populace of Mansfield, certainly, but that of peripheral areas would appear to.

QUESTION: Do you think many, some, or none of the local white residents would abide by the Supreme Court decision to the extent of not using force against desegregation processes? ANSWER: Some, but this depends entirely on the groundwork. The people will follow strong leaders whether those leaders are on the wrong or right side. This has been proved. The Methodist minister in his letter to the editor pleads for respect for the Supreme Court. But for over a year such respect has been systematically destroyed locally by editorials and letters to the editor . . . It is impossible to foretell. It would depend on whom they followed.

QUESTION: Will the students at the school accept desegregation? ANSWER: If properly presented to them, and if their parents and others allow them to, they would certainly accept it. At the present time they would not—not because of convictions about the issue but because of pressures and prejudices.

QUESTION: Were there outside forces involved in the organization of resistance to desegregation? ANSWER: I can find no evidence that there were. However, they were in evidence almost immediately afterward, and certainly were involved in the latter part of the crisis period.

QUESTION: Were there outside forces involved in the Negroes' attempts to desegregate? ANSWER: Unquestionably, yes. It is significant that the N.A.A.C.P. lost all of its local supporters within the month. . . . It is significant, too, however, that the Negroes behaved with perfect dignity and did nothing in any way untoward during the entire period on the local level. They made themselves invisible, gave no answer, displayed no intention to use force to gain entry to the school, and behaved with perfect tact. . . . They showed up far better than those who demonstrated against them.

QUESTION: Do most youngsters of high-school age really fear that they, as individuals, will be involved in social mingling with the Negro if he is accepted into the school? ANSWER: I have asked this of many high-school students of both sexes, and they all think it is too ridiculous. They fear it for others, yes, but for themselves impossible—they have not the slightest fear they will be involved in social mingling or in any form of mongrelization. Each feels that it would be bad for others, but each feels thoroughly insulated against the danger himself.

Main Building and Library —
University of Texas

15 Eeny, Meeny, Miney, Mo

Since May 17, 1954, Southern states have had to develop some things that other states do not have or separating the races might become a concern of historians alone. These things include white citizens councils and legislators who do not mind bucking the oath of office in which they swear to uphold the Constitution of the United States. If a state happens to have an attorney general who can catch the N.A.A.C.P. doing some things, so much the better. If it also has a governor who is not going to let the innocent excite the guilty (Chapter 14), the odds are that mixing the races is not going to bother anybody for a while. Texas has some citizens councils, it has many legislators who are willing to find out what is and what is not constitutional, and until 1957 it had an attorney general and a governor who measured up to the requirements above. The majority of Texans do not favor mixing the races if they can help it, but in Will Wilson, a former state supreme court justice, the state has an attorney general who has said he will support decisions made by the United States Supreme Court and who said so when he campaigned for the office. Governor Price Daniel has acted in the main on the principle of letting sleeping dogs lie as long as possible.

The first citizens council was organized in Mississippi in 1954; gradually the resistance plan spread to other Southern states. The first in Texas was organized at Kilgore in July 1955, and by mid-1957 nearly a dozen councils were spread through the eastern part of the state. Their thinking and methods are shown in a round robin of quotations from interviews published in the Houston *Post* and the Dallas *News* in August 1955; quotations from one of Lynn Landrum's columns in the *News* a year later reflect opposition to the councils. The men quoted are Ross Carlton, a lawyer, president of the Texas Citizens Council of Dallas; B. E. Masters, president emeritus of the Kilgore Junior College, a founder of the Kilgore Citizens Council; A. G. Morton, Jr., an oilman-farmer, president of the Kilgore council; G. L. Florence, a lawyer, member of the Gilmer Citizens Council; and Landrum.

CARLTON: "We believe in segregation. It's the only system where two races of people have lived side by side in peace."

MASTERS: "I got into this field for the sole purpose of trying to keep our nation from mongrelization."

MORTON: "We are just a group of white people who are solidly united as being opposed to . . . integration in our school system or at any other level."

LANDRUM: "It is the policy of the column to have no truck with the Citizens Councils which are blossoming out all over. The Columntator has learned to distrust mass thinking."

CARLTON: "We are nonpartisan and nonsectarian. We are not preaching any religious or racial intolerance."

MORTON: "Our activities will be carried on by legal means and without force, threats or other forms of intimidation."

FLORENCE: "Public opinion, properly guided and crystallized, can change any law by any court."

MASTERS: "They [Negroes] do not recognize the sanctity of the home. Look at their divorce rate and you will see that. They are humble and friendly until they get the upper hand, when they become arrogant and domineering."

LANDRUM: "Citizens Councils number in their ranks many upright, God-fearing folk. And that was true of the Ku Klux Klan, too."

CARLTON: "We will not tolerate any violence or any talk of it. We want to use every legal means to preserve segregation. This organization is flat against activities like those of the Ku Klux Klan."

MORTON: "The big majority of council members are not Negro-haters. There may be some former Klansmen among us, but I don't know who they are."

MASTERS: "We had as much right to organize as the NAACP. Our object is to show the Negroes we're a unit against integration. We have no fight against the Negro— we're friends to them personally—but we're fighting to the bitter end against the NAACP and the ruling by the Supreme Court."

FLORENCE: "If they would keep out the wild-eyed agitators, and let our Negroes alone, we wouldn't have any question of integration."

MASTERS: "Other parts of Texas were running wild, going pell mell for integration, and the State Board of Education has dodged the issue, so we felt we should set an example of opposition."

LANDRUM: "With whatever good there is in the councils, there is a deal of bad, it seems to the Columntator."

In September 1956, after investigating the N.A.A.C.P. in several Texas cities, Attorney General John Ben Shepperd asked for an injunction banning the Negro organization from Texas. "This suit . . . is no different from any other suit brought by the attorney general to determine if a Texas organization is complying with the laws of Texas," Shepperd said. "We allege that the NAACP has exceeded the bounds of propriety and law." The state's petition to the court said: "This action is not, in any manner, a suit against the Negro citizens of Texas . . . In no event does [the state] intend to infer any attempt to deny the rights of Negroes or others to belong to any organization fully complying with the constitution and laws of the State of Texas." The suit charged the N.A.A.C.P. with eight offenses, the principal one being barratry—inciting lawsuits. Shepperd was later to offer the testimony of Negro students or their parents to prove this charge. Otis T. Dunagan, a state district judge, granted a temporary restraining order and set a hearing for a temporary injunction.

The scene of the hearing was Judge Dunagan's courtroom in the new Smith County Courthouse at Tyler, a city in East Texas. The courtroom, with 120 seats, was crowded with around three hundred people, more than half of them Negroes, during the seventeen days of the hearing. Many more stood in the hall, unable to get in the courtroom. Two Texas Rangers, several uniformed state highway patrolmen, and deputy sheriffs were in the courtroom throughout the hearing, but they had nothing to do except to prompt a few whites who tried to take Confederate flags into the courtroom.

Judge Dunagan summarized the suit at the end of the hearing: "This is not an integration or segregation suit but is one to determine if the defendants are operating and conducting their business within the laws of this state. . . . When the courts of this land base their decisions and judgments on anything other than the Constitution and the written law it will be a sad day for constitutional government. This nation will then cease to be a government of law and become a government of men." So saying he granted a temporary injunction.

In May 1957 he made it permanent, enjoining the N.A.A.C.P. from other than "educational and charitable activities within the state."

Following Alabama and Louisiana, Texas was the third state to restrict the N.A.A.C.P., but Texans were not of one mind in wanting it restricted. The same Landrum column quoted earlier opposed restricting the Negro organization and represented to a large extent the thinking of white Texans who opposed Shepperd's action: "NAACP is barging in and making all sorts of trouble in Texas now. But it would be a sorry sort of Texas in which a citizen, be he high yellow, white, black, brown or red, can not let out a loud demand for his rights—as he conceives them to be. . . . The colored people have as much right to hard-headed, uncompromising leadership as have the white folks."

The attorney general, however, played second fiddle to the Texas legislature in scourging the N.A.A.C.P. In March 1957 the House of Representatives argued a bill to make it unlawful for a member of the Negro organization to hold a job with state, county, or local governments, including school districts. Introduced by Representative Reagan R. Huffman, of East Texas, the bill would require all employees to sign sworn statements that they did not belong to the N.A.A.C.P. "Any person refusing to supply a statement shall be summarily dismissed. . . . We can take care of our Negro citizens. . . . They don't want trouble caused by the NAACP," Huffman told the House.

"Has the NAACP ever been adjudicated a subversive organization?" asked Representative George Thurman.

"No, sir," Huffman said. "But I'm going to answer with this. . . . We have evidence that NAACP is infiltrated with members of the Communist Party."

Representative Bob Mullen, of the Rio Grande Valley, was one who opposed Huffman and the segregation bloc. "Many are voting for this bill because they expect it to be knocked out the first time it comes up in court," he told the House.

"I cannot vote to punish members of any organization for pursuing what they think is right. If they were subversive it would be covered by present law." The bill passed the House by a vote of seventy-five to forty-nine.

The House passed seven more bills intended to preserve racial separation in the schools. All were introduced by legislators from East Texas, where 80 per cent of the state's Negroes live. The other seven bills:

§ Set up standards for assigning students to schools. Not mentioning race in the list of factors to be considered, it said no child would be forced to attend an integrated school. It denied school boards authority to carry out "any order" to admit a student unless the board approved. Probably unconstitutional.

§ Exempted from the compulsory attendance law any child withdrawing from an integrated school if he then enrolled in a segregated school—meaning only that a child is not compelled to go to one school if he goes to another. It said "forced integration" is "contrary to rights of the individual." Possibly unconstitutional.

§ Required schools to be labeled "white," "Negro," or "integrated" and required students to be tentatively assigned by race pending later assignment on the basis of other factors. Almost surely unconstitutional.

§ Authorized grants to students withdrawing from integrated schools to pay their tuition at segregated private schools. Probably unconstitutional.

§ Directed the attorney general to defend all lawsuits attacking segregation in the schools. Probably constitutional.

§ Required anyone working for or against integration to register with the Texas secretary of state. Later, when the bill was before a Senate committee, it was the only one to be referred to Attorney General Wilson, who said it was unconstitutional.

§ Prohibited future integration of any school district with-

out approval by the voters—local option. Undoubtedly unconstitutional.

Most of the bills reflected proposals made by the Texas
Advisory Council on Segregation in Public Schools, appointed in 1955 by Governor Allan Shivers. The commission,
whose proposals were supported by Governor Shivers, asked
school officials to "utilize every legal means at their command
to avoid and circumvent compliance [with Supreme Court
decisions] and to maintain a dual school system so long as
the people of this State and the local communities desire it."

The bills met determined opposition in the Senate, where
two senators, Henry Gonzalez, of San Antonio, and Abraham
Kazen, Jr., of Laredo, filibustered to a record thirty-six hours
and two minutes to oppose, in vain, the first of the House
bills to reach the Senate floor—the bill setting up standards
for assigning students to schools. They filibustered again,
also in vain, when the Senate took up a second House bill—
the one requiring local option elections on integration. Each
bill was passed, but coming at the end of the session the de-
laying tactics hamstrung the East Texans. Largely as a result
of the filibusters, the other bills died in the Senate. Senators
Gonzalez and Kazen were supported by Senators Charles
Herring, of Austin, Hubert Hudson, of Brownsville, Bruce
Reagan, of Corpus Christi, and Frank Owen III, of El Paso.

Governor Daniel later signed the two bills without asking
the attorney general for an opinion on their constitutionality.
"It is my conclusion that the bills do not violate the Constitution of the United States or the State of Texas or the court
decisions which have been referred to by those questioning
the measures," the governor said. There is no question that
the local option bill is a victory of consequence for segregation forces. Introduced by Representative Jerry Sadler, an
East Texas lawyer who was a member of the Texas Railroad
Commission in the late 1930s and was twice an unsuccessful
candidate for governor in the 1940s, the bill does not affect
school districts integrated before August 1957, but it pre-

vented planned integration in Galveston and Port Arthur, whose school boards had voted to begin integration in the fall of 1957. The law gave the boards the alternatives of a court test or an election, which can be called only by petition of 20 per cent of the voters. If the bill proves to be unconstitutional it will nevertheless have delayed further integration by two years.

More than a hundred Texas school districts have been integrated without trouble, including San Antonio, El Paso, Austin, and Corpus Christi. Most of the integrated districts have comparatively few Negroes. Late in 1956 the Texas Association of School Boards passed, with only one dissenting vote, a resolution: "No matter what the final outcome of the integration question may be, this body urges each district and its educators and administrators to practice and teach by example the fundamental American policy of tolerance in racial and religious matters. We urge each local district to approach the question of integration with the dignity befitting an institution dedicated to the teaching of American principles."

V TEXAS IS ITS OWN REWARD

DOWNTOWN SAN ANTONIO AND THE RIVER

Sam Houston's "Steamboat House"—Huntsville

16 The Texas Neurosis

"Dear Sir: I have been hearing for a long time about what a big place Texas is and what wonderful people Texans are, and I have started to wonder. . . . Is there any such place as Texas?" The letter, signed "Virginia," began a newspaper column written for the Associated Press, in 1952, by Ed Creagh. The column was a parody on the old New York *Sun's* reply to a child who had asked if there were a Santa Claus.

"No, Virginia, there isn't any Texas," Creagh wrote. "Texas is just one of those good-natured myths—like Paul Bunyan, George Washington's cherry tree, or Brooklyn—that has been handed down, generation after generation, until many people have come to believe that it is true. It would be nice, wouldn't it, if there really were a Texas? . . . But you're getting to be a big girl now, Virginia, and the truth must not be kept from you. . . . Figure it out for yourself, Virginia: There couldn't

be a Texas. No nation on earth, not even this rich and powerful land of ours, could afford a Texas. If Texas really existed,
there wouldn't be room for the rest of us. Before you knew it,
the whole country would be overrun by Texans. And that way
lies madness."

The Texan spirit is not often spoofed so merrily. The state's
ebullience incites others, who enjoy it or raise Cain with it
or deplore it but are seldom indifferent to it. *Fortune* has expressed the wish "that Texas could be friendly on a neighbor-
hood basis instead of a state basis." It is not an unheard-of
plaint, for the state has civic pride on a regional scale. Texas
abounds in vivid patriotism, in the conviction that Texas
synthesizes the earth's advantages—and that even this good
must be improved. Many Texans size up their state as an ante-
room to heaven, the cornucopia of the universe, and a com-
pendium of the excellences all rolled into one. Texas, "the
mecca, the land of promise, to which all eyes are turned,"
said a pamphlet published by the state, in 1875, to attract
immigrants. The quotation has more dimension now than
then, but some Texans see only this one image.

The state's jubilation at being Texas attracts more interest
than anything except its millionaire legend. "Being a Texan
would be embarrassing to anyone except a Texan," a Colum-
bus (Ohio) *Star* columnist wrote in 1950. The winner of a
Houston contest to write the most beautiful sentence in the
Texan language was Costanza Schafer, a former Californian,
whose entry was, "Daddy gave me Texas for Christmas." In
1954 John Rosenfield wrote in the Dallas *News:* "In vaude-
ville days the automatic gag was 'Hoboken.' A ritzier joke
was 'Philadelphia' . . . Now, so help me, Broadway au-
diences fall to pieces at the mere mention of 'Texas' . . ."
This ready identification has come to be more a penalty than
a good, a penalty of excess.

People in other states, though sometimes entertained by
the Texas neurosis, often come to think of Texas as being the
site of a permanent American Legion convention, a stage for

a continuing travesty of a Gilbert and Sullivan burlesque. The Texan spirit, fertilized by high hearts and a fancy for an older Texas that lost touch with reality before the First World War, is the state's most widely known symbol. In the long run the *joie de Texas vivre* has estranged more than be-friended outsiders, especially since the public accepted the illusion that Texas is populated almost entirely by million-aires. "The unpopularity of Texas is probably at its all-time high," the historian Walter Prescott Webb, a native Texan, wrote in 1952. "I trust it is not increasing, but I find it even in the western states. . . . Texans should learn silence."

Most Texans become possessed, to varying degrees, when they leave their state, trying to please by acting the role strangers expect of them. Paul Crume, of the Dallas *News*, wrote of a Dallas man who drove to Los Angeles: "He started out . . . with a Lincoln Continental and maybe $6,000. By the time he reached the coast, his holdings had increased to 150 oil wells, two refineries, two big cattle ranches, an island in the Gulf of Mexico . . . This is the way a lot of Texas fortunes are made." Such inflation affects other than fortunes. "Texas things and people, when they leave the state, seem to expand in size," Crume wrote. "Every Texas figure grows at least three zeros behind it whenever it pops up outside of Texas. Piper Cubs become B-36 bombers in out-of-state talk." Yet Texas, as a state, cannot officially blow its own horn. A provision of its constitution prohibits the state from spending public funds to advertise itself. One of only three states that does not promote itself, Texas has not felt the need to rescind this constitutional ban.

The Texan spirit rewards and subtracts from the state in nearly equal parts. Something of a puzzle in its contagion for newcomers through all the state's history, its substance is state confidence and self-esteem. Both owe their long life to a history that is as much of a piece, in miniature, as that of the United States, and to the tranquilizing influence of a type of superlative arising from physical rather than cultural bigness. Concern for superlatives of all kinds, though it is often a pose, waylays the state's sense of proportion. In 1956 William Donald Cross, of Dallas, began preparing a book listing "several hundred of the most . . . costly products regularly available on the American market"—a dictionary of extravagance. Some conclude that Texans are more taken with size for size's sake than with the state itself. Paul M. Butler, national chairman of the Democratic party, was surprised at the number of Texans he met on a trip to Alaska. "I think some of them have moved there so they will still live in the biggest state when Alaska is admitted to the Union," he said.

The Texan spirit bemuses others because of its daydreams of grandeur and a characteristic that is the opposite of Missouri's popular name—not "Show Me" but "Let's Show Everybody." Many valid ingredients of the Texan spirit enrich the state in flavor and competence, but the folly growing with the spirit has the effect of weeds on a lawn. A type of Texan unconsciously changes from being himself to being the state's Mr. Hyde, striving to fulfill the legend whenever he gets a chance to play "Texan." Mr. Hyde suffers from a malignant form of Texan spirit that may be called Texas fever—megalomania, the insanity of state-exaltation, the passion for big things. Newcomers, if infected, are apt to get the hang of being Texan in a way that stuns a native. One can become a Texan quicker than anything else. A melancholy Texas sight is an indelibly urban male wearing conventional clothing except for stripes at both ends and in the middle—cowboy boots, hat and belt. Natives have not cornered the artificial wearing of the Western badge.

The Texan spirit is made of exaltation, zeal, and faith—defined in the Bible as "the substance of things hoped for, the evidence of things not seen." Texas fever is made of exaggeration, enthusiasm, and error—an adding machine can manufacture it. The undiluted Texan—he is thought of as typical but is not—is sustained by fever more than spirit, and he is the bait for critics. Critics—how that word hounds the Texas story!

Texans are the only "race of people" known to anthropologists who do not depend on breeding for propagation. Like princes and lords, they can be made by "breath," plus a big white hat—which comparatively few Texans wear. J. Frank Dobie, 1952, Dallas *News.*

Texans sincerely believe that all other Americans are envious of them. J. B. Priestley, 1955, *Journey Down a Rainbow.*

Illusions about Texas were prophesied by a legend nearly three centuries older than the state, that of Coronado's hopes as he set out from Mexico. In the poet Townsend Miller's words:

And my lords

The streets were of beaten gold, the young maidens
As copper, the gardens jasper and they dance in them
The doors studded with turquoise the porches silver
The boughs hung with golden bells and they clash in the
    breeze
The feathers, the strange fruit and it lies to the east.[1]

Some Texans take comfort in the fiction of Coronado's dream even if they know of his disillusionment. By magnifying certain aspects of the state's mythology—some genuine, some false—one can make omitted aspects seem inconsequential in spite of their relevance. Thus many Texans, living in a cocoon of utopian fantasy, are unaware of their extraordinary state's wants and of the necessity of its role in nation and world. The result, besides creating a state patriotism hostile to critics who are themselves Texans, is that reality is met a quarter of the way. Many Texans are lulled by the same illusions that deceive outsiders, illusions having scant or no touch with the

[1] *A Letter From Texas,* Neiman-Marcus, Dallas, 1939.

facts of Texas history or the moment. Once public fancy has fixed on an interpretation, however, facts can do little to correct the fixation.

Probably no one can say how much of the illusion was created by Texans and how much by others. Texans, at any rate, have done little to arrest the absurdities, and they must often pay the piper for tunes called by others. "Asa Jones, a cowman of Alpine, Texas, was telling me of an experience he had in New Orleans before farm tractors were invented," J. Frank Dobie wrote in 1952. "He was on a horse-trading expedition and was stopping at a small hotel run by a widow. One night, soon after he had gone to bed, she called him in great excitement. Putting on his pants and boots hurriedly, he opened the door. 'A drunk man is downstairs,' she said, 'cutting up and swearing he is going to lodge here. We won't have him, but he won't go away. I see on the register that you are from Texas, and I know you can handle him.'" Asa Jones was not called to protect a widow because he was a prize fighter or a giant killer; he was called because he lived in Texas. In 1919, when Boston police went on strike, a Texan at Harvard University was called in and commissioned an emergency policeman for no other reason than that he was a Texan.

By no means all Texas nonsense originates with Texans. In 1953 Graham Greene, the British novelist, and a friend of his named John Sutro started the Anglo-Texan Society. A letter from the secretary of the society to the Houston *Post*, in 1956, said the society was inspired by Greene and Sutro when the two Englishmen "met a small party of Texans who were feeling alone and friendless in a strange country." The society's subsequent revelries, including a blood-letting contest between a member of Parliament and a British woman to see which was "the most blue-blooded American," did not involve Texans but affected the public as being Texan. The word "Texan" in the society's name cued the public. Yet reports of the society's activities in two London newspapers, the *Daily*

Mail and the *Evening Standard,* left the impression that the society's only decorum was attributable to the few Texans at the parties. The English are having a good time with their Anglo-Texan Society; Texas gets credit for the high jinks.

Dobie has written that the public is like the hero in Hoyt's *Texas Steer,* at one time a popular play. Somebody in the play mentions Texas, at which the hero pulls both six-shooters and empties their blank cartridges into the ceiling, crying, "At mention of that grand old name I always sa-lute!" And the public is world-wide. Andrei Vishinski, the Soviet Minister of Foreign Affairs from 1949 to 1953, was snared by the myth. "Ah, Texas! Russia is the Texas of Europe—the biggest and best, you know," Vishinski once told Dick West of the Dallas *News.*

In the main, however, the public is only a nuisance. The trouble lies with those Texans afflicted with Texas fever, a state of withered curiosity causing suspicion of anything not Texan. In 1953, when Luther H. Evans, a native Texan, was Librarian of Congress, he told a University of Texas audience: "Texans have the attitude that if the rest of the world would act like them everything would be all right. But the rest of the world doesn't want to be like us." It is hard for many Texans to escape the state's image. Texas Independence Day (March 2) and San Jacinto Day (April 21) are state holidays. The Lone Star flag has come to be flown with the Stars and Stripes as a rule, but it still flies alone at times. Texas history is studied in the state's elementary schools, high schools, and colleges. More than a hundred organizations exist for the study, or just the recall, of Texas history. Possibly in no other state are signed stories of state worship published in some newspapers and regional magazines; the uniform theme of these stories is "Thank God I Am a Texan," which is often their title.

Important historic shrines, of which the Alamo is the best known, are sometimes used to prompt chauvinism. In 1952, when Adlai Stevenson, the Democratic presidential candi-

date, was to make a campaign speech at the Alamo, his opponent's supporters protested to the Daughters of the Republic
of Texas because Stevenson favored federal ownership of
the tidelands. "Let him speak in Texas if he must," the protest
said, "but let us preserve the Alamo for those who respect and
revere her traditions." Texas patriotism is used to camouflage
politicians' aims and issues. "[Allan] Shivers, with more courage of the real Texas brand, has taken his stand," concluded
a Dallas *News* editorial in 1954. Campaign literature for Thad
Hutcheson, a Republican candidate for United States Senator
in the special election of 1957, was mailed in envelopes
marked "A Note from a TRUE Texan." The word "TRUE"
was in letters more than half the height of the envelopes.

"The State of Texas continues to profit by its half-serious
pose that it is only an affiliate rather than a member of the
United States," the Montreal *Gazette* said in 1954. The pose,
if it is no more than that, is instinctive. "The only issues . . .
will be Americanism and pure Texanism," said Beauford
Jester, in 1946, when he was making a successful campaign
for governor. "There is not going to be any Communism in
this country or in Texas," said Senator Tom Connally, in 1949,
in a Houston speech. The Texan illusion of being a separate
nationality, a race apart, is dying, but very slowly.

The extreme Texan spirit approves of anything Texan and
is hostile to all else. The Dallas chapter of the American Institute of Architects once hired a lawyer to protest the action
of the Dallas County Commissioners Court in awarding a
design contract to a firm in St. Louis rather than to one in
Texas. In 1938, in a report on Texas public-health problems,
the United States Public Health Service said, "The best results
cannot be expected until Texans can realize without shock
that someone from Maine or California might do a specific
health job a little better than anyone available from within
the state."

"Whenever the time comes . . . that Texans are not regarded abroad as giants of one kind or another, they will be

a people of dilapidated hearts," Dobie wrote. "When the time of neglect arrives and [Texans] can no longer enjoy being misinterpreted, millions will be too dispirited to nurture the myth that generations have habitually both denied and encouraged."

One great fault of the Texians is that [they] try to do every-thing at once, & having done very little & that badly, they imagine they have succeeded . . . Francis C. Sheridan, 1840, *Galveston Island.*

Texans have done too much bragging about their state. Texas is the biggest state in area but the biggest and best of any single thing will be found somewhere else. . . . Texans ought to be content with the variety of loveliness, the pictur-esqueness of what they actually do have. Hubert Mewhin-ney, 1955, Houston *Post.*

Commercial opportunism has caused no other state to seem so foolish and provincial as Texas. If Texas could copyright its name and sell the right to use it commercially, it is con-ceivable that in a few years it would have enough proceeds to build and fill with books a number of state libraries in small towns, where they are needed, or build several state parks, which are also needed. Both Texans and others depend on the state's name for profit.

Among frivolous products using Texas themes as a lure are Texas Bucks in denominations up to $5,000,000, Texas Buck coins, Texas passports, Texas citizenship certificates, Texas ambassador cards, Texas insurance policies, Texas greeting cards, Texas boast cards, Texas maps so drawn that the state is larger in area than the United States, Texas menus ("Sliced Breast of Chaparral with sauté of Boiled Lizard Tongues" and the like), Texas wrapping paper, a Texas Millionaire game with a total of $256,000,000 in Texas Bucks, a one-page Texas dictionary of superlatives, a booklet titled *Texas Brags* that sold more than half a million copies in its first decade,

Texas land deeds in which the buyer is legally deeded a square foot or a square inch of land, and Texas oil-well deeds —"The Texas Millionaires Oil Co. certifies that [name of purchaser], along with Jane Russell, Frank Sinatra, Dorothy Lamour, Dinah Shore and 15 other Hollywood Stars, owns a legal interest in a real Texas Oil Well, the Marik No. 1, in Austin County," says a gift card accompanying the deed, price $1.00.

Texans have shown so little interest in these products of flagging imaginations that nearly all would have been instant failures were there a law prohibiting them from being sent out of the state. They succeed, when they do, because the rest of the world buys them. L. U. Kaiser, originator of Texas Bucks, the most successful of these products, was at first unable to keep up with the world-wide demand for the play money in his own print shop and had to hire other firms to help print them. The largest single order for Texas Bucks— 1,250,000—came not from Texas but from Kansas City, Missouri.

The Texas trademark is also used to stimulate more orthodox commercial hopes. The Retail Merchants Association of Houston once arranged for buyers of Western hats to be given membership certificates in the "Royal Texas Order of the Western Fedora." At the head of a Dallas department store's daily newspaper ads is the phrase " 'Texas-Size' Titche's" or " 'Texas-Size' Clearance." Every Ford car assembled in Dallas bears a sticker on its rear window: "Built in Texas by Texans." One of the Dodge Automobile Company's 1956 models was called the Texan. The same car was called the Coronet in other states, but the Texas version had different upholstery and a "Texan" insigne, and it was priced at fifty dollars more than the Coronet.

Journalists, book publishers, movie producers, and manufacturers make use of the Texas trademark, whose commercial use is not confined to the United States. In 1952, hoping to get two thousand or so well-to-do Texas tourists in South

France, the Riviera sponsored a Texas Week. The festival included the novelty of an "aquatic rodeo," Texas fashion
shows at Cannes and other cities, a choir of French children
singing "Deep in the Heart of Texas" and "The Eyes of Texas,"
and, by mischance, a band playing "Marching Through
Georgia." One of two minor officials of the French government who came to Texas three months beforehand to pep
up interest in France's Texas Week said this was the first time
France had so honored any country or state. The Riviera's
Texas Week, however, may have been a disappointment to
the Riviera; it was not repeated in following years.

*If Texas is annexed "we are not to be great gainers when
compared to the United States. . . . We surrender everything and in reality we get nothing, only protection. . . .
When we once become a part and parcel of the United States
we are subject to all their vicissitudes. . . . [But if Texas is
not annexed] the Glory of the United States has already cul-
minated. A rival power will soon be built up, and the Pacific,
as well as the Atlantic, will be component parts of Texas in
thirty years from this date."* Sam Houston, 1844, in a letter
to William S. Murphy, United States chargé d'affaires to
Texas.

The hero of Eugene Manlove Rhodes's short story, "The
Tie-Fast Men," is asked, "Who's the hardest [of men], Mr.
Bates?" He replies: ". . . Well, the Tejanos, and them that
holds with Texas ideas, they use a short rope and they tie it
hard and fast to the horn of the saddle. Now the California
man and his neighbors, they use a long rope and take their
dallies. Then if they get in trouble they let the dally come
off. It's a heap safer . . . But the Texas man, he's done fixed
himself so he can't let go. . . . There ain't goin' to be no
half-way measures. What he drops his loop over is his, or he's
its. . . . And that habit influences them in other things be-

sides ropin'. It ain't only a habit. It's a religion, sort of. You're never quite sure what a sensible man will do."

Rhodes was a New Mexico man. Another interpretation of the Texan is that of John Knott, a cartoonist for the Dallas *News*, who created the character of Old Man Texas for his cartoons. In 1939 Walter Prescott Webb described the appearance of Knott's Texan as "a composite of many fathers of this generation. He is tall, angular, shrewd, and kindly. He wears a broad-brimmed hat, a drooping mustache, and around his eyes are those wrinkles made by looking long distances over a windy, sunlit land. Two things Old Man Texas is good at: seeing through people to their motives and asking penetrating questions. His kindly exterior covers but does not wholly conceal great power, not only for discrimination but for action once he decides that action is necessary. He has in him something of Stephen F. Austin, Sam Houston, Colonel Charles Goodnight, Jack Hays, and L. H. McNelly. He has a little of the weariness of the farmer and the coolness of the cattleman."

Knott's Texan never existed except as an ideal, a dream, a composite of some of the better characteristics of a faded era. Rhodes's profile—stubbornness, directness, foolhardiness, and daring—was more to the point, but it, too, belongs most to the past. Both interpretations, however, deal with themes which have influenced the shaping of the Texan spirit. The picture is filled in when the folly is added, plus the chore of living up to the legend. "The trouble is that the Texan is so afraid the world will think his state—or himself—does not measure up that he goes to any lengths to put on a big front —often too big," Stanley Walker, author of *Home to Texas*, a sensible book about the state, wrote in *Look* magazine in 1952.

Daily, in every medium of public expression, the Texan spirit is the subject of reproof, of humor, of exaggeration, and of burlesque. "Nearly every youngster born in Texas gets a thorough schooling, before he reaches his 'teens, in the peculiar morals of his state," John Fischer, editor of *Harper's*, wrote in 1954. "This code of behavior usually is imparted in brusque, infrequent remarks from male relatives, ranch foremen, rig bosses, or other adults who feel some responsibility for his spiritual guidance. . . . This kind of upbringing leaves an impress which some Texans are never able to outgrow. It is true that in recent years the native-born have begun to shun the traditional, outward marks of their race. . . . But the sense of moral superiority which was ingrained in childhood frequently sticks for life. Quite naturally, outsiders find this intolerable, and anti-Texas sentiment sometimes can be almost as virulent as anti-Semitism in Hitler's Germany."

The intolerability Fischer mentioned was the motive for a song in the Broadway musical comedy, *Look, Ma, I'm Dancin'*, of 1948. The chorus of the song, titled "I'm Tired of Texas," began,

> I'm tired of Texas,
> So tired of Texas.
> I'm gonna head out, spread out
> Away from Texas.
> I'm so darn fed up
> That I can hardly hold my head up.

Whatever the reason may have been, "I'm Tired of Texas" was the hit song of the show.

The ubiquity of Texas jokes has caused them to become an American monotony, and their subject is uniform—excess of Texan spirit. A presumably new joke in 1956 was the measure of many: a Texan in heaven was dismayed because there was no hymn singing. He asked Saint Peter if he might organize a choir, saying that he would need a thousand sopranos, a thousand contraltos, and a thousand tenors. Saint Peter inquired about basses. "Oh, I'll sing bass myself," the Texan said. An Associated Press story from Bermuda, in 1956, illustrated how the whole cloth of Texan spoof may be presented as fact. The news service quoted a message from the

commissioner of the United States Housing Administration to
a convention of the National Savings and Loan League. "I
recently visited a part of Texas where a lot of building
was taking place," the commissioner was quoted as saying.
"Homes were rising in all directions, and among them was a
fine, modern church. I gazed with admiration at this structure
and naturally asked what was the denomination. The answer
from the builder was unexpected. He said, 'It hasn't got any
denomination. I'm building it on speculation.'"

In 1952, during the Texas State Fair, the first Texan of
Distinction award was given to Eugene Holman, a native
Texan who was president of the Standard Oil Company
(New Jersey). Holman made a talk at the time, "What Is a
Texan?" "I particularly admire these four virtues of a Texan
as I see them—his sense of adventure, his sense of individual
responsibility, his true appreciation of bigness, and his respect for moral law," he said. There is something to be said
for Holman's points—a great deal to be said for Texans' "true
appreciation of bigness"—and there is no question about his
feeling that "Texans are oil-minded people." But the conclusion of his talk was a point some Texans overlook: "So the real
answer to the question, 'What Is a Texan?' is, 'He is an
American.'"

The Texan thinks of himself as belonging to an indestructible freemasonry, membership in which is required of anyone
who lives in Texas, or ever did. More and more, however,
Texans are shrinking from excesses of the Texan spirit, a
withdrawal encouraged from within the state. William H.
Kittrell, of Dallas, has described himself as a registered lob-
byist and peanut farmer; enlightened and courageous, he is
one of the most entertaining men in Texas. That his people
were in Texas before Sam Houston arrived makes him a Texas
authority of consequence even to those who use the Texan
spirit as an intoxicant. In 1948 Kittrell and three of his friends
applied for a state charter as Professional Texans, Inc., an
organization described in the incorporation papers as "Phil-

anthropic, Benevolent, Patriotic, and Educational." The emphasis, it developed, was to be on education, and it is a misfortune that the organization languished as soon as the charter was granted.

"It was our particular purpose to issue rebukes and reprovals to the people who were, or pretended to be, Texans, and as Texans committed oafish deeds in far-off places," Kittrell wrote in 1956. "We particularly objected to excursionists from Dallas and Houston who went to New York night spots and slipped the leader of a band a two-dollar bill, asking him to play 'I've Been Working on the Railroad' so they could arise and sing, publicly, 'The Eyes of Texas.' It is particularly painful to see some knock-kneed fellow wearing cowboy boots that hurt his flat feet, and a Texas Ranger gunbelt with a gold-plated buckle that is almost hidden by folds of fat, talking with seeming modesty about his non-existent daily allowable [oil production], his herds of white faces, and implying that he won the war unaided by Eisenhower, MacArthur, or Nimitz. It was a wonderful project, and a patriotic duty, and I am sorry we never got around to performing it." Possibly as a warning, Kittrell added that Professional Texans, Inc., "is still a legally constituted body."

For years another Texan—a distinguished scholar—has toyed with the idea of organizing a secret society to exploit the state's rugged past at considerable profit. It would be called the Sons of the Six-Shooter Toters of Texas. Its initials, SSSTT, would be its password—Ssstt!—and its obvious emblem would be made of brass, washed in gold, and sold for the price of the Ku Klux sheet—$16. At last, little by little, Texans are learning to laugh at themselves—as in "The Timid Texan," by Annie Grey Young:

> One day I met a Texan who
> Was talking of his state.
> While sitting in the park he said,
> "This place is not so great.

A lot of states have cattle
And a lot of states have oil,
Other states grow better crops
For they have richer soil.

"Our girls aren't always prettier,
Our men aren't always tall
And often we say things are big
When they are really small."
I met this man in Austin
And I talked to him all day,
But then two men in white came up
And led the man away.

Intracoastal Canal at Brazosport

17 What Rogues and Peasant Slaves!

"Why does Texas always withstand [civilization]?" Gutzon
Borglum asked his friend J. Frank Dobie in 1936. Borglum,
one of America's eminent sculptors, did not query with a traveler's quick judgment; he lived in Texas at the time, the year
of the Texas Centennial. In the beginning the state did not
withstand but embraced civilization. One of the first colonists
said and most believed that "the cultivated mind is the guardian genius of democracy." Stephen Austin used a provision of
the Spanish charter granted to his father to draw educated
people to his colony; artisans, stone carvers, doctors, and engineers got much larger grants of land than uneducated men.
As such concerns gradually melted in the heat of growing materialism, the cultivated mind atrophied or went into hiding.

Texas has long been measured by H. L. Mencken's description of the South, in 1920, as "the Sahara of the Bozart"—an intellectual and literary desert. Till the 1950s, at least, educated men have thought of Texas as a colony of perpetual Philistines, provincials, and materialists.

Texas has always honored success in politics and fortune-making. Only as great cities emerged after the Second World War has the creative mind impressed the state's consciousness—and that only in the cities. For so large an area, for a state not less than sixth in population in every census since 1900, Texas has produced little literature of distinction except folklore. Its best architecture—virtually its only indigenous architecture—is more than a century old. Not until the 1940s did its painters begin to surpass regional interest. Not until the 1950s was it possible to take into account the state's composers. With two or three exceptions, notably Elisabet Ney, who came to Texas from Germany in 1872, its few sculptors have been mediocrities.

In general one must talk about the state's creative minds by comparing them with each other rather than with national figures. No Texas novelist or poet—orthodox delineators of the creative spirit—has affected the nation as have several writers of the Deep South. But since the Second World War—the war may prove to divide the state from almost every aspect of its past—creative minds have been doing things with effect. In the same period Texans in cities came to be as cultivated as urban Northerners in taking in the arts—going to concerts, theaters, and art museums, reading books, buying paintings. So dismal has been the past, however, that few outsiders care to acknowledge these developments for fear they will be thought of as were people in the fifteenth century who said the world was round.

Though Texans are vexed by constant reminders of their want of mentality, they stand to gain from this irreverence and ought to encourage it. If a renaissance of sorts is possible in one state, Texas is having one—a notable one compared with its creative life before the war. It will not have more of one if others should acknowledge and praise this perhaps unexpected circumstance, and it is possible for the condition to grow better for being unknown. Such optimism is not new. Writing in the *Southwest Review* in 1924, Jay B. Hubbell said the Southwest "has an unsatisfied appetite for good poetry, drama, fiction, criticism, pictures, music, science, ideas. . . . Many southwesterners have waited long for such an awakening as has come about in the last ten years." Hubbell meant Texas as much as the rest of the Southwest, but he also saw that "the older picturesqueness of the Southwest is rapidly giving way to a cultural stage which stands for ready-made clothing, education, ideas, manners, and literature."

Hubbell's second observation turned out to have more meat to it than his first, so what of the newer optimism for the state's mentality? Its source is one of this book's themes—that liberalism is becoming a contender of effect in Texas. "In the United States at this time [1950] liberalism is not only the dominant but even the sole intellectual tradition," Lionel Trilling says in the Preface to his *The Liberal Imagination,* a collection of essays on literature and society. "The conservative impulse and the reactionary impulse do not, with some isolated and some ecclesiastical exceptions, express themselves in ideas but only in action or in irritable mental gestures which seek to resemble ideas.

". . . If between sentiment and ideas there is a natural connection so close as to amount to a kind of identity, then the connection between literature and politics will be seen as a very immediate one." Trilling did not mean "the narrow but the wide sense of the word politics . . . the politics of culture, the organization of human life toward some end or other, toward the modification of sentiments, which is to say the quality of human life." His analysis helps explain the failure of the state's creative mind at the time of Hubbell's quotations, when liberalism was unheard of in Texas, and the quickening of it now.

This evaluation of the state's creative mentality is limited to writing, mainly because the author is intellectually incapable of measuring aesthetic achievement in every field. It is a pity that it would be unseemly to call in another writer to evaluate the state's painters, for painting may lead the state's creative work. Critics other than Texans find from seven to twelve Texas painters—a large number for one state—who may be considered in the national sense, all but Robert Preusser still living in the state. Even considering writing alone prompts the bother of fences. As with so many of this book's subjects, one is treed by limiting literature to one state. Abstractions pay no heed to political boundaries. Texas laps over into everywhere as everywhere blends with Texas. What of Katherine Anne Porter? She was born in Texas, spent some of her early life in the state, and some of her work includes this background. Adding Miss Porter to the list of Texas writers would add prestige, but only a chamber of commerce would do so. What of Henry Nash Smith? His *Virgin Land* called for no less creative power than Faulkner's *Light in August*. Having spent most of his first forty years in Texas, Smith may be called a Texas writer, yet California, where he now teaches, calls him a California writer. Most of the writers considered here are Texans at the moment and have been for most or all of their lives. The focus is since the Second World War; only a few Texas writers who signify died before that time.

The excess of historical, cowboy, badman, and other types of fact, memoir, and fiction overwhelming the state's writing for more than a century is omitted here. Most of the books written by Texans and by others about Texas are material for literature, not literature itself. Some of the historical and range writing is valid, and a few of these books are important, but most reward only those who have no wish to encounter the present except in comic strips, or the past except in romance and gunplay. "No informed person would hold that the Southwest can claim any considerable body of *pure literature* as its own," Frank Dobie says in his *Guide to Life and Literature of the Southwest.* Narrowed to Texas, and thus excluding Willa Cather and others of power, the effect of Dobie's statement is redoubled. "Free play of mind upon life is the essence of good writing," Dobie wrote. "Among historians of the Southwest the general rule has been to be careful of facts and equally careful in avoiding thought-provoking interpretations." Free play of mind burdened few Texas writers until after the Second World War. Whether Texas is maturing must be decided by someone looking backward on today, but its writers, many instead of a few of whom are now seeing their state in terms of life more than fancy, prove that Texas is growing.

Texans are still so close to the past and so busy with the present that very few of them bother to write. . . . Texas literature is ripe for the picking, but there just are not enough writers in the state to do it justice. Edward Weeks, 1955, *The Open Heart.*

The new citizen who comes to Texas to make his fortune . . . will receive all possible help, be he an American or a foreigner. But I wonder if the same help would be given to the man of wisdom and classical characteristics who should go there with the purpose of living without adventure. Guido Piovene, 1954, *De America.*

One suspects that everything America already believed about Texas writing was confirmed, in 1952, when *Sironia, Texas* was published. Winning the Houghton Mifflin Literary Fellowship Award, whose other winners include books by Robert Penn Warren and David Cornel DeJong, Joseph Wechsberg and Anthony West, the novel promised much. The work of Madison Cooper, a wealthy, pinchpenny eccentric of Waco, the two-volume novel runs to 840,000 words on 1731 pages, the longest American novel ever published—nearly twice as long as *Gone with the Wind,* one and a half times as long as *War and Peace*, longer than the Old and New Testaments combined. Its length is its distinction. The *Christian Science Monitor* reviewed it with "unequivocal condemnation." Granville Hicks, reviewing Cooper's second novel, *The Haunted Hacienda*, in the New York *Times*, concluded "that the crudity of his writing matches the crudity of the [Texas] life he writes about." His first novel published when he was fifty-eight, Cooper died four years later. He was artless, immature, and lacking the sensitiveness and experience that tune the creator's mind. He was obsessed with the animal extremities occupying William Faulkner without being fortified by Faulkner's talent, and he needed an editor conscious of economy's advantages.

Cooper was an extension of the condition Texas writing is showing signs of escaping. That his work was praised by Lon Tinkle, literary editor of the Dallas *News* and a professor of French at Southern Methodist University, may owe to Tinkle's willingness to respond to any Texas writer who has some claim, however vague, to thought processes. Tinkle is the calm petrel of Texas letters, and a more civilized man is hard to imagine. Notables of New York publishing houses, to most of whom Tinkle is well known, find it hard to believe that he is a native Texan, born on a farm. In any event, though he often writes of his state's literary work with an enthusiasm that would speak well for Southern letters, he is of more journalistic service to the writing craft than any other Southerner. His urbanity, cultivated mind, and inclination have made him the central figure of Texas writing—a governor and a stimulus but more a road than a bridge to critical consciousness. He founded, and virtually runs, the Texas Institute of Letters, through which is awarded an annual prize of $1000 for what is judged to be the best Texas book of the preceding year. One of many anomalies of Texas life is that the donor of this award is Carr P. Collins, an insurance executive and a disciple of the anti-literary mentality advocated by another subject of his benefaction, W. Lee O'Daniel.

Tinkle continues part of a tradition started by John H. Mc-
Ginnis, also an S.M.U. professor, a dedicated literary missionary who was the first to prod Texas writers upward. Literary
editor of the Dallas *News* for several years before he became
editor of the *Southwest Review*, in 1927, McGinnis was a gen-
ial disciplinarian who tolerated no fluff or excess in writing
and whose effects are felt long after the sixteen years he
edited the *Review*. He made the *Review*, founded at the University of Texas in 1915 by Stark Young and others, a regional magazine by no means limited to regional concepts.
He gave it a character and an integrity that have since been
enlarged by Allen Maxwell and Margaret L. Hartley, now the
editor and assistant editor. The *Review* cannot be pegged as
only a literary quarterly because, with S.M.U., its sponsor, it
leads enlightenment at the cost of sometimes virulent criticism by Dallas patrioteers.

Maxwell is also director of Southern Methodist University
Press, for years the only book publisher of consequence in
Texas. In 1950, however, when Frank H. Wardlaw became
director of the University of Texas Press, the state advanced
again, though in a somewhat different way than the *Review*
has benefited the region. The *Review* has many meanings, but
foremost in the 1950s has been guarding what Maxwell calls
"the condition of intellectual freedom" in Texas. One value of
the University of Texas Press is scholarship, nettling those
Texans who feel that such a press should concentrate on publishing Texas lore and history. The press does publish those
subjects: *The Word on the Brazos*, a collection of Negro
preacher tales, by J. Mason Brewer, a Negro writer; *Sam Houston: The Great Designer*, by Llerena B. Friend; *The Silver
Cradle*, by Julia Nott Waugh, a story of San Antonio's Mexican people; and *Life on the Texas Range*, a collection of photographs by Erwin E. Smith, the Matthew Brady of the cattle
country, are among outstanding examples. Perhaps a fourth
of its books concern Texas, but it has also published the four-
volume *Byron's Don Juan, A Variorum Edition*, the most sig-

nificant piece of Byron scholarship in the twentieth century; C. Judson Herrick's notable *The Evolution of Human Nature;* and *The Life of David Hume,* by Ernest Campbell Mossner, the superior work on the Scotch philosopher. In August 1957 it published the first complete English translation of *Platero and I,* by Juan Ramón Jiménez, the Spanish poet who won the Nobel Prize for literature in 1956. Wardlaw, a South Carolinian of heritage, intellect, and wit, distinguished the press in less than five years.

Within my children's lifetime—by 2000 A.D.—I see a Texas with riches of the mind and spirit to match today's material wealth. . . . I see growing from this . . . a political system completely responsible to . . . the people. Former Texas Governor W. P. Hobby, 1955, Houston *Post.*

The *Review,* the two university presses, and the writers below are coaxing Texas away from the arid mentality of its past, goading it toward that necessity of the adult mind, self-inquiry. The difference is not so much that there are more writers; enough Texans with a concern for superficial history or sugared life have been writers. What differs is that many postwar writers are evaluating the state or whatever subject with critical rather than Pollyanna values.

Foremost in distilling life into fiction, and in the promise of it, are Horton Foote, William Goyen, and Tom Lea. Living in New York longer than Texas, Foote got no glory with a Broadway play, *The Chase,* in 1952, but was praised for several television plays produced in the next two years. When these works were published in two books on the same January day in 1956—*Harrison, Texas,* eight television plays, and a novel, *The Chase*—Foote proved to be an important creative writer. In the novel and in three of the plays, especially *The Trip to Bountiful,* he showed that he may become the first Texas imaginative writer of national significance. The novel and all the plays are set in the Gulf coast country, as is his

home town of Wharton. Goyen, a Houstonian most of his life,
penetrates small-town Texas life in a novel, *House of Breath*,
and later wrote a volume of short stories, *Ghost and Flesh*.
Both are impressionistic and unique in Texas writing. Lea was
a painter of distinction before 1949, when his first novel, *The
Brave Bulls*, was published. With the magnificence of that
book, a story of death and the fear of it cast in Mexico's bull-
fighting, he eclipsed one talent with another. Lea, of El Paso,
has since written *The Wonderful Country*, a historical novel
of the frontier, and a two-volume history of the King Ranch
that hobbled his future during the four years of its writing. None of this trio—none of the fiction writers below—has
yet written enough to line up a sure comparison of talents
but only of expectation.

Next to those three in the evidence of creative talent are
George G. Williams (*The Blind Bull*), David Westheimer
(*Summer on the Water* and *The Magic Fallacy*), and John
W. Wilson (*High John the Conqueror*) for novels interpreting
Texas life with reality rather than smokescreens, and John
Howard Griffin, discussed in Chapter 14. Other imaginative
writers who signify are William A. Owens (*Walking on Bor-
rowed Land*), Sikes Johnson (*The Hope of Refuge*), and
Eugene McKinney, a playwright of remarkable impression-
istic talent. Fred Gipson (*Hound-dog Man, The Home Place,
and Old Yeller*) is important in spite of lacking the evaluation of the others, and George Sessions Perry signifies for
two early novels, *Hold Autumn in Your Hand* and *Walls
Rise Up*. Some would add another fiction writer to this list,
the humorist Dillon Anderson (*I and Claudie* and *Claudie's
Kinfolks*), a wealthy Houston lawyer and a former aide to
President Eisenhower.

Chief among non-fiction writers are the three great figures
of Texas writing, J. Frank Dobie, Walter Prescott Webb, and
Roy Bedichek. After them come Henry Nash Smith, Frank E.
Vandiver, J. Evetts Haley, and Joe B. Frantz, important for
widely varying reasons. Leaders in gathering and writing

folklore are John A. Lomax, Mody C. Boatright, and J. Mason
Brewer, the state's one Negro writer of importance. Depend-
ing on critical values, between six and nine more writers
could be added to all these. Though neither is a writer but
serves writing, Carl Hertzog and Paul Baker are important to
American art. Baker, a giant of intellect, head of the Baylor
University Theater, is a world figure in experimental drama;
Hertzog, of El Paso, is one of America's eminent book de-
signers.

Dobie, Webb, and Bedichek contradict every popular notion about Texas. They do not typify the state or any state.
Of these three leading Texas thinkers, one is not well known
even to Texans. His richly stored mind a benediction, his talk
a natural art of grace and wisdom, Roy Bedichek may come
to live in the minds of men after he dies. Gentle, but a man
of gusto, contemporary, but appalled by what the world pays
for contemporariness, he has a Rousseauan fondness for the
savage: "In many ways, it seems to me, civilization is deca-
dence." After leading a double life for forty years—"promoter
of [Texas] interschool sports and contests on week days and
a naturalist during Sundays and other vacations"—he wrote
his first book, *Adventures with a Texas Naturalist*. It was published in 1947, when he was nearly seventy. A work of substance and attraction for the people of any state or country,
it distills a lifetime of observation and philosophy by a field
naturalist, a book in many ways the equal of Thoreau's *Wal-
den*. In it and, to a lesser extent, in his second book, *Karánka-
way Country* (1950), he telescopes and relates all life—po-
etically, as in describing meadow larks on a spring morning
and in telling of the mockingbird, and grimly, as in an astonishing essay on factory-raised chickens. Liberal in the word's
devalued meaning of freedom and individuality, protesting
but not rebelling his own time, steeped in the grain of classic
knowledge, Bedichek is a rarity of any age, a man made
whole.

If any Texan has created a universal of culture, if any has

altered the mind of man, he is Walter Prescott Webb, historian, of the University of Texas. Time will tell, but the hypotheses are not eccentric. He takes what everybody already knows and puts it together with meanings that escaped detection before. That is called thinking. In 1931, after he had thought about and written it for ten years, his *The Great Plains* was published. *The Great Frontier*, Webb's Everest, came twenty-one years later. Two books, two ideas: "A man is not likely to have three such ideas," he has said, but later, in the May 1957 *Harper's* ("The American West, Perpetual Mirage"), he planted the extremely controversial seed of a third such book and idea. Controversy has salted reaction to *The Great Plains* and *The Great Frontier*. Geoffrey Barraclough, the British historian, has a chapter appraising *The Great Frontier* in his *History in a Changing World*. "Whatever reservations we may have to formulate as to its positive results," he says, "Webb's work deserves recognition as a bold attempt to re-examine along new lines the fundamental postulates of modern history; even where, we may think, it fails to convince, it helps us to clarify the issues, and above all else to see the present not as a continuation of, but as a break with past development."

Harkness lecturer in American history at London University in 1938, and later Harmsworth professor in American history at Oxford University, Webb is not accustomed to Barraclough's praise. *The Great Frontier*, its portent ill suiting the optimism of the American temper, was condemned with vim when it was published. "There will be a thousand voices raised to dispute Mr. Webb's assumption that the physical frontiers are gone," said the reviewer for the *Christian Science Monitor*. Describing a frontier as "a vacancy inviting occupancy," Webb shows that since 1492 history has been shaped mainly by the expanding frontier, which created a four-hundred-year boom ending early in the twentieth century. The frontier resulted in the institutions of democracy and capitalism, but the frontier is now gone, with the result that capitalism as we know it will fade and democracy, though still possible, will be altered as individual freedom becomes "corporate individualism." He shows what he thinks the world is now up against, and his theory is winning respect.

Born in East Texas, in 1888, his family moved to the state's western frontier six years later. "The fact that I grew up on the frontier, and was a child among the first residents there, gave me some advantages in understanding the thing itself and the books about it," he wrote, in the New York *Herald Tribune,* in 1952. "If my views about the frontier are unconventional, that may be explained by the fact that I never had a course on the subject. I arrived at those views by looking at the subject directly and not through the eyes of another." Webb looks and talks very much like a West Texas cattle breeder come to town in his store clothes. Stern of face and hale of disposition, an iconoclast of theory, Webb weaves dreams and pragmatism to bridge to the mind's glory.

Dobie is the state's conscience but is not compressed by state or region. Nonconformist in not bowing the knee to prejudice, superstition, or habits of thought, to anything waylaying the intellect, he prompts and goads and freshens a state needing him as lethargy needs the spiriting of rain and the outdoors. He air conditions the state without manufacturing air, rebelling from fixed ideas and ideas fixed by demagogues, attacking anything—dogma or man—aimed at fooling the people. He is the bane of humbugs, pedagogues, and coverers-up. Unconscious of having a personal stake in anything, of what the mass may think of him, he attacks against the odds of materialism's appeal. The passion for being himself—sincere—applies to little things as well as big. "The other day a charming woman . . . was inviting Dobie and me to dinner, after which she engagingly promised to show us some slides she made of her trip last summer," Bedichek said at a Texas Folklore Society dinner, in 1955, honoring Dobie. "'I'd like to come for the company, but I sure as hell hate pictures,' drawled Dobie in reply. . . . To an invitation to join a liter-

ary club, Dobie replied, 'Dear Bill, I can't work up any enthusiasm about a literary club. I wouldn't want to hear anyone
read his writing for an hour or two.' Just like that—no weasel-
words, no cushioning phrases."

"The rhythms of nature and the rhythms of both prose and
poetry are a part of my nature," Dobie wrote in 1952. "A kind
of pervading purpose in my writing has been to make human beings aware of natural harmonies. I want to be an artist, but facts often get in the way. . . . There have been
three stages to my thinking: when I did not think at all and
the pageant of the past was all sufficient; when, about 1940,
I became a contemporary of myself; more recently, when I
decided that cultivation of the beautiful and of intellectual
integrity is more important, in so far as a writer is related
to society, than all else." Toned from childhood in the nearly
matchless prose of the King James version of the Bible, reared
on a ranch in the brush country below San Antonio, educated
at the University of Texas and Columbia University, he is
above all things a teacher but an enemy of formalized teaching. He lives in the minds of thousands of Texans for teaching
a course, "Life and Literature of the Southwest," at the University of Texas. In 1943 he was visiting professor of American history at Cambridge University, but on returning to the
University of Texas he found it being taken over by reactionary politicians, and in 1949 "we parted company."

Of his nearly twenty books, and as many more edited by
him for the Texas Folklore Society, the best is either *The Mus-
tangs*—the classic on its subject, "a book with love and fire
in its heart," the *Christian Science Monitor's* reviewer wrote
—or *Tongues of the Monte*, a fantasy of beauty and fact about
northern Mexico and Mexicans. His best known work is
Coronado's Children, a collection of legends about the
Southwest. The meaning of his help to other writers will never
be known; even Dobie could not estimate that. "I suppose in
the last thirty years he has read sympathetically and criticized with the patience and tenderness of a skilled surgeon

during an operation, hundreds of manuscripts of young, un-practiced, but aspiring writers," Bedichek said in his talk. As much could be said of older, more practiced writers, whose lucidity, economy, and diction have been improved—some-times created—by Dobie's giving of self. "I am called a folk-lorist, but I care little about scientific folklore," he has written. "I have done hard research on range history, but I care more for the beautiful and picturesque than for facts." His mobile face capped with white hair wonderfully awry, his mischie-vous, wide-awake, dust-blue eyes estranged from malice even in ire, Dobie lives to help live, never homogenized by his time.

He, Webb, and Bedichek have in common a slew of common sense, individualism, and hospitality. They have a tendency to graze away from the herd but enjoy associating with their fellows. Rebels in resisting the one-mindedness that would make all men the same in their approvals and rejections, they coax the fates a little. They are the state's chief gifts to en-lightenment.

The Big Bend and Chisos Mountains

18 Coda

John it is a strange land. John it is hard to describe.
But perhaps like this: hold up your right hand, palm outward
And break the last three fingers down from the joint
And there I think you have it. The westering thumb
The beautiful bleak land, the silent mesas
Big Bend and the great canyons at its end
El Paso, the Northern Pass, and they came down through it.
Southward and east the slow hot river moving
River of Palms, Grande del Norte, and over the wrist
To Brownsville and it empties in the vast blue waters.
Upward the long coast curving and far above it
Over the bent joints the red bordering river
Red River, land of the Washita and the Tejas
And last the index, Panhandle, the high plains

The bleached bone laid on the huge heart of the continent.
This is the empire.[1]

So the poet Townsend Miller mapped Texas.

"It is openness, bigness. It is the cloud-accented blue sky
above the coastal prairie. It is the velvet night along a thousand miles of the Rio Grande. It is the bracing Panhandle
morning, the breeze running as free as a young stallion across
oceans of space. It is the hills running nearly a thousand miles
from east to west. The red iron hills of San Augustine, the
post oak hills of Athens, the round, bald, rich swells of the
Temple country, the hills circling Austin like ramparts, the
great and heart-lifting hills running on through Dripping
Springs and Johnson City and Fredericksburg and Junction,
the rugged highlands of Ozona and Sonora, the mesas of the
Fort Stockton country, and then the real mountains, the
brown Davises, the up-ended Guadalupes, the far and lonely
Chisos."

So the editor W. D. Bedell profiled the state.

Man has been traced through thirty-seven thousand years
of the state's prehistory, but historically—the time in which
people of European origin have known the land that is now
Texas—the state is four and a quarter centuries old. The
Spaniard Cabeza de Vaca opened this period when he and
three companions, sole survivors of a wrecked ship, washed
up on the Gulf coast in 1528. Years later he wrote an account
of this adventure—the first written record of the land. Of the
four and a quarter centuries, the first three belonged to the
Spaniards, then a brief interval to the Mexicans, and the rest
is American. Three hundred American families, led by Stephen F. Austin, twenty-seven-year-old heir to his father's
dreams, began colonizing the land late in 1821. Other groups
followed, until thirty thousand Americans—four times the
number of Mexicans—were living in Texas by 1830. Six years
later they rebelled; their new nation, the Republic of Texas,
endured for ten years. After Texas was annexed to the Union,

[1] *A Letter From Texas*, Neiman-Marcus, Dallas, 1939.

in 1846, a war with Mexico ended the contest for the land.

Time and again the United States had spurned the land. Aaron Burr, partner of misfortune, was the first to go after it. Jefferson, his country rich in Louisiana Purchase land, embittered by Burr's rivalry for the presidency in 1800, was not much concerned whether America's western boundary was the Sabine or the Rio Grande. Between the rivers was Texas, claimed but not quite secured by Spain, and there Burr dreamed of creating a new American frontier. His dream came a cropper when he was betrayed by a cohort, a scoundrel named James Wilkinson, and ruined by Jefferson's vengeance. A decade later the land was rebuffed again when James Monroe, trading for title to Florida, relinquished to Spain America's claim to Texas. Next Andrew Jackson schemed with his friend Sam Houston to get the land for the United States, and gradually Texas became one of the great political issues of the time. Opposing President Tyler's hope of taking Texas into the Union, Daniel Webster resigned as Secretary of State. The issue was not so much Texas as slavery: Texas would be another slave state. Sam Houston, by all odds the most extraordinary figure in the state's history, triggered his goal of annexation by flirting with Great Britain. The British, though they had no wish to acquire Texas, opposed American annexation and at one time thought of using force to prevent it. The American Congress, fearing Britain's motives, narrowly approved annexation in 1845. The Senate was deadlocked on the issue, twenty-six to twenty-six, when Senator Edward A. Hannegan, of Indiana, switched his vote to favor annexation. Thus Texas became the twenty-eighth state.

Frederick Law Olmsted, in *A Journey through Texas*, the second volume of the Northerner's Southern trilogy of the 1850s, opposed the charge that the United States got Texas through guile: "We saw the land lying idle; we took it. . . . When the history [of the state's rebellion, independence, and annexation] is candidly re-read, the story that the whole

movement was the development of a deliberate and treach-
erous plot for the conquest of Texas, appears a needless
exaggeration of influences that really played a secondary
part. . . . The land was fertile; that was the kernel of the
matter." One peculiarity of the state's annexation is its right
to divide itself into more states. The Joint Resolution of Annexation says: "New States of convenient size, not exceeding
four in number, in addition to the said State of Texas . . .
may hereafter, by the consent of said State, be formed . . ."

Texas, a land of many climates, tilts to the southeast, as if
propped up against the western mountains. Thus the streams
run from the northwest to the southeast, almost parallel with
each other. Eight of them—the Sabine, Neches, Trinity,
Brazos, Colorado, Guadalupe-San Antonio, Nueces, and the
Rio Grande, all named by the Spaniards—empty into the
Gulf of Mexico. The Rio Grande, longest of the group, forms
the southern boundary of the state. The Red River, which
forms part of the northern boundary, is the second longest
in the state and the only one of importance not bearing a
Spanish name.

While visiting Walter Prescott Webb, the historian, at the
University of Texas in 1953, Arnold Toynbee was driven
through the sheep and goat country near Austin. The hills
and green of Austin, closing in on a bend of the Colorado
River, make it the beauty of larger Texas cities, but there is
a shock of nearby contrast; the Balconnes Fault cuts the area
into two environments. The east of Travis County is humid,
buoyant; the west is arid, hard up. Toynbee saw the west,
a broken, scrub-oak, *caliche* country, nursed by a series of
dams. Guided by Joe B. Frantz, historian and university
professor, Toynbee said the area made him feel he was back
in Turkey: the dryness, the dams, the stunted growth, the
sheep and goats, the heat.

Visitors of Toynbee's stripe, measuring with perspectives
of mind and travel, compare the state to many lands—which
one depends on where they see Texas. Preoccupation with

the state's size hides its variety of land, climate, and attitude
from the run of travelers, and from many Texans, too. The
land's variety excites extremes of pleasure and disgust when
part of it is taken for the whole. Alistair Cooke, of the Manchester *Guardian,* stung the landscape—a "dreadful marvel"
—after crossing the state from east to west in 1955: "There
are more petrified and godforsaken landscapes in the United
States, but none more evenly inhabited, none which the natives so imperturbably assume to be a reasonable and 'mighty
pretty' place to live." However that may be, one stigma of
the land's enormity—distances—has not been melted by the
air age's drawing-in of space, and it may never be. El Paso
and Amarillo, cities of consequence, are in Texas but do not
feel they are of it politically. Amarillo is closer to Denver,
Colorado, and Wichita, Kansas, than to Austin; El Paso is
nearly twice as far from Austin as from Santa Fe, capital of
New Mexico. Dalhart, north of Amarillo in the Texas Panhandle, is nearer to five other state capitals—New Mexico,
Kansas, Colorado, Oklahoma, and Nebraska—than to Austin.

*At this moment [Texas] is doubtless the most confident
spot on earth. There is a sense in which Texas is the last
American frontier. That same boundless belief in the future
which bore our pioneering fathers from the Atlantic to the
Pacific may be found everywhere today in Texas.* 1952,
Christian Century.

*Texans, it is said, are different. But Texans, anyway, would
never agree they were a minority, and Texas is a nice joke.
. . . Texas, to the stranger, is a huge, friendly, school-boyish
state. The brag has a grin. . . . More significant is the fact
that whereas, as you move through the deep south, everyone
asks you "How are you feeling?" in Texas it at once changes
to "How are you doing?" . . . One day even Texas will be
assimilated.* Sir William Haley, 1956, *The Times,* of London.

The land and past are fixed, but Texas life is a mobile

balanced in haste. Texans stew in issues and antipathies, in habits of thought and action which are not peculiar to the state but often seem to be aggravated beyond compare. Texas has a knack for conflict, for seasoning principles to an *en garde* status, and hence the intensity of fighting over issues of the time. In any battle between property rights and human rights, the odds are on property rights, as they are in all states, but the victor is never spoiled by getting a chance to rest. In an early chapter of *Home to Texas,* the wise and mellowed memoir of an arch-conservative of large gifts and weaknesses, Stanley Walker compressed his private Texas of a generation ago—a state some Texans see today:

"Most of the time, as a youngster, I looked upon Texas and many things Texan with feelings pretty close to hatred and disgust. Texas was a place to get away from. These feelings, of course, came in part from lack of knowledge and perspective, but there is no need to apologize for them; they were real, honest, and I do not intend to prettify them. As an eager but perpetually frustrated youth, I looked upon Texas as a place essentially coarse and brutal. Its humor was either silly or offensive. Its so-called heroic figures were mostly fakers. Its politicians were ridiculous, either ignoramuses, zealots, demagogues, or plain asses. . . . The preachers tried to run everything, and came very near doing it. The wrong people got the respect and the money. Hard, killing labor, for its own sake, was rated much too highly as a virtue. The free souls, the sensitive men and women, the scholars, the dreamers, the independent thinkers were regarded with suspicion, as cranks and menaces. . . . My feeling was shared by many another boy and girl of my own period. That is one reason you will find Texans scattered all over the world, doing big and little jobs. Some of them may lift a glass to dear old Texas on Texas Independence Day, March 2, but they have no hankering to go back and settle down." Still, after years of success in Gotham, Walker came home to Texas.

Marguerite Johnston, who moved to Texas from Washington, D.C., in 1946, later wrote of a newcomer's reaction to the state. Reared in Birmingham, Alabama, and afterward a newspaper woman in Washington, she had been on the staff of the Houston *Post* since 1947. A woman of intellect and the wisdom of proportion, she wrote in part of her reaction to habits and customs rather than to the larger concerns of the Walker quotation.

"It was surprising to see stop signs on four corners instead of the customary two, and to watch high powered automobiles pausing at the intersection for a courteous little minuet before shooting on down the street. It was surprising to learn that 'houseparty' in the local newspapers did not mean having several people to visit in one's home for a week or two, but meant the ladies who help the hostess serve at a tea. And that the 'Senate' and 'House' were in Austin instead of Washington. . . . It was puzzling to notice that even the best-paved streets through a long-established part of town might have a sudden rectangle of unpaved earth and gravel on one side or the other, and to have it explained as a right of the homesteader.

"It was startling, coming from a Washington that is supposed to be the cocktail-drinkingest city in the country, to hear a college girl ask casually for 'bourbon over ice' and to see elegantly dressed men and women carrying a bottle of whisky in a paper bag to an expensive table. It was dismaying to discover that the felt hat, wool suit and silver bracelets which would have seen me through an informal evening in Washington were painfully sturdy amid the veils, furs, jewels and feathers of a Houston luncheon and 'style show.' It was puzzling that in the state where land comes in measurements of infinity, houses should be jammed together on lots smaller than those of a New England village—until we learned about the price of land in these parts [Houston]."

Other customs, though fading, reflect vestiges of the state's past. One day in 1953 a tall, simply dressed woman in high-button shoes asked a clerk in the china section of a Houston department store to show her the "ranchware"—dinner service with border designs of cattle brands. She bought nearly a hundred dollars' worth of the service and the clerk asked if it were to be charged. "When I buy anything I pay for it," she said, taking a roll of currency from her purse. As the purse lay open on the counter while she peeled off the bills, the clerk could see its contents: side by side were a small Bible and what he took to be a .45-caliber pistol. But no matter Texans' reluctance to lose the Western color of the state's past, it is being overwhelmed in the growing urban pressures. "The frontier Texan figures in fiction and in factual descriptions with a 'drawl' and as a man of few words," Roy Bedichek wrote in *Adventures with a Texas Naturalist*. "Of course, now, with a generation of urbanization, as much chatter falls from the composite mouth of Texas as from that of any other state . . . Outdoor living not only softens speech but slows its tempo, reflecting quieter nerves and mental reactions surer if somewhat slower on the trigger." The indoors has been closing in on Texans since the First World War.

Distinctions of Texas life owing to the state's frontier past were nearly melted down in the rising cities and economy of the Second World War and after. Remnants of cattle-country and ranching customs endure from Texans' determination to keep them going and because the state continues to lead in raising beef. But ranching's hold on Texas was scant compared with oil's, and the state's cattle industry, unlike oil, had little effect on the nation. "In the economic and social history of the United States the rise and fall of 'the Cattle Kingdom' had been no more than a brilliant flash in the trigger-pan," Arnold Toynbee says in Volume 8 of *A Study of History*, terming the industry's zenith an "amply recorded history of an abortive pastoral civilization in North America" between 1866 and 1877.

Paul Bunyan got to Texas—in oil, of course—but most of the state's own folk heroes are in ranching. Pecos Bill choked a rattlesnake to death with his bare hands when he was an infant. Later he owned every rancher's dream, the Perpetual Motion Ranch—let it alone and it ran itself. Another source of legend, though still quite alive, has disappeared far more than ranching from effect on Texas life. The Texas Rangers, organized during the Revolution to hold back the Indians, is now the oldest force of its kind in the world, having had a more or less continuous existence for nearly a century and a quarter. But the Rangers' legends and romance are in the past, though not yet out of sight to some living men.

John Fischer, the editor of *Harper's* magazine, was born on the Oklahoma side of the border village of Texhoma, a mischance that may account for his latter-day peeve with and concern for Texas. Dining with a Texan in 1954, Fischer talked of Texans' plight. "Texas, some parts of it, is jumping five hundred years in twenty," he said. "It was a good world —just, quiet, healthy—when today's men were boys. It was more fun before big industry and oil, and many Texans would like to keep it that way." Two years earlier, in his Range Ridin' column in the Amarillo *News-Globe*, Mason King reflected Fischer's conclusion: "Boy, those good old days when you could safely go to sleep with all the doors open or eat with a neighbor without an engraved invitation are gone forever." Of the Southern states, only North Carolina and Texas have not baited new industry with tax exemptions for specified periods. But Texas is a paradox in wanting the boom economy of more and more industry while hoping to shun industrialization.

I want no monument of stone or marble, but plant at my head a pecan tree and at my feet an old-fashioned walnut. And when those trees shall bear, let the pecans and walnuts be given out among the plain people of Texas, so that they may plant them and make Texas a land of trees. James Stephen Hogg, 1906, a few hours before his death.

The state's intimations of greatness are badgered by a number of obstacles. The source of most of these obstacles is the complaint of Chapter 12: eight million urban Texans are partly disfranchised by less than a million rural Texans. The Texas legislature of the 1950s deals in solutions that succeeded in the 1890s. The following evidence is greatly abridged:

The notion that murder is a petty crime in Texas is exaggerated, but the exaggeration is not without substance. In May 1940 a Houston man murdered another in a tavern brawl; he was given a suspended sentence. In January 1946 he murdered a second man, for which he was penalized with six months in jail. In 1954 he pleaded guilty to breaking an automobile windshield. He was sentenced to six months in jail, equaling the price he paid for killing two men. In 1952 another Houstonian shot a man to death in a tavern. The killing was ruled justifiable homicide because it took place at night, plus one other circumstance. An old Texas law reads: "In cases of burglary and theft by night the homicide is justifiable at any time while the offender is in the building . . . where the theft is committed." Witnesses said the dead man had picked up $4.75 in change belonging to the killer and refused to return it, thus making him a thief and his murder justified. Higher state courts have sustained the law; its repeal is a function of the legislature. A man charged with a crime in Texas need but hire a lawyer who is a member of the legislature to get his case postponed if the legislature is in session, stimulating some lawyers to serve as lawmakers. A legislator can have any case postponed while the legislature is in session.

The cost of a station-to-station telephone call from Austin to Texarkana, Texas, is one dollar for three minutes on Sundays, but a call across the state line to Texarkana, Arkansas, costs twenty-five cents less—a comparison of federal control of interstate calls and the absence of state control. Texas is one of two states that do not regulate telephone service, one of four that do not regulate telegraph service, one of six that do not regulate electric light and power service, and one of nine that do not regulate water service. Such controls are a function of the legislature.

An automobile-inspection law, the first in the state's history, was passed by the Texas legislature in 1951. The law's effect was to reverse a trend of many years by substantially reducing the number of deaths and injuries from auto accidents in 1952, when total mileage increased 9 per cent. No matter the result, no matter that most other states with large populations have had such laws for years, Texans raised Cain. The law was an issue in the governor's race of 1952; Governor Allan Shivers promised to ask the legislature to amend or repeal the law. Some candidates for the legislature based their campaigns on opposition to the law. Two of the law's sponsors, Representatives J. K. Aynesworth and J. A. Steward, a retired admiral, were defeated for re-election. The law was revised—a euphemism for "killed" in this case—in 1953. Steering gears, exhaust systems, and other equipment affecting safety were inspected under the old law; horns, lights, brakes, rear-view mirrors, and windshield wipers are inspected under the new law, which does not require a driver to comply with the inspection to buy his license plates. Such does not end the convenience of Texas driving laws. While other states make a boy wait until he is sixteen to get a license to drive, while many states with big cities and complex freeways hold him back until he is eighteen, Texas licenses children at age fourteen in some cases.

No child can be charged with or convicted of a crime in any Texas court until he is seventeen. The Texas court system itself is an object of justice's concern. Writing in 1956, W. St. John Garwood, an associate justice of the Texas Supreme Court, said "a jury trial in Texas is not infrequently a battle of wits . . . between lawyer-gladiators, with the judge sitting as a sort of modest referee, afraid that any vigorous action he might take in the interest of justice will be invading the jury's domain or (still worse) will earn him an opponent at the next election and require him to spend all of his meagre salary for political purposes." Only Texas and Oklahoma have separate "supreme" courts for civil and criminal cases. Yet in spite of the fact that Texas law favors the criminal, Texas is the only state whose prison population is growing faster than the state's population, and it is one of only three states without a department of probation and paroles. With the exception of full prisons, these are all concerns of the legislature.

Texas is the only state that prevents a married woman from selling or borrowing on property she owned before she was married without her husband's consent, and she cannot bring suit of any kind, except for divorce, without her husband's consent. Texas is the only state permitting cities to annex surrounding areas without the consent of the people to be annexed, a power making it legally possible for a city to take into its limits all of Texas that is not incorporated. Each of seven Texas cities appropriates more money to care for its parks than the legislature appropriates for the fifty state parks.

Texas puts its bylaws into its constitution. The state has needed a new constitution since a few years after the existing constitution was ratified in 1876; it has been amended 108 times since then. And a revision of statutes is needed with as much urgency as a new constitution. Stuart McGregor, of the Dallas *News,* took up the problem in 1956, listing four causes of the state's clumsy government: "First, the State Constitution . . . is so detailed that it obstructs both needed reform and needed new action . . . Second, the state's administrative system, with its more than 150 agencies of every structural type, makes difficult a co-ordinated state policy even after one has been enacted. Third, there are many corporate, professional and trade pressure groups that have learned to take advantage of this confused situation. They do not want an efficient State Government because they get what they want more easily now. Fourth, conflicting economic self-interests growing out of Texas' great diversity of natural resources and material production add to the difficulty of getting co-ordinated action for the good of the state as a whole."

Texas statutes were last revised in 1925—"and that job was rather poorly done," the Dallas *News* editorialized in 1956. "Both state and local government in Texas are loaded down with involved, conflicting and obsolete legislation," the editorial said. The gangsterism and corruptions of George B. Parr's dictatorship in Duval County, though waning in the middle 1950s from the pressures of opposition in the county and lawsuits by the state and federal governments, were attacked by John Ben Shepperd, then attorney general, in 1956. He said Duval County's rottenness was made possible by the inability of the state's statutes to cope with such injustices, and he warned that similar situations are possible unless the statutes are revised.

Some of the state's room for improvement is shown through the tedium of statistics. The life expectancy of a child born in Texas is sixty-eight years, one less than the national average. The state's infant mortality rate is two higher than the average for the forty-eight states. The state's spending for health and hospitals was ninth in the nation in 1955; Texas needs ten thousand more hospital beds. The state with a reputation for riches was twenty-seventh in per capita income in 1955. A year earlier it was seventh in the nation in public-school spending and sixteenth in schoolteachers' salaries, but it was first in spending for public assistance. In 1955 its maximum workmen's compensation benefit was lower than that for every state except Alabama; its average weekly unemployment payment was forty-sixth in the nation. Though Texas professes to oppose federal aids, it stars in receiving them: in 1955 it was second in federal payments to individuals and institutions and third in federal grants-in-aid to state and local governments.

Texas would seem to be at the world's mercy in its state finances, a result of its dependence on oil taxes. In a speech at Wichita Falls, in 1957, Waggoner Carr, Speaker of the

Texas House of Representatives, said the state would do well to find other tax sources of consequence. "The entire revenue situation . . . could change drastically almost overnight," he said. "We are more or less at the mercy of foreign dictators. Their whims can easily determine how much tax revenue the State of Texas will collect during the next two years." He said Texas must "broaden our tax base in order to at least reduce the effects which foreign powers can exercise over the finances of our state. For years we have sidestepped the unpleasant chore of completely overhauling our tax structure." His reference to foreign influence presumably meant imports of foreign oil, much of which is owned by American firms. When imports are small, Texas production—and tax revenue from it—is larger, and hence the effect of imported oil on the state's finances. A strike of oil workers once imperiled state finances when refineries were shut down and unable to take production from Texas wells.

In 1953 the Texas Poll, a public-opinion survey, asked five hundred Texans what they thought of their state. The survey's conclusion was that "a majority of Texans are openly critical of Texan ways." It attributed this surprise to one of two things, either "that recent propaganda of certain out-of-state magazines and books has penetrated into the minds" of Texans or "that no one ever took a good look before at the composite opinion of Texans about Texas." One question was "What would you say are some of the bad qualities of people in Texas?" Heading the list of more than forty criticisms was bragging, listed by 15 per cent. Second were "drinking, gambling, cursing, carousing, shooting, fighting, killing," 13 per cent, and third was "mistreating other races," 5 per cent. Asked "What would you say are some of the good qualities of people in Texas?" 70 per cent answered "friendly, neighborly, hospitable."

"What's Wrong with Texas?" was the title of an article written by Stanley Walker for *Look* magazine in 1952. Some of his complaints were: Texans have an inferiority complex;

a Texan who strikes it rich in oil "becomes an authority on theology, geology, Texas history, economics, ceramics, Bang's disease in cattle, and what to do about juvenile delinquency"; the state's generosity is not only exaggerated but most Texans "could show Vermonters how to cut corners and save pennies"; and "Public office, on the lower levels, is bestowed on the . . . theory of 'to each according to his needs.'"

A new possibility, leadership of the South, now threads the weave of the state's strengths and weaknesses. Such a position is confused by the South's latterly grown conviction that Texas is not a member state. W. J. Cash does not refer to Texas in the 429 pages of *The Mind of the South*. Francis Butler Simkins, in the Preface to *A History of the South*, another work of importance, says "there are doubts about the true Southern character" of Texas and five other states. "The changes of nine decades [since the Civil War] have weakened the heritage of southern traditionalism, revolutionized the economy, and made Texas more western than southern," V. O. Key, Jr., says in *Southern Politics*. These opinions are shared by many Texans, but the Civil War in the past and segregation in the present, plus the tie of geography, give Texas a liaison with the South.[2]

Speaking at commencement exercises at Rice Institute in 1952, Douglas Southall Freeman said Texas cannot be separated from the South intellectually or economically, that Texas has an obligation to the rest of the South. The wealth and resources of Texas are so out of proportion to those of other Southern states, he said, that a danger exists that Texas may develop one self-contained standard while the rest of the South develops a lower one. Bicknell Eubanks, of the *Christian Science Monitor*, wrote in 1955 that "Texas will

[2]No conclusion in this book, not even those dealing in issues and controversy, aroused opposition from readers of the manuscript—mostly men of intellect and open minds—as did my belief that Texas is tied to the South. It is still my belief, but a belief posted with the notice that several formidable minds think I leaped before I looked at the facts.

be even more important [in the national political scene] because of its strategic position in the South. As the largest state south of Mason and Dixon's Line, populationwise and economically, Texas exerts influence on other southern states." In any event, it appears that political and economic leadership of the South has been thrust on Texas by circumstances. The circumstances are the power of the state's position in congressional posts, the state's role as a hostage to certain Southern realities, notably segregation of the races and the Solid South tradition, and the state's wealth.

Since an English plough first broke the virgin sward of the sea-slope of Virginia, Saxons have not entered on so magnificent a domain [as Texas]. Many times, while making these notes, I have stopped to seek a superlative equal to some individual feature of the scenery . . . and one is more than ever wanting to apply to the country as a whole. . . . Texas has an Arcadian preeminence of position among our States, and an opulent future before her, that only wanton mismanagement can forfeit. Frederick Law Olmsted, 1857, *A Journey through Texas.*

In many respects Texas is to the rest of the United States as the United States is to the rest of the Western world: younger, full of pep, an irritant, annoying in its self-assurance, and thought by older and perhaps wiser regions to need counsel. The state is as eager to be counseled by the rest of the United States as the nation is to be counseled by the Continent. Texas is a remnant of the American dream of the nineteenth century. It is a place where men expect to do well, one of the last known addresses of Horatio Alger. The mirage of the frontier lingers, even in the cities, but is as false as other mirages. The state excels in the newer frontier of automation: the most automated industries are oil and chemical. Texas is Uncle Sam's gray sheep, his Scotland, his Gascony. The state's gusto for the moment, its boldness make it fairer

game than it means to be. "Pious but Hopeless Request for
Humility in Texas" was the title of an editorial in the Baltimore *Sun* early in 1945. Little about Texas is safe to say. The
state remains an improbable place to all save romantics—children, dreamers, and pilgrims of hope, to whom it is a land in
the sunset, a mecca, an illusion.

Muting its merits, eloquent in its deficiencies, ignored
when it is wise and scorned when it is not, too new for history's perspective, too old to be allowed its exuberances, too
rich too recently to be accepted socially, producing billions
in wealth that are spent elsewhere, Texas has need of a resource that is lightly valued: it is self-restoring. The state will
be envied, apart from its economic riches, so long as it has
its thrustiness and its luxury of spirit, both common traits of
the West but outmoded in the North and impossible for the
South. Texas will be criticized until it matures.

The Texan today feels that he is singled out for a special
place in the world and yet mocked by fate. Industry and
growing cities are contracting some of the state's distinctions,
filling the vacant space with reforms. Texas will not move on
without draining off some of its singularities. The state is an
extravagant place in a sober world, giving American life a
touch of fantasy. There is an excitement here. The state is un-
predictable and undisciplined in a world liking pattern and
order. As Texas grows its nonconformity will melt to some
extent, though the nonconformity by no means consists of a
society of nonconformists. Texans, though hopeful of being
a separate race, also want to be thought of as normal. Texas
is partly make-believe, a playlike place, in the modern world,
and unconsciously Texans want to change that. The state has
been something of a drama, one that no longer convinces, is
not quite believed, in the changes of time. The Texas myth is
diluted with each decade because the myth could not hold
forever the willing suspension of doubt that is vital to dra-
matic success.

On the other hand, of what use is it to be like everything

else? Why should anything conform for conformity's sake?
The mind of Texas is shifting, slowly, in the stacking of years
on top of the Second World War, but neither the state nor
America would gain if Texas shed its individuality. It is as
apt to do so as it is to divide into five states. "But if America
is so thoroughly standardized, how do you explain Texas?"
asked the Briton John Allan May, after surveying the United
States for the *Christian Science Monitor*, in 1953. "Texas is
pretty well a country in its own right, and to Texans it usually
is right. Compared with people in the rest of the States, Texans . . . look different, talk different, live different, and act
different. Not only different, but bigger. And frequently
better."

Briefly, in the state's first hours as a republic, its motto may
be said to have been "Try Me," the words on a cuff link
used by President Sam Houston as a substitute for the great
seal of the republic. The Texas legislature adopted "Friendship" as the state motto in 1930, and friendship is a Texan
characteristic. But "Try Me" is a dare, confident and without
the belligerency of a chip on the shoulder. The accidental
motto was more apt.

The Varner Plantation — West Columbia

INDEX

Sharp, Mrs. Walter B., 102
Shell Oil Co., 94
Shepperd, John Ben, 21, 214–16, 265
Sheridan, Francis C., 231
Sherman, Tex., 95
Shiro, Tex., 191
Shivercrats, 56
Shivers, Allan, 21, 45, 55, 56, 59, 60, 63, 66–67, 70, 130, 160, 196, 197, 205, 218, 230, 263
Shore, Dinah, 115, 232
Simkins, Francis Butler, 178, 267
Sims, E. A., 81–82
Sinatra, Frank, 115, 232
Sironia, Texas, 243–44
Smith, Al, 125
Smith, Erwin E., 245
Smith, Gerald L. K., 139
Smith, Henry Nash, 242, 247
Smith, Lloyd Hilton, 35
Smith, Lonnie, 194
Smith, Margaret Chase, 47
Smith, Robert E., 43
Sonnenberg, Ben, 84–85
Sons of the American Revolution, 64, 185
Sons of the Republic of Texas, 93
Sons of the Six-Shooter Toters of Texas, 237
Southern Baptist church, 177, 178–79, 182, 184
Southern Baptist Theological Seminary, 182, 184
Southern Manifesto, 158–59, 197–98
Southern Methodist University, 103, 114, 138–41, 187, 245
Southern Methodist University Press, 245
Southern Politics, quoted, 57, 267
South Texas College of Law and Commerce, 66
Southwest Book Fair, 94
Southwest Review, 138, 139, 245; quoted, 199, 241
Southworth, Ray M., 82
Spinks, Brian, quoted, 196–97
Standard Oil Co. (Indiana), 111
State Democratic Executive Committee (Texas), 71
State Fair of Texas, 129, 175, 236
States' rights, 26–29, 49
Statler Hilton Hotel (Dallas), 132

Stevens, Risë, 115
Stevenson, Adlai, 56, 59, 70, 71, 116, 161, 229–30
Steward, J. A., 263
Stokowski, Leopold, 121
Strake, George W., 76–77, 188
Streeter, Thomas W., 19
Strout, Richard L., 110
Study of History, A, quoted, 260
Superior Oil Co., 107
Supreme Court, U.S., decisions of, 28–29, 79, 116, 117, 130, 190, 194–95, 197, 199, 200, 202, 206, 213
Sutro, John, 228
Sweet, Alexander E., 125

Tarrant County, 202
Tate, Willis M., 141
Taylor, Tex., 200
Tejas Club (Houston), 124
Tennessee Gas Transmission Co., 117
Texas, annexation of, 18–19, 117, 233, 254–55; "Big Rich" fantasy in, 31–45, 50–52, 86; chauvinism of, 19, 223–38; economic colony, 29–30; festivals and customs, 51–52; House of Representatives, 162–63, 164, 216–18; Jim Crow laws of, 199; labor laws of, 63–64; materialism in, 19–20; mineral production of, 21; philanthropy in, 34, 47, 97–104, 201; politics in, 20–21, 53–72; poll tax in, 21, 66; press, views of, 20, 24, 49–50, 54–55, 60; religion in, 19, 175–88; rural-urban conflict in, 17, 72, 162–71, 262; scandals in state government, 21, 62, 67; Senate, 163, 218; size and variousness of, 24–25, 67–68; South, the, and, 21, 27–30, 169, 267; state revenue and oil, 21–22, 91, 265–66; unpopularity of, 18, 22–24, 45–50, 223–38
Texas A. and M. College, 201
Texas Advisory Council on Segregation in Public Schools, 218
Texas Almanac, quoted, 89–90
Texas and Pacific Railroad, 131
"Texas Association for the Advancement of Millionaires," 59–60

Cottonseed-Oil Mill—Memphis, Texas

LIST OF DRAWINGS

AUTHOR'S NOTE: In no sense of the word did Schiwetz "illustrate" the text of this book. He was asked to make a series
of sketches on modern Texas, independent of the book's text.
Outside of a discussion or two, the only specific planning we
did together was on the endpapers. Any other method, we
thought, would limit the artist to some extent.